FREE AT LAST

Selected List of Other Books by Arna Bontemps

STORY OF THE NEGRO

WE HAVE TOMORROW

CHARIOT IN THE SKY

GOLDEN SLIPPERS *(Anthology)*

BLACK THUNDER

GOD SENDS SUNDAY

100 YEARS OF NEGRO FREEDOM

AMERICAN NEGRO POETRY *(Anthology)*

FAMOUS NEGRO ATHLETES

HOLD FAST TO DREAMS *(Anthology)*

GREAT SLAVE NARRATIVES *(Anthology)*

With Jack Conroy

THE FAST SOONER HOUND

THEY SEEK A CITY

Edited by Langston Hughes and Arna Bontemps

THE BOOK OF NEGRO FOLKLORE

THE POETRY OF THE NEGRO (1746-1970)

FREE AT LAST

The Life of Frederick Douglass

ARNA BONTEMPS

ILLUSTRATED WITH PHOTOGRAPHS

DODD, MEAD & COMPANY
NEW YORK

ISBN 0-396-06308-X

Library of Congress Catalog Card Number: 76-143285

Printed in the United States of America
by The Cornwall Press, Inc., Cornwall, N. Y.

For

AVON NYANZA WILLIAMS, JR.

CONTENTS

CONTENTS

ILLUSTRATIONS

(following page 118)

ix

I

THE JOURNEY

T HE PAPERS he carried were not forged. They were borrowed. But the clothes, the red shirt, the tarpaulin hat,
the loosely knotted black tie, worn to impersonate a sailor,
had been bought in a Balitmore shop. Standing nervously
on the platform of the old depot by Bowly's Wharf, he tried
to keep one eye on the waiting train while the other
watched for the arrival of a hack now due on Pratt Street.

The other passengers had already climbed abroad. Even
the coach at the tail end, the one designated for "colored,"
had its load. The Indian-like brown youth, twitching un-
comfortably in his strange get-up, moved toward that final
coach. He was within a few yards when the train whistle
blew. At the same instant a horse-drawn carriage swerved
and stopped at the curb. Presently a hackman came running with a large, crudely tied bundle. The train was moving when the tall youth snatched the luggage and hopped
onto the step. A moment later he was in his seat, the bundle
beside him.

How long would it be before he had to face the conductor? Among the other passengers in the coach, whose
glances he now avoided, was there anyone who might
recognize or betray him? Frederick Bailey knew the risks.
He had known them when he made his decision.

While this day, Monday, September 3, 1838, had been circled on no visible calendar, it had been marked for weeks in his mind. This train had been chosen, its schedule noted. Even the collaboration of Isaac Rolls, the hackman, had been timed to the second. Escape from slavery was no careless matter. The stakes were tremendous, the penalty for failure brutal. Nobody knew it better than young Fred. He had tried before.

The savage aftermath of that earlier dream of freedom was still hot in his memory, but it was not on this that his mind dwelt as the train sped. Nor had it figured directly in the decision to take today's action. At twenty-one Fred Bailey was sufficiently mature to take a long view of his own adolescent longings and the impetuousness of his nature. But he was not looking backward. As a boy he had tried to jerk himself out of the trap in which he was caught. His aim had been to escape the tortures of slavery on Maryland's Eastern Shore. Now the thing he felt was less a push than a pull.

Slavery still repelled, but his treatment had been much less harsh since he learned the trade of a calker and could be hired out by the day to earn wages for his master. The other calkers with whom he labored in the shipyards, pounding tarred oakum into the seams of vessels under construction and paying the lines over with melted pitch to insure against leaks, were all free men, however, and the inequality between his status and theirs was soon apparent to the new hand. In the yards together they were all calkers, carrying the same tools, walking with the same pride. No ship went down a way till they had done their work. And in the presence of the paymaster at the week's end they were not different one from the other. Fred's wage was a dollar and a half a day like any journeyman calker's. It was after work, in the insubstantial twilight, that the spirit of the slave-laborer was bashed.

While the free men, his partners and companions of the week, returned to their homes and families on Saturday night, Fred Bailey went to a house on Fell Street, knocked on the door of a white man named Hugh Auld and meekly surrendered the nine dollars he had been paid for his toil. On the dark street again, unhurried and scarcely tired at all after the day's exertions, a crushing loneliness suddenly fell on him. Was there any good reason, before God or man, why one calker should be free while another, who could match him by any test of manhood, should be bound? Was it more just for Fred Bailey to give his wages to Hugh Auld than for Hugh Auld to turn his over to Fred Bailey? Surely it was *not* that Hugh Auld was a better man.

Once or twice Fred was tempted to clarify that point by smashing his master's face, but he had tried fighting with his fists before. He didn't care to review that episode with the slave-breaker, even though the outcome had provided a revelation of his own growing manhood. It had failed to win him freedom, and he knew that nothing short of freedom would console him now. So he bowed instead and turned his face from the man inside the doorway.

To purge this insult he attended meetings of the East Baltimore Mental Improvement Society, an association of free Negroes on Fell's Point. It had not been contemplated by the organizers of the group that slaves would be included, but an exception was made in the case of Fred Bailey. He could read and write as well as most of the members. In stature and in general appearance he caught the eye immediately. More important, his speech was excellent, and public address and debating were among the principal activities of the Society. Soon he was taking a prominent, if not a leading, part in the programs of the group. Occasionaly he walked home with a young woman he met at these gatherings. Her name was Anna Murray, and she worked as housekeeper for a well-to-do white family. She appeared to be older than Fred. Like other members of the East Baltimore Mental Improvement Society, other than Fred Bailey, Anna was free, but she promptly fell in love with the deep-voiced copper-colored slave.

Fred's heart melted too, though not enough to cause him to forget the shame of his condition. There is little doubt that Anna was ready to accept him as he was without reservations. But for Fred the passion of the heart was just another element in the growing complication of his life. He would not be drawn into a slave marriage. He pondered a little longer and then narrowed the problem down to a simple formulation. If he could not be completely free, he might just as well be in a pit. If he made a break for it, attempted to escape, two possibilities lay ahead. He might reach Philadelphia, if he were lucky, and move on farther into free territory beyond the reach of the agents of the slave power that operated across the line to bring back fugitives. If he failed, the pit would claim him all right; he would be sold. The next owner would be one accustomed to dealing with unwilling bondsmen. Perhaps it would be a rice planter.

The friends he met in the Society were not prepared to help Fred escape. They willingly shared their knowledge of the problem involved, for many of them were in touch with runaways, but the Free Negro as such had not yet been brought into the fight against slavery. Among the folk of this class were some who went so far as to support the position of the South. A small number were themselves slaveowners. A still smaller group served slaveowners as informers on the activities of dissatisfied bondsmen. Most of them avoided the dangers to themselves of involvement in assisting fugitives. The penalties for this were harsh.

Nevertheless there were always some who were ready to take risks, and the sailor friend who let Fred Bailey borrow his seaman's protection was one. Fred remembered the fellow gratefully as the conductor appeared in the Negro coach. By then the train was nearing Havre de Grace. Fred also recalled, as he blessed his benefactor, that the sailor did not look much like himself. That description on the papers called for a dark Negro. Fred's skin was light brown. His thick hair was incorrigible, but the texture left little doubt that his ancestry was only partly African. A close examination of the subject by the conductor would certainly disclose—

But there he was now, snatching tickets scornfully and growling questions as he examined passengers in front of Fred. When Fred failed to show the obsequiousness expected of passengers in this coach, when he neither hurried nor fumbled for the precious evidence of his right to travel, the conductor's manner suddenly changed. Their eyes met briefly. Fred studied the lines in the man's face. Was he one who might be expected to share the prevailing sentimentality about men who work in ships? Had the popular agitation for "free trade and sailors' rights" left a soft spot in the heart of this railroad man? Fred waited and the shadow of a smile appeared.

"I suppose you have your free papers, sailor."

Fred shook his head. "Never carry my free papers to sea with me, sir."

That seemed to satisfy the conductor. "But you must have something to show you're a free man?"

Fred's smile broadened. "I have a paper that will carry me around the world." He paused, reaching into his deep sailor's pocket. "I have a paper with the American eagle on it," he beamed.

The conductor unfolded the borrowed seaman's protection, gave it a quick glance and then folded it again. "Your ticket?"

Fred Bailey paid his fare, explaining as he did so his failure to buy a ticket in the station. The conductor returned the paper and moved on to the next passenger. And the most anxious moment in the already stormy career of this runaway slave slowly faded. He had no way of knowing, of course, that in the same moment his unique personality was slipping into American history.

Insofar as the escape of Fred Bailey from Maryland slavery was concerned, however, anxious moments did not end at Havre de Grace. A second one followed on the Susquehanna River. Standing among passengers and crew members aboard the ferryboat by which the crossing was made, Fred became aware of persons who might have recognized him had he not been rigged out as a sailor, and at least one fellow, employed as a hand on the boat, was not put off by the disguise. Indeed he was so glad to discover that his old friend was now following the sea he could not pass the opportunity to identify himself and ask a few questions.

How long had Fred been sailing? Where was he going now? How soon did he expect to return? Fred muttered and stammered till he could withdraw, as inoffensively as possible, to another part of the boat. But another kind of fear had arisen now, and it was still with him when he returned to his seat in the coach. There were other people on that train who had seen him before. Would they betray him by misguided friendship as Nichols, the ferryboat hand, had almost done? Fred turned his face toward the window.

A southbound train was standing on the track opposite. Presently it started to move slowly, and a moment later a familiar face floated past. Fred recognized the skipper of a revenue cutter whose vessel he had helped to calk only a few days before. The Captain could scarcely have failed to identify the fugitive had he bothered to look out of his window, but the moment passed and he lost his chance.

A still better opportunity to uphold and sustain the institution of slavery in America was presented to a German blacksmith who happened to be riding the same train on which Fred Bailey was a passenger. Fred saw Frederick Stein, by whom he had once been employed, standing on the platform, and he saw the look of recognition in the man's eyes. Again the familiar Baltimorean was at the doorway of the Negro coach and looking intently at Fred. Why did he stare so hard? And why did he turn away eventually and walk slowly back to his own coach?

"He knew me," Fred almost whispered. "I'm sure he knew me. He saw me running away and held his peace."

But all dangers were not yet passed. Every fugitive knew that the border lines between slavery and freedom were the perilous ones, and the one Fred Bailey dreaded most in the journey between Baltimore and New York was Wilmington. It was here that train passengers took the steamboat for Philadelphia. The change from one to the other would expose him again in a city fairly leaping with slave catchers and kidnappers. But the worst experience he had there was a pounding heart and a tormented mind. He boarded the vessel without incident and when the voyage began, he was calm enough to notice the beauty of the Delaware River and to think of Philadelphia as the Quaker City.

Marcus Hook came into view on the west bank, but Fred Bailey did not know when the steamer left the slave waters of Delaware and entered the untainted stream that belonged to Pennsylvania. It was not till he stepped ashore in the late sunlight that eloquent phrases about freedom began to crowd his mind. Here a man could live "more in one day than a year of . . . slave life." It was the feeling a man might have "upon escape from a den of hungry lions." And the air—yes, that was what all fugitives from slavery discovered—the air itself was different in a free state, unpolluted. "Anguish and grief, like darkness and rain, may be depicted," he composed softly, "but gladness and joy,

like the rainbow, defy the skill of pen or pencil." Fred
Bailey left the wharf walking with great strides.

He paused only long enough to ask a question of a black
man he saw on the street. "How do I get to New York?"

The stranger directed him to the Willow Street depot. A
few hours later Fred bought a ticket and boarded the train
without being asked to show papers that permitted him to
travel.

Not till he had crossed the Hudson River by ferryboat
the next morning and planted his feet on the New York
waterfront did it dawn on the fugitive that the life of freedom had its problems too. Where to go and what to do
were questions now. While fumbling for answers, he
walked. A few hours later he stopped suddenly, a familiar
figure facing him on the sidewalk. The man carried a
whitewash brush and a pail, and Fred recognized the Negro
as a Baltimore slave he had known.

"Jake; Allender's Jake!"

The ex-slave flinched. "I'm William Dixon—*now*," he
whispered.

The flash of recognition was followed by a softer glow
of understanding. Fred recalled a hullabaloo that had followed the escape of Dr. Allender's slave. He remembered
talk about efforts by the Doctor's son to secure the runaway's return. Somehow or other young Tolly Allender had
failed to establish his father's claims of ownership, and Jake
had remained in New York. More exactly, Jake had vanished in New York, and William Dixon, free man, had
begun walking the streets in search of odd jobs.

The whitewasher still showed nervousness. He seemed
eager to get away. Fred blocked his way. Had freedom
made William Dixon jumpy? Where could a newcomer
find a place to stop, something to eat? What about work?

To all these questions Dixon shook his head hopelessly.

No, it wasn't freedom that had broken his nerve. It was the Southerners. New York was full of them right now. They were returning in droves from Saratoga Springs, Lake George and other fashionable watering places in the upper part of the state, and the city as a whole was coddling them disgustingly. A runaway slave was as harried here as he would have been in Baltimore. Spies and kidnappers lurked in every nook and crack. That was why he was not anxious to prolong this conversation. Someone might be watching.

If Fred wanted advice, however, Dixon could give a little. The first thing was to stay away from the waterfront.

But calking was Fred's trade. It was by this work that he hoped to earn his living as a free man.

He would have to change his plans. The shipyards and wharves were among the first places in which a fugitive would be sought. Especially a fugitive who had previously worked in shipyards. Certainly that made sense.

Fred agreed. Equally dangerous to the runaway were all colored boarding houses. Some Negroes had been known to inform on others for a consideration. In a big city like New York you came across all kinds. Slave catchers themselves kept close watch of boarding houses patronized by Negroes. William Dixon hoped all this would explain why he didn't want to be seen talking to a stranger like Fred. Would Fred excuse him?

Fred turned slowly as the poor whitewasher hurried away with his brush and pail. There was nothing he could do now but keep moving. When darkness fell that evening, he was still walking. He had eaten nothing. Despite the warning, he stumbled back toward the wharves, drawn perhaps by the greater familiarity of that part of the city and a vague sense of belonging there. He found a spot among barrels, rested his luggage and went to sleep.

At daybreak the next morning he started again. He had reached the Tombs and paused to look around when a sailor came out of a shack, crossed Center Street and approached Fred. The fellow seemed friendly. Fred decided to ask for help.

The sailor turned out to be a good risk. A few moments later, having listened sympathetically to Fred's story, he opened his door and offered the fugitive the hospitality of his squalid rooms. Fred Bailey took off his shoes and slept in a bed that night for the first time in three days. Early the following morning he went with the sailor to an address on the corner of Lispenard and Church.

At twenty-eight David Ruggles' health was already ruined, his eyesight failing. He had been in the hands of physicians for a year, and by them he had been, in his own words, "bled, leeched, cupped, plastered, blistered, salivated, dosed with arsenic, nux vomica, iodine, strychnine and other poisonous drugs." He had not yet lost all faith in the medical profession, but his trust was wavering. A net result of his treatments to date included "enlargement of his liver, the worst kind of dyspepsia, irritation of the lungs, chronic inflammation of the bowels, piles, nervous and mental debility," and a strange numbness of the skin which left him insensitive to pin pricks and to extreme heat.

None who knew him would deny, however, that his suffering was in a large measure the result of his antislavery activities. The young free Negro was working himself to death in the cause of freedom. As secretary of the New York Committee of Vigilance he seldom rested; his duties included around-the-clock aid to fugitives and free Negroes passing through the city, advice and legal help to slaves and kidnapped persons on ships whose captains were suspected of defying the antislavery laws of New York, the rescuing from jail of free people detained on trumped-up charges with a view to having them claimed as fugitives, fighting a running battle with officials and prominent New Yorkers thought to be assisting the slaveholders of the South, working for the extradition of free black people unjustly held in slave states, and trying to recover property and legacies illegally withheld from blacks. In addition to these stipulated activities of the Committee, in most of which Ruggles was the man who met the enemy, put his foot in the door, stood up to the bullies and did the talking, the secretary had the discouraging job of finding places for meetings. Few halls were avaliable to interracial groups of abolitionists, and the basements which were occasionally secured required much larger fees than for all-white meetings of almost any other character. More often than not the secretary would have to fall back on one of the black churches for the place of assembly. The even more discouraging job of raising funds to keep the work going also rested in part on the shoulders of the secretary. But it never occurred to David Ruggles to complain about the load he carried. Instead he cursed his symptoms and upbraided the doctors who failed to cure him.

Though he fed and clothed and otherwise assisted more than six hundred runaways in the years he lived at Lispenard and Church, Ruggles greeted Fred Bailey as warmly as if the tall stranger were the first to find haven in his house. At the same time the wavering, dimly peering Ruggles made a deep impression on the fugitive. Though the Underground Railroad had been operating for more than a decade, speeding its passengers from one secret station to another, this marked Fred's first contact with an agent of the system. But he didn't have to be told that he had found a friend. The young man's unselfishness, his dedication to the cause of his oppressed brothers were too obvious to question. When the sailor left them, Fred rested his luggage and told his story.

Yes, he was a fugitive, running for his freedom. He was hungry. His money was almost gone. He didn't know where to go. He had set his mind on the shipyards, but now —now it seemed unsafe. Meanwhile, in Baltimore, there was Anna to whom he had promised to write as soon as he reached freedom.

Ruggles listened approvingly. When Fred finished talking, the secretary of the Committee of Vigilance showed him to a room—Fred never said whether it was in the attic, the cellar, or elsewhere in the house—where he could remain hidden a few days, a room reserved for fainting wayfarers, for hunted folk, for the newborn, the infants of freedom. He might, if he wished, direct Anna to this address. Since she was free, no problem was involved.

Fred wrote the letter to Anna. Then a few days passed, days in which Ruggles carried on the routine work of the Committee of Vigilance. Perhaps he also put in a few licks on his pet project of the moment, a *Slaveholders' Directory*, in which he was undertaking to list the names and addresses of all members of the bar, police officers, city marshals, constables and other persons who "lend themselves to kidnapping" in New York City. Fred remained in hiding, of course, but this did not prevent him from learning a good bit about Ruggles' life and character. It was not too long afterward that the fugitive slave wrote, recalling the experience:

> He was a whole-souled man, fully imbued with a love of his afflicted and hunted people, and took pleasure in being to me, as was his wont, "Eyes to the blind, and legs to the lame." This brave and devoted man suffered much from the persecutions common to all who have been prominent benefactors. He at last became blind, and needed a friend to guide him, even as he had been a guide to others.

While the partial blindness which Fred noticed at the time Ruggles befriended him was new and did not become total till later, the life of suffering was already an old story. David Ruggles had been born in Norwich, Connecticut, in

1810. His parents were among the 152 free black people in a total of less than 4,000 in Norwich at that time. It was perhaps in this town, some of whose Negro inhabitants had fought bravely in the Revolutionary War, that he acquired his passion for freedom. His childhood there had been happy. More than four years before he met Fred, when Ruggles was himself in his early twenties, he had written nostalgically of the "by-gone days in New England, the land of steady habits where my happiest hours were spent with my playmates in her schools and in her churches."

Negroes in Norwich worked as domestics, whitewashers, confectioners, sextons, farmers and seamen, but perhaps New York promised more to a boy of seventeen. At any rate it was at that age that David Ruggles made his way to the city. He became a "butter merchant" and later expanded his trade into a full line of groceries. These were of "excellent quality," but even at that date ideology began to complicate the boy's existence. He decided to sell only that sugar that was manufactured by *free people*.

Perhaps it was natural, given such twitchings of conscience, that in 1833 David Ruggles should give up the grocery business in favor of selling subscriptions to *The Emancipator*, the New York antislavery paper. His work thereafter included talks before organizations and groups in Pennsylvania as well as New York an soon projected him into the fight against the colonization movement and on the side of equal rights for Negroes in the free states. His earnings from these labors were inadequate for his needs, however.

In the following year he opened a bookshop and circulated antislavery papers and books while selling stationery and doing job printing, letterpress work, picture framing and book binding. Another service he offered was the composing of letters. Later on he added a reading room, since blacks were excluded from other reading rooms as well as public lectures in the city, and placed current periodicals, tracts and pamphlets within reach of the Negro public at a subscription fee of $2.75 per year, $0.25 per month or $0.0625 per week. But of more concern to him than this income was his aim to provide a "centre of literary attraction for young men whose mental appetites thirst for food" and thus win them away from the "allurement of vice which surrounded them on every side."

An unexpected fire on the premises destroyed the bookshop and closed the reading room after about a year and perhaps served to warn the young proprietor that his activities had come to the attention of proslavery elements in the city. And just two months later at a large mass meeting of "Friends of Human Rights" Ruggles was asked to act as secretary. The meeting was called to consider "measures to ascertain, if possible, the extent to which the cruel practice of kidnapping men, women and children is carried on in this city, and to aid such unfortunate persons as may be in danger of being reduced to slavery in maintaining their rights." A small committee of both whites and blacks was appointed to retain legal counsel and carry out the purposes of the meeting. It was in this way that Ruggles had become the paid executive secretary of the New York Committee of Vigilance and a full-time operator of a key station on the Underground Railroad.

Anna Murray was not blessed with good looks. Nor had she found time or felt an incentive to teach herself to read and wirte. She was a plain dark woman, inclined toward stoutness and accustomed to wearing a bandanna handkerchief about her head. But she possessed a glamour that no slave or ex-slave could fail to recognize. She was free. Her parents, Bambarra and Mary Murray, had achieved freedom in Denton, Maryland, just before her birth, and in her late teens she had left them to find work as a domestic in Baltimore. Since there were eleven other children in the family, four of them younger than herself, her readiness to get away is understandable. The older brothers and sisters remained in slavery.

When she arrived at David Ruggles' place in New York in response to Fred's letter (which had to be read to her), her bundles were enormous, for she had brought along some household furnishings, but her money had run out, as had Fred's. They had nothing with which to pay a preacher or to continue their journey together if that were decided. They had come to the end of their string.

Apparently, however, this was just the kind of situation that stimulated the half-sick, half-blind young man who had given them shelter. The preacher whom Ruggles found to marry them was a Presbyterian named J. W. C. Pennington, himself a fugitive who had been a blacksmith in slavery. The Reverend Pennington was neither surprised nor disappointed to discover that the couple had no money, and, to Fred, "he seemed well-pleased with our thanks." After the ceremony in Ruggles' house, which was also witnessed by a vague Mrs. Mitchell who never reappears in Fred's career, Ruggles slipped a five-dollar bill into the bridegroom's hand.

The point of this gift was, as Ruggles explained, his conviction that New York was not the place for the couple. Fred's trade was calking, and all agreed that he couldn't afford to seek work on the New York waterfront. Slave catchers would snatch him quicker than a cat could wink. New Bedford, on the other hand, was more promising. There was a different attitude toward fugitives there. In New Bedford many ships were fitted out for whaling voyages, and Ruggles was sure that Fred would be able to find work and make a good living. Equally important, there was a colored family there that Ruggles knew, a Mr. and Mrs. Nathan Johnson. He could provide a letter to them, and the Johnsons would help Fred and Anna find work and get settled.

Two days after the marriage Fred and his bride boarded the paddle-wheel steamer *John W. Richmond,* a vessel operating between New York City and Newport, Rhode Island. Since Negro passengers were not allowed in the cabin nor behind the paddle wheels, the two spent the night on the foredeck. But it was not till later that the injustice of this exposure made an impression upon them. Next morning they reached Newport and went ashore with their motley luggage.

A stagecoach came down to the wharf as the steamer docked. Painted on its sides in large yellow letters were the words *New Bedford.* Fred looked at it wistfully, fingering the change that remained from his five dollars. As he hesitated, looking first at Anna and then at the waiting stagecoach and finally at the coins in his hand, he heard a man's voice with a strange inflection. "Thee get in."

Fred didn't quite leap into the waiting stagecoach. He only stepped right fast. All he wanted was a little encouragement, and this direction was it. Anna followed close behind. Then two Quaker gentlemen, one of whom had spoken the words that touched off all this activity, climbed into the coach and introduced themselves. They were Friends William C. Taber and Joseph Ricketson, the latter the proprietor of a candle works in New Bedford, and one glance had been enough to clarify in their minds the predicament of the dark travelers.

Not till the stage reached Stone Bridge and the other passengers went into an Inn for breakfast did the question of fare arise. Fred explained the situation to the driver, paid what he could toward the passage and promised to make up the difference when they reached New Bedford. To his surprise, the driver raised no objection. At New Bedford, however, he calmly set the couple's luggage aside, explaining that he would hold it till they returned with the balance of the fare.

The baggage was soon redeemed, as it happened, because the Nathan Johnsons were kindly old people who responded immediately to the needs of the wayfarers. The Johnsons began by advancing to Fred and Anna the two dollars they needed to put themselves straight with the stagecoach driver. Their generosity did not end till they had made the strangers their guests, provided them with food and lodging and finally bestowed upon the fugitive the new name "Douglass." If this last favor seemed to those concerned "comparatively unimportant," it was because they had no way of knowing that a time would come when it could be said of Frederick Douglass that with the exception of the President and the Vice President of the United States, it was the most widely known name in Washington, D. C.

The naming came about pleasantly, almost on the spur of the moment. Nathan Johnson had been reading Scott's *Lady of the Lake* when the question arose. No free man could publicly carry the name he had borne in slavery. Partly it was a security measure. While Nathan Johnson and his wife gave the newcomers every assurance that Fred would be in no danger of recapture in New Bedford, still a name was a necessity, and Fred and Anna would have to decide how they would like to be known. Fred agreed and related to his host his experiences to date with names.

He had been given by his slave mother a name commensurate with her immodest dream for his future. But Frederick Augustus Washington Bailey soon became an embarrassment to a boy sensitive to ridicule. When he was brought into Baltimore to work in the shipyards, he quietly dropped the two middle names. In New York he had called himself Johnson, and this is the name that appeared on his marriage certificate.

Nathan Johnson took a moment to indicate how many colored Johnsons there were in New Bedford and then urged Fred to spare himself the confusion this situation was already causing. When Fred agreed, the older man suggested the name of Scott's hero about whom he had just been reading with much pleasure and of whom the fugitive somehow reminded him.

And so began the life of Frederick Douglass, free man, resident of New Bedford, age twenty-one.

On March 29, 1839, scarcely more than six months after Nathan Johnson gave him the name, the world began to be aware of Frederick Douglass. It was on that date that the first mention of him appeared in William Lloyd Garrison's *Liberator.* Two years later at least one editor was ready to credit the young fugitive with having given "a fresh impulse to anti-slavery." Another who heard him speak was reminded of Spartacus, the Thracian revolutionary leader. Spartacus too had been a slave. Sold to a school of gladiators in the century before Christ, he had escaped to Mount Vesuvius where he rallied a large force of runaways, struck successful blows against the armies of Rome, caused slaves everywhere to rise in revolt against their masters, sacked many cities, overran all of southern Italy and eventually threw the whole empire into an uproar. Then, in defeat finally, he had won the approbation of history by proving himself more noble than the Romans against whom he fought.

Of course Douglass had done nothing to merit such a comparison. Nor was his gift of oratory as remarkable at that date as some proclaimed. Reading one of his choice early bits now, a satire on a slaveholder's sermon to his slaves, for example, one wonders why Northern audiences were so unfailingly convulsed. The "wit, argument, sarcasm, pathos" that these hearers extolled shine less brightly on the printed page. But perhaps their estimate of the "highly melodious and rich" voice can be accepted along with the compliments so generally paid to his appearance. The young Douglass was undoubtedly a treat to the eye, and there were also other reasons why the abolitionists may be excused for getting excited.

Douglass was the best catch the crusade had made since Wendell Phillips joined it. He was a great public attraction in a movement which, like woman suffrage, temperance and birth control, depended on the pulling power of its proponents. But the young Douglass was more than just good box-office. He actually made converts. It was the opinion of James Russell Lowell that "the very look and bearing of Douglass are an irresistible logic against the oppression of his race." The fact that his public career began with an assignment to raise money for the American Anti-Slavery Society does not imply base motives on the part of the abolitionists.

In the short interval between his own servitude and his brave, David-and-Goliath challenge to all slavery, Douglass had to learn to live as a free man. He had to finish saving himself, for escape from the actual chains was only the first phase of personal emancipation. The next began the fifth day after his arrival in New Bedford.

On Union Street he saw a pile of coal that had been unloaded in front of an attractive home. Douglass was dressed for dirty work, and this seemed to be an opportunity. He went around to the back door and asked the woman in the kitchen if he might put the coal away for her.

"What will you charge?" she asked.

"I'll leave that to you, madam."

She nodded, and Douglass went to work. While the job did not detain him long, he had time to consider and compare standards of life in New Bedford with what he had seen in Maryland. The advantage was overwhelmingly on the side of the Northern city. Both Ruggles and Nathan Johnson had commented on the wealth and prosperity of the city which in that very year was sending out nearly two hundred whalers and bringing in one hundred and sixty thousand barrels of oil, and they had indicated that in proportion to its population New Bedford was probably the richest city in the nation, but these facts surprised Douglass less than an observation he made himself.

The thing he saw was that common working people in New Bedford lived in better, more elegantly furnished and more comfortably and conveniently arranged homes than did the slaveholders of Maryland's Eastern Shore. This was not only true of a house like the one in which he was putting away coal—which incidentally belonged to the Reverend Ephraim Peabody, the Unitarian minister—but applied equally to the dwelling of a colored family like the Johnsons with whom the Douglasses continued to lodge. Nathan Johnson kept a nicer house, set a better table, owned more books, read more newspapers and knew more about public affairs and cultural matters than nine-tenths of the slaveholders in all Talbot County.

When the work was finished, the Reverend Peabody's housekeeper placed two silver half dollars in Douglass's blackened hands, and he drifted away on a cloud. He was never able to describe adequately the emotion he felt after receiving his first wage as a free man. He could not stop blessing the woman who had paid it to him or telling himself that the coins were his—his own—and that the hands that held them were his. Nobody could take his wages away from him. It seemed unreal, but how wonderful! In a sense he had been a free man more than two weeks. Now he was a free *laborer*. This was the crowning glory.

Even a sudden and ironic reversal of fortunes failed to bring his spirit down. Someone mentioned a ship which Rodney French, a wealthy antislavery man, was fitting out for a whaling voyage. A big job of calking and coopering remained to be done on the vessel, work for which Douglass was amply qualified and for which the prevailing wage in New Bedford was two dollars a day. The owner, to whom Fred applied, agreed to hire the newcomer and directed him to the float-stage where the work was in progress. It was here in the shipyard that Douglass learned from the white workers the second and more painful lesson in freedom.

Heads began to wag ominously as he approached the ship. Though no objection was raised in New Bedford when Negro children attended public schools with whites, though a warm and friendly attitude existed toward black people generally, though a Negro who informed on a runaway slave had recently found it advisable to leave town to escape public indignation, and though many of the most influential citizens were outspoken advocates of the slave's cause, another attitude—less talked about in public, pehaps came to the surface when Douglass met the white men of his trade in the shipyard. He couldn't work there as a calker, they informed him bluntly. He couldn't do any skilled work on French's vessel or any other. If he struck one blow at his trade, every white man engaged on the ship would walk off and leave it unfinished. They had no personal objection to the black man, but he would have to do unskilled work for which the wage was one dollar a day instead of two.

Douglass was shocked, of course, but not as much as he might have been except for the savage enormities of slavery from which he had escaped. He accepted unskilled work for Rodney French and continued to rejoice in his freedom. The discrimination bothered him no more than that which he later discovered in the New Bedford Lyceum, which refused to admit Negroes to lectures in its hall. It was just an unpleasantness and a reminder that there were new strug-

gles for the black man beyond emancipation. It was something like slavery but it wasn't slavery, and the battles—
well, they did not seem impossible. Indeed the time soon
came when the Lyceum changed its policy, thanks to
Charles Sumner, Theodore Parker, Ralph Waldo Emerson
and Horace Mann, all of whom refused to appear in the
lecture courses from which Negroes were excluded. But
Douglass lived long enough to acquire new insights into
the problems involved in his shipyard experience in New
Bedford and to learn why it was that the fight for equality
in employment opportunities for free Negroes was bound
to be a long and bitter one.

Other unskilled jobs followed. Douglass shoveled more
coal, dug cellars, moved rubbish from back yards, loaded
and unloaded vessels on the wharves, scoured the cabins
of ships and sawed wood. There was plenty of odd work at
that season, especially wood to be sawed, for seagoing
whalers stored a great deal of it before putting out. Douglass borrowed a frame saw and a buck from Nathan Johnson and began wrestling with logs. When the frame that
held the saw weakened as a result of heavy use, he went
into a general store to buy cord with which to brace it.

How much cord did he want?

Douglass shrugged. The smallest amount certainly. "A
fip's worth, say."

The clerk spun around sharply. "You don't belong
around here."

Douglass was as much terrified by the man's tone as his
words. Had he said something wrong? Had he betrayed
himself to a slave catcher or an informer? He stood erect
and tried to hide his alarm. Presently he noticed a change
of expression on the face of the man behind the counter.
The storekeeper explained. The Maryland "fip" or "fip-
enny-bit," valued at six and a quarter cents, was called

fourpence in New England. A considerable relief for Douglass followed this moment.

Odd jobs could be found in New Bedford, if you looked
for them, but it did not take Douglass many weeks to
realize that much time was lost when one had to find a new
job every day or two and that the uncertainty of not having
steady, continuing employment was a drag on the mind.
The prices of food and clothes seemed outrageously high.
Anna's efforts were a help, even though she became preg-
nant almost immediately, but she too found only day's
work in domestic service at first, and the life of freedom
was never easy that winter.

It took an encouraging turn later on, however, as a result of another meeting with Joseph Ricketson, one of the
two Quakers who had spoken to Fred and Anna on the
wharf at Newport and then ridden into New Bedford with
them at the time of their arrival. This time Ricketson
offered the young man temporary work in the oil refinery
of his candle works. Douglass accepted readily and was in
turn accepted by the other men employed in the establishment, even though all the rest were white. Perhaps the fact
that his duties called for much lifting of large casks of oil
had something to do with their attitude, but this failed to
trouble Douglass. He was a young giant.

When he was no longer needed in the oil refinery of
Ricketson's candle works, Douglass returned to the waterfront for another spell as laborer on vessels under repair,
and this led to a steady job in a nearby brass foundry which
specialized in shipwork. His foundry work involved blowing the bellows, swinging the crane and emptying flasks in
which castings were made. In this situation, according to
Douglass, he was on several occasions indebted to a foreman named Cobb for protecting him from "abuse that one
or more of the hands were disposed to throw upon me." By

this time, however, an outsider might have been justified in asking if Douglass himself were not partly to blame.

The flight to freedom had been a tremendous emotional experience to a high-strung youth who had passed through extreme tortures of slavery. Douglass's life in bondage had been no ordinary servitude. Parker Pillsbury, hearing the details a year or two later, called it a "terrible apocalypse." Perhaps some emotional sag was to be expected. Marks of the ordeal must have remained on his personality for a while at least. Douglass had been a problem slave, and at the brass foundry that pattern seemed about to be repeated when the foreman intervened.

By that time, too, another element had been introduced into the life of the fugitive. A young man came around selling subscriptions to William Lloyd Garrison's *Liberator*. Douglass tried to ged rid of the agent. When the fellow persisted, he had to reveal that he had just escaped from slavery and was still hard pressed to earn enough money to support himself and his wife. On the strength of this the young man decided to enter a subscription for the foundry worker without payment of the fee.

Douglass was entranced by Garrison's paper. Not only did he pour over it in his spare time at home, but at the foundry he devised ways of propping a copy before him as he worked the bellows. The picturesque denunciations of oppressors, the passionate cries for human brotherhood, the rebukes to hypocrisy in church and state, the undercurrent of solemnity—everything about the *Liberator* stirred Douglass's blood. Garrison became his teacher, his hero, his idol. When he finished with a copy of the *Liberator,* its contents had been practically memorized.

How this new zeal affected Douglass's work and his home life can only be surmised, but he left no doubt that Garrisonianism promptly became his religion. In a very short time he had a clear understanding of the principles of the

Anti-Slavery movement. He learned about antislavery meetings of Negroes in New Bedford and attended, leaning forward eagerly in his seat as the speakers paced the platform, weighed arguments carefully and broke into strong applause when a telling point was made. The enlightenment of these Negroes, compared to those he had known in slavery, was a revelation that filled Douglass with pride. But he took no leading part. He was satisfied to listen and to follow their deliberations approvingly. It was thus that on March 12, 1839, he was present at the Christian Church to add his name to the list of those who adopted a resolution condemning slavery and African colonization and praising Garrison "as deserving of our support and confidence." Three weeks later the event was noted in the columns of the *Liberator*.

Less than two weeks after the *Liberator* carried this news note Garrison himself came to New Bedford to lecture, and Douglass was in the audience sitting well back in the gallery of the old Liberty Hall. The place was dilapidated and in bad odor. It had long been deserted for other purposes, but it was the only auditorium in New Bedford in which antislavery meetings of mixed audiences could be held. Douglass noticed the defaced woodwork, the unhinged doors, the broken glass of the windows and the smears left on the walls by bad eggs with which such gatherings had occasionally been pelted. But the condition of the hall and the evidence of stormy sessions in behalf of freedom only served to sharpen his perceptions. It all seemed in keeping. The setting was right.

The speaker was right too. When the thirty-three year old Garrison took the platform, Douglass was convinced that "the hour and the man were well met and well united." In Garrison, as he appeared to the youthful fugitive, "there was no contradiction between the speech and the speaker, but absolute sympathy and oneness. The faces of millions of men might be searched without finding one just like his." It was a "singularly pleasing countenance" in which Douglass saw "the resurrection and the life of the dead and buried hopes of my enslaved people." Such earnestness and depth of feeling as Garrison exhibited seemed more than remarkable in a man of his age.

Garrison's style of address did not strike Douglass as eloquent. The words were not fancy, and there was nothing about his sentences that called attention to themselves. The effectiveness of the speech came from Garrison's inner fire, his stern principles, his insistence on "sinless perfection." Not only was Sunday a Sabbath, he held, "but all days were Sabbaths, and to be kept holy." Sectarianism was "false and mischievous—the regenerated throughout the world being members of one body." Ministers who defended slavery were sons of the devil. Churches that welcomed slaveholders were synagogues of satan. Color prejudice was rebellion against God. Our nation was a nation of liars for upholding the institution of slavery.

Douglass was thrilled. It seemed to him that Garrison was uttering "the spontaneous feeling of my own heart." He was so transported by the ideas and the personality of the speaker, in fact, that the next two years of his life passed in a kind of blur. From his own account one would think that nothing happened between that April evening in 1839 and the summer of 1841.

Actually, of course, things did occur, and at least two of them cannot have escaped his notice, despite the dazzling light and wonderful excitement of intellectual awakening. It was during this time that their first two children were born to Anna and Frederick Douglass, Rosetta in June of 1839 and Lewis sixteen months later. Between these events Anna continued to supplement the family earnings by day's work over washtubs or at housecleaning, and Fred kept his job at the brass foundry.

He also heard other speeches at Liberty Hall and continued to attend antislavery meetings held by Negroes in the city. By June 30, 1841, he had become a leader in this group. On that date he served as chairman of a meeting called to censor the Maryland Colonization Society for threatening to remove free colored people from that state by force. Douglass's group urged the Maryland folk to stand firm and not let themselves be pushed around. The meeting also took note of another assault on the sickly, half-blind David Ruggles. He had been roughly handled on the steamboat between New York and Nantucket when he defied the segregation policy. Douglass and his New Bedford friends condemned the attack in a resolution which later turned up in the columns of the *Liberator*.

Garrison returned to New Bedford six weeks later to attend the annual meeting of the Bristol Anti-Slavery Society, and Douglass went back to Liberty Hall to listen to his hero. Again he was not disappointed. Garrison's words touched something in Douglass that vibrated like a violin string. But by now Garison was more than just a mouthpiece uttering thunderous words. To Douglass he was the very soul of protest.

Here was the young crusader who had been thrown into a Baltimore jail for accusing a shipowner of carrying slaves in his vessel, who ten years ago, while still in his twenties, had begun publishing the *Liberator* in a dingy third-floor room in Boston, setting the old secondhand type himself and running it on a press he had bought at a bargain. Here was the American who for his convictions had been dragged through Boston streets and with a rope tied around his neck and for whose arrest and conviction the state of Georgia was ready to pay $5,000. He it was who had given words to ageless human agony when he put the following paragraph in the first issue of his paper:

> I am aware that many object to the severity of my language; but is there not cause for severity? I *will be* as harsh as truth, and as uncompromising as justice. On this subject, I do not wish to think, or speak with moderation. No! No! Tell a man whose house is on fire to give a moderate alarm; tell him to moderately rescue his wife from the hands of the ravisher; tell the mother to gradually extricate her babe from the fire into which it has fallen;—but urge me not to use moderation in a cause like the present. I am in earnest— I will not equivocate—I will not excuse—I will not retreat a single inch—AND I WILL BE HEARD.

On this day, however, Douglass did more than listen with tingling spine. The meeting was thrown open for discussion, and the twenty-four-year-old Douglass stood up. Somehow he had begun to feel that he too must be heard. His words on this occasion are not preserved, but in the report of the meeting which Garrison sent back to the *Liberator,* he took occasion to mention "several talented young men from New Bedford, one of them formerly a slave whose addresses were listened to by large and attentive audiences with deep interest."

Perhaps Garrison missed hearing all the names. That made no difference to Douglass. He didn't expect anybody present to know his name. But the following day when a group of forty abolitionists from New Bedford, including both whites and Negroes, decided to go along with Garrison and other leaders to a convention at Nantucket, Douglass began to think that this was a good time for him to take a short vacation. He had not had one since he came to New Bedford. With no other thought in mind, he followed the delegation down to the dock where the steamboat *Telegraph* waited.

When all the abolitionists were aboard, however, the

Captain announced that the vessel would not move till the Negroes in the group went to the segregated quarters provided for them. This was the wrong group to which to make that kind of suggestion. The passengers included not only Garrison but William C. Coffin, New Bedford's leading abolitionist. Some of the delegates promptly left the boat in disgust. The rest decided to argue. After long and heated contention a compromise was reached. *All* the abolitionists would go to the quarters designated for blacks. This arrangement turned out to offer unexpected advantages. It gave the group a fine chance to hold a spirited antislavery, antisegregation meeting under the chairmanship of Francis Jackson during the sixty-mile voyage.

It also keyed them up for the meetings in Athenaeum Hall in Nantucket that evening and the next morning. The evening meeting as it happened was not remarkable, but at the morning session Coffin was struck by a sudden hunch. The statuesque fugitive—why not bring him to the platform to speak for the New Bedford delegation? He located Douglass in the back of the auditorium and whispered the suggestion to him.

Douglass was reluctant. He hadn't expected to talk. Leading Anti-Slavery people from several states were there. What could he say to these educated people, these public figures? Coffin insisted. He had heard Douglass. He was sure the convention would enjoy the story of his life in bondage. Douglass began trembling, but finally he agreed to say a few words if called upon. A few moments later Coffin led him to the platform and introduced him as a delegate whose diploma was written on his back.

Douglass felt his knees knocking together, his hands shaking and his mouth constricted as he began to talk.

II

SONG OF THE SON

I WAS BORN in Tuckahoe, in Talbot County, Maryland. I have no accurate knowledge of my age. By far the larger part of the slaves know as little of their ages as horses know of theirs. I do not remember to have ever met a slave who could tell of his birthday. They seldom come nearer to it than planting-time, harvest-time, cherry-time, spring-time or fall-time. The nearest estimate I can give makes me now between twenty-three and twenty-four. I come to this from hearing my master say sometime during 1835 I was about seventeen years old."

Gradually he gained confidence before the audience in the crowded hall. Soon his voice took on a rather remarkable quality. It was a strong voice with an organlike range and many natural shadings, a voice which could be described in different ways by people who heard it on the same occasion. No one there, however, and no one who heard it afterward, ever left the smallest doubt that there was something special about it. Few failed to note the strange melancholy which it awakened.

His bearing was equally striking. Some of those present noticed his hair. It was long, but neither straight nor wooly. Others regarded his head, his eyes, his stature. A British woman novelist, visiting in the United States, perhaps summed up their comments when she said, "I found him to be a light mulatto . . . with an unusually handsome exterior, such as I imagine should belong to an Arab chief. Those beautiful eyes . . ."

He spoke extemporaneously of course, but he had probably told his experience before and he certainly told it many times afterward, so many times in fact that he was finally persuaded, two or three years later, to write it down just as he was in the habit of telling it; and the testimony of those who read it and of those who heard it at Nantucket that day is that it was essentially the same story.

"My mother was named Harriet Bailey. She was the daughter of Isaac and Betsey Bailey, both colored and quite dark. My mother was of a darker complexion than either my grandmother and grandfather.

"My father was a white man. He was admitted to be such by all I ever heard speak of my parentage. My mother and I were separated when I was but an infant. It is a common custom in the part of Maryland from which I ran away to part children from their mothers at a very early age. Frequently before the child has reached its twelfth month it is placed under the care of an old woman too old for field labor.

"I never saw my mother to know her more than four or five times in my life, and each of these times was very short in duration and at night. She was hired by a Mr. Stewart who lived about twelve miles from my home. She made her journeys to see me in the night, traveling the whole distance on foot after the performance of her day's work. She was a field hand, and a whipping is the penalty for not being in the field at sunrise. I do not recollect of ever seeing my mother by the light of day. She was with me in the night. She would lie down with me and get me to sleep, but long before I waked she was gone. Very little communication

ever took place between us. She died when I was about
seven years old. I was not allowed to be present during her
illness, at her death or burial. Never having enjoyed her
soothing presence to any considerable extent, I received the
tidings of her death with much the same emotions I should
have felt at the death of a stranger.

"She left me without the slightest intimation of who my
father was. Slaveholders have ordained that the children of
slaves shall in all cases follow the condition of their
mothers. This is done to administer to their own lusts and
make a gratification of their desires profitable as well as
pleasurable. By this cunning arrangement the slaveholder,
in cases not a few, sustains to his slaves the double relation
of master and father.

"Such slaves are a constant offence to their mistress. She
is never better pleased than when she sees them under the
lash, especially when she suspects her husband of showing
to his mulatto children favors which he withholds from
his black slaves. The master is frequently compelled to sell
this class of his slaves out of deference to the feelings of his
white wife. Unless he does this, he must not only whip
them himself but must stand by and see one white son tie
up his brother of but a few shades darker complexion than
himself.

"I have had two masters. My first master's name was
Anthony. I do not remember his first name. He was called
Captain Anthony, a title which I presume he acquired by
sailing a craft on the Chesapeake Bay. He was not considered a rich slaveholder. He owned two or three farms
and about thirty slaves. His farms and slaves were under
the care of an overseer. The overseer's name was Plummer.
Mr. Plummer was a miserable drunkard, a profane swearer
and a savage monster. I have known him to cut and slash
the women's heads so horribly that even master would be
enraged at his cruelty and would threaten to whip him if

he did not mind himself. Master, however, was not a humane slaveholder. It required extraordinary barbarity on the part of an overseer to affect him. He was a cruel man hardened by a long life of slaveholding. He would at times seem to take great pleasure in whipping a slave. I have often been awakened at the dawn of day by the most heart-rending shrieks of an own aunt of mine whom he used to tie up to a joist and whip upon her naked back till she was covered with blood. No words, no tears, no prayers from his victim seemed to move his iron heart. The louder she screamed, the harder he whipped. Where the blood ran fastest, there he whipped longest. He would whip her to make her scream and whip her to make her hush. I remember the first time I ever witnessed this exhibition. I was quite a child, but I well remember it. It was the blood-stained gate, the entrance to the hell of slavery through which I was about to pass.

"It took place soon after I went to live with my old master. Aunt Hester went out one night and happened to be absent when my master desired her presence. He had warned her that she must never let him catch her in company with a young man who was paying attention to her. The young man's name was Ned Roberts, generally called Lloyd's Ned. She was a woman of noble form and of graceful proportions, having few equals in personal appearance among the colored or white women of our neighborhood.

"Aunt Hester had not only disobeyed his orders in going out but had been found in company with Lloyd's Ned. I learned this from what he said while whipping her. Before he commenced whipping Aunt Hester, he took her into the kitchen and stripped her from neck to waist. After crossing her hands he tied them with a strong rope and led her to a stool under a large hook in the joist put in for the purpose. He made her get upon the stool and tied her hands to the hook. Her arms were stretched up at their full length so that she stood upon the ends of her toes. He then said to her, 'Now you unmentionable, I'll learn you how to disobey my orders!' After rolling up his sleeves he commenced to lay on the heavy cowskin, and soon the warm, red blood came dripping to the floor. I was so terrified and horror-stricken that I hid myself in a closet. It was all new to me. I had always lived with my grandmother on the outskirts of the plantation where she was put to raise the children of the younger women.

"My master's family consisted of two sons, Andrew and Richard; one daughter, Lucretia, and her husband, Captain Thomas Auld. They lived in one house upon the home plantation of Colonel Edward Lloyd. My master was Colonel Lloyd's clerk and superintendent. He was what might be called the overseer of the overseers. I spent two years of childhood on this plantation in my old master's family, and as I received my first impressions of slavery on this plantation, I will give some description of it and of slavery as it there existed. The plantation is about twelve miles north of Easton, on the border of Miles River. The principal products raised upon it were tobacco, corn and wheat. With the products of this and other farms belonging to him Colonel Lloyd was able to keep in almost constant use a large sloop in carrying them to market at Baltimore. This sloop was named the *Sally Lloyd* in honor of one of the colonel's daughters. My master's son-in-law, Captain Auld, was master of the vessel. She was otherwise manned by the colonel's own slaves Peter, Isaac, Rich and Jake. These were esteemed very highly by the other slaves and looked upon as the privileged ones. It was no small affair in the eyes of the slaves to be allowed to see Baltimore.

"Colonel Lloyd kept from three to four hundred slaves on his home plantation and owned a large number more on the neighboring farms belonging to him. The overseers

of these farms received advice and direction from the managers of the home plantation. This was the great business
place. It was the seat of government for the whole twenty
farms. All disputes among the overseers were settled here.
If a slave was convicted of any high misdemeanor or
evinced a determination to run away, he was brought immediately here, whipped, put on the sloop, carried to Baltimore and sold to Austin Woolfolk or some other slave
trader.

"The home plantation of Colonel Lloyd wore the
appearance of a country village. All the mechanical operations for all the farms were performed here. The shoemak-
ing and mending, the blacksmithing, cartwrighting, coopering, weaving and graingrinding wcrc all pcrformcd by
slaves on the home plantation. It was called by the slaves
the Great House Farm. Few privileges were esteemed
higher than that of being selected to do errands at the
Great House Farm. A representative could not be prouder
of his election to a seat in the American Congress than a
slave on one of the out-farms would be of his election to do
errands at the Great House Farm. The competitors for this
office sought as diligently to please their overseers as the
office seekers in the political parties seek to please and
deceive the people. The same traits of character might be
seen in Colonel Lloyd's slaves as are seen in the slaves of
the political parties.

"The slaves selected to go to the Great House Farm for
the monthly allowance for themselves and their fellow-
slaves were peculiarly enthusiastic. While on their way they
would make the dense old woods for miles around rever-
berate with their wild songs, revealing at once the highest
joy and the deepest sadness. Into all their songs they would
manage to weave something of the Great House Farm.

> I am going away to the Great House Farm!
> O, Yea! O, Yea! O!

I have sometimes thought that the mere hearing of those songs would do more to impress some minds with the horrible character of slavery than the reading of whole volumes of philosophy on the subject.

"I did not when a slave understand the deep meaning of those rude songs. I was myself within the circle. I neither saw nor heard as those without might see and hear, but those songs still follow me, and I have been astonished since I came to the North to find persons who could speak of the singing among slaves as evidence of their contentment and happiness. Slaves sing most when they are most unhappy. The songs of the slaves represent the sorrows of his heart. He is relieved by them as an aching heart is relieved by its tears. I have often sung to drown my sorrow but seldom to express my happiness.

"My own treatment while I lived on Colonel Lloyd's plantation was similar to that of other slave children. The most I had to do was to drive up the cows at evening, keep the fowls out of the garden, keep the front yard clean and run errands for my old master's daughter, Mrs. Lucretia Auld. Most of my leisure time I spent helping Master Daniel Lloyd in finding his birds after he had shot them. Master Daniel became quite attached to me and was a sort of protector. He would not allow the older boys to impose upon me and would divide his cakes with me.

"I was seldom whipped by old master and suffered little [except] from hunger and cold. I suffered much from hunger but much more from cold. In hottest summer and coldest winter I was kept almost naked, nothing on but a coarse tow linen shirt reaching only to my knees. I must have perished with cold but that the coldest nights I used to steal a bag which was used for carrying corn to the mill. I would crawl into this bag and there sleep on the cold clay floor with my head in and my feet out.

"I was probably between seven and eight years old when

I left Colonel Lloyd's plantation. I shall never forget the
joy with which I received the information that my old
master Captain Anthony had determined to let me go to
Baltimore to live with Mr. Hugh Auld, brother to his son-
in-law, Captain Thomas Auld. I received this about three
days before my departure. I spent the most of these three
days in the creek washing off the plantation scurf and preparing myself for my departure. I spent the time in washing not so much because I wished to but because Mrs.
Lucretia had told me I must get all the dead skin off my
feet and knees before I could go to Baltimore, for the
people in Baltimore were very cleanly and would laugh at
me if I looked dirty. Besides, she was going to give me a
pair of trousers which I should not put on unless I got all
the dirt off me. The thought of owning a pair of trousers
was great indeed. It was almost sufficient to make me take
off the skin itself.

"I had the strongest desire to see Baltimore. Cousin Tom
had inspired me with that desire by his description of the
place. I could never point out anything at the Great House,
no matter how beautiful or powerful, but that he had
seen something in Baltimore far exceeding it. We sailed
out of Miles River on a Saturday morning. In the afternoon
of that day we reached Annapolis. It was the first large
town that I had ever seen. I thought it a wonderful place,
more imposing even than the Great House Farm.

"We arrived at Baltimore early on Sunday morning. We
had on board the sloop a large flock of sheep, and after aid-
ing in driving them to the slaughter house on Slater's Hill
I was conducted by Rich to my new home in Alliciana
Street, near Gardner's shipyard on Fells Point. Mr. and
Mrs. Auld met me at the door with their little son Thomas,
to take care of whom I had been given. And here I saw
what I had never seen before: a white face beaming with
the most kindly emotions. It was the face of my new mistress,

Sophia Auld, and it was a new strange sight to me. Little
Thomas was told [that here] was his Freddy. I was to take
care of little Thomas.

"My new mistress proved to be all she appeared when I
met her at the door, a woman of the kindest heart and finest
feelings. She had never had a slave under her control previously to myself. Prior to her marriage she had been dependent upon her own industry for a living. She was by
trade a weaver. I was astonished at her goodness. I scarcely
knew how to behave towards her. The crouching servility,
usually so acceptable in a slave, seemed to disturb her.

"Very soon after I went to live with Mr. and Mrs. Auld
she commenced to teach me the A, B, C's. After I had
learned these, she assisted me in learning to spell words of
three or four letters. At this point of my progress, Mr. Auld
found out what was going on and at once forbade Mrs.
Auld to instruct me further, telling her among other things
that it was unlawful as well as unsafe to teach a slave to
read. It would make him discontented and unhappy. These
words sank deep into my heart and called into existence an
entirely new train of thought. I now understood the white
man's power to enslave the black man. From that moment
I understood the pathway from slavery to freedom, and I
set out with high hope and a fixed purpose, at whatever
cost of trouble, to learn how to read. Thus in learning to
read I owe almost as much to the opposition of my master
as to the aid of my mistress. I acknowledge the benefit of
both.

"I lived in Master Hugh's family about seven years. During this time I succeeded in learning to read and write.
[Meanwhile] slavery proved as injurious to [my mistress]
as it did to me. When I went there, she was a pious, warm
and tender-hearted woman. Slavery divested her of these
qualities. The first step downward was in her ceasing to instruct me. She finally became even more violent in her op-

position than her husband. Nothing seemed to make her more angry than to see me [reading]. I have had her rush at me with a face made all up of fury and snatch from me a newspaper.

"From this time I was most narrowly watched. If I was in a separate room any considerable time, I was sure to be suspected of having a book and was at once called to give an account. All this, however, was too late. Mistress, in teaching me the alphabet, had given me the inch, and no precaution could prevent me from taking the ell.

"The plan which I adopted and the one by which I was most successful was that of making friends of all the little white boys whom I met in the street. As many of these as I could I converted into teachers. With their aid, obtained at different times and in different places, I finally learned to read. When I was sent on errands, I always took my book with me and by going one part of my errand quickly I found time to get a lesson before my return. I used also to carry bread with me—enough of which was always in the house, and to which I was always welcome, for I was much better off in this regard than many of the poor white children in our neighborhood. This bread I used to bestow upon the hungry little urchins who in return would give me that more valuable bread of knowledge. I used to talk this matter of slavery over with them. I would sometimes say to them that I wished I could be as free as they would be when they got to be men. These words used to trouble them. They would express sympathy and console me with the hope that something would occur by which I might be free.

"I was now about twelve years old, and the thought of being a slave for life began to bear heavily upon my heart. Just about this time I got hold of a book entitled *The Columbian Orator*. Every opportunity I got I used to read this book. Among much of other interesting matter I found in it a dialogue between a master and his slave. The slave was represented as having run away from his master three times. The dialogue represented the conversation which took place between them when the slave was retaken the third time. The whole argument in behalf of slavery was brought forward by the master. All of it was disposed of by the slave.

"In the same book I met with one of Sheridan's speeches in behalf of Catholic emancipation. These were choice to me. I read them over and over again. The more I read the more I was led to abhor and detest my enslavers. I could regard them in no other light than a band of robbers who had left their homes and gone to Africa and stolen us from our homes and in a strange land reduced us to slavery. I loathed them as the meanest as well as the most wicked of men. As I read I would at times feel that learning to read had been a curse rather than a blessing. It had given me a view of my wretched condition without the remedy. In moments of agony I envied my fellow-slaves for their stupidity. I have often wished myself a beast. Anything, no matter what, to get rid of thinking! It was this everlasting thinking on my condition that tormented me.

"I often found myself regretting my own existence and wishing myself dead, and but for the hope of being free I have no doubt that I should have killed myself or done something for which I should have been killed. While in this state of mind I was eager to hear anyone speak of slavery. Every little while I heard something about the abolitionists. It was some time before I found what the word meant.

"The light broke my degrees. I went one day down on the wharf. Seeing two Irishmen unloading a scow of stone, I went unasked and helped them. When we finished, one of them came to me and asked me if I were a slave. I told him I was. He asked, 'Are ye a slave for life?' I told him that I

was. The good Irishman seemed to be deeply affected by
the statement. He said to the other that it was a pity so fine
a little fellow as myself should be a slave for life. They
both advised me to run away to the North, that I should
find friends there and that I should be free. I pretended not
to be interested in what they said and treated them as if I
did not understand, for I feared they might be treacherous.
White men have been known to encourage slaves to escape
and then to get the reward by catching and returning them
to their masters. I was afraid of this, but I remembered
their advice. I was too young to think of escaping immediately and besides I wished to learn to write, since I might
have to write my own pass. I consoled myself with the hope
that I should one day find a good chance. Meanwhile I
would learn to write.

"The idea as to how I might learn to write was suggested
to me in the shipyard [where I saw] ship carpenters after
hewing and getting a piece of timber ready for use write
on the timber the name of that part of the ship for which
it was intended. When a piece of timber was for the larboard side, it would be marked 'L.' For the starboard side
it would be marked 'S.' Starboard side forward would be
'S. F.' Larboard aft, 'L. A.' I soon learned the names of
these letters and for what they were intended. I immediately commenced copying them. After that when I met with
any boy who could write, I would tell him I could write as
well as he. I would make the letters and ask him to beat
that. My copy book was the board fence, brick wall and
pavement. My pen and ink a lump of chalk. With these and
in this way I learned. By this time my little Master Thomas
had gone to school and learned to write and had filled a
number of copy books. These had been brought home.
When left alone I used to spend the time in writing in the
spaces left in Master Thomas's copy book, copying what he
had written. Thus I finally succeeded in learning to write.

"After I went to live in Baltimore, my old master's youngest son Richard died. After his death my old master Captain Anthony died, leaving only his son Andrew and daughter Lucretia to share his estate. He left no will as to the disposal of his property. It was therefore necessary to have a valuation of the property that it might be divided between Mrs. Lucretia and Master Andrew. I was sent for to be valued with the other property. I took passage in the schooner *Wild Cat* and after about twenty-four hours found myself near the place of my birth.

"We were all ranked together at the valuation. There were horses and men, cattle and women, pigs and children, all holding the same rank in the scale of being. After the valuation, then came the division. Our fate for life was now to be decided. In addition to the pain of separation there was the horrid dread of falling into the hands of Master Andrew. He was known to us all as being a most cruel wretch who had already wasted a large portion of his father's property. We all felt that we might as well be sold at once to the Georgia traders as to pass into his hands, for we knew that that would follow.

"I fell into the portion of Mrs. Lucretia and was sent immediately back to Baltimore to live again in the family of Master Hugh. It was a glad day for me. Very soon after my return to Baltimore my mistress Lucretia died leaving her husband and one child, and in a very short time after her death Master Andrew died. Now all the property of my old master, slaves included, was in the hands of strangers, strangers who had had nothing to do with accumulating it. Not a slave was left free. If any one thing in my experience more than another served to deepen my conviction of the infernal character of slavery and to fill me with loathing of slaveholders it was their base ingratitude to my poor grandmother.

"She had served my old master faithfully from youth to

old age. She had been the source of all his wealth. She had
peopled his plantation with slaves. She had become a great-
grandmother in his service. She had rocked him in infancy,
attended him in childhood, served him through life and at
his death wiped from his brow the death sweat and closed
his eyes forever. She was nevertheless left a slave—a slave
for life—a slave in the hands of strangers. And in their
hands she saw her children, her grandchildren and her
great-grandchildren divided like sheep without being grati-
fied with the privilege of a single word as to their or her
destiny. To cap the climax of their base ingratitude and
fiendish barbarity, my grandmother, who was now very old,
having outlived my old master and all his children, having
seen the beginning and end of all of them, her present owners finding she was of little value, her frame already racked
with the pains of old age, complete helplessness fast stealing
over her once active limbs, they took her to the woods,
built her a little hut, put up a little mud-chimney and
then made her welcome to the privilege of supporting herself there in perfect loneliness. Thus they turned her out
to die. If my poor old grandmother now lives, she lives to
suffer in utter loneliness.

"The hearth is desolate. The children, the unconcious
children, who once sang and danced in her presence are
gone. She gropes her way in the darkness of age for a drink
of water. Instead of the voices of her children she hears by
day the moans of the dove and by night the screams of the
hideous owl. All is gloom. The grave is at the door. And
now, when weighed down by the pains and aches of old age,
when the head inclines to the feet, when the beginning and
ending of human existence meet and helpless infancy and
painful old age combine together—at this time, this most
needful time, the time for the exercise of that tenderness
and affection which children only can exercise toward a declining parent—my poor old grandmother, the devoted

mother of twelve children, is left all alone in yonder little hut before a few dim embers. She stands—she sits—she staggers—she falls! She groans—she dies. And there are none of her children or grandchildren present to place beneath the sod her fallen remains. Will not a righteous God visit for these things?"

Before Douglass could leave the platform, thunder broke in Athenaeum Hall. In a moment the Abolitionists were beside themselves. In the midst of the uproar Garrison sprang to his feet. "Is this a man or a *thing?*" he shouted.

"A MAN! A MAN!" they boomed in a deafening chorus.

What miracle was this? The noblest slave of them all had escaped the black dungeon to plead the cause of his brothers. The convention was overcome with emotion. But Douglass hadn't finished his story, Garrison reminded them. Though the meeting had run overtime, he hadn't yet brought them to the time of his escape. Would they like to ask him to continue it at the evening session? Of course, they would.

Word spread quickly in Nantucket. A wonder had happened. A bigger crowd came that night and jammed every inch of standing room. The abolitionists could scarcely wait for Douglass to resume his story. When he took the platform again, they did not wait to applaud and demonstrate. They started in immediately and kept it up throughout the evening, causing him to interrupt himself frequently and wait for the cheering to subside. It was all most encouraging to an inexperienced speaker, and his delivery improved as his confidence grew. Once or twice he even indulged his talent for mimicry and thereby provoked waves of laughter.

"About two years after the death of Mrs. Lucretia, Master Thomas married his second wife," be began calmly. "Master now lived in St. Michael's. Not long after his marriage a misunderstanding took place between himself and

Master Hugh. As a means of punishing his brother, he took me from him to live with himself at St. Michael's. I sailed from Baltimore in the sloop *Amanda*. On my passage I paid attention to the direction which the steamboats took to go to Philadelphia. I found that instead of going down on reaching North Point they went up the bay in a north-easterly direction. My determination to run away was revived. I resolved to wait only so long as the offering of a favorable opportunity.

"It was now more than seven years since I lived with Master Thomas Auld on Colonel Lloyd's plantation. We were now almost entire strangers to each other. He was to me a new master and I to him a new slave. A very short time brought us into full acquaintance with each other, however. I was made acquainted with his wife not less than with himself. They were equally mean and cruel. Not to give a slave enough to eat is regarded as the most aggravated development of meanness among slaveholders. Master Thomas gave us enough of neither coarse nor fine food. There were four slaves of us in the kitchen, my sister Eliza, my aunt Priscilla, Henny and myself, and we were reduced to begging and stealing.

"Captain Auld was not born a slaveholder. He had been a poor man, master only of a bay craft. He came into possession of all his slaves by marriage. Adopted slaveholders are the worst. He was cruel but cowardly. He found himself incapable of managing his slaves either by force, fear or fraud. In August, 1832, my master attended a Methodist camp-meeting and there experienced religion. If it had any effect on his character, it made him more cruel and hateful in all his ways. Prior to his conversion he relied upon his own depravity to shield and sustain him in his savage barbarity. After his conversion he found religious sanction and support for his slaveholding cruelty. He prayed morning, noon and night. His activity in revivals was great. His house was the preachers' home. They used to take great pleasure in coming there to put up. While he starved us, he stuffed them. We have had three or four preachers there at a time. The names of those who used to come most frequently while I lived there were Mr. Storks, Mr. Ewery, Mr. Humphry and Mr. Hickey. I have also seen Mr. George Cookman at our house. We slaves loved Mr. Cookman. We believed him to be a good man. We thought him instrumental in getting Mr. Samuel Harrison, a very rich slaveholder, to emancipate his slaves. When he was at our house, we were sure to be called in to prayers. Mr. Cookman could not come among us without betraying his sympathy for us.

"I have seen my master tie up a lame young woman and whip her with a heavy cowskin upon her naked shoulders [while quoting] this passage of scripture, 'He that knoweth his master's will and doeth it not shall be beaten with many stripes.'

"Master would keep this young woman tied up in this situation four or five hours at a time. I have known him to tie her up early in the morning and whip her before breakfast, leave her, go to his store, return at dinner and whip her again. The secret of master's cruelty toward Henny is in her being almost helpless. When a child she fell into the fire and burned herself horribly. She could do very little but bear heavy burdens. She was to master a bill of expense and a constant offence to him. He gave her away once to his sister, but being a poor gift she was not disposed to keep her. Finally he set her adrift to take care of herself.

"My master and I had quite a number of differences. He found me unsuitable to his purpose. My city life, he said, had almost ruined me. One of my greatest faults was that of letting his horse run away and go down to his father-in-law's farm, which was about five miles from St. Michael's. I would then have to go after it. My reason for this kind of carelessness, or carefulness, was that I could always get something to eat when I went there. Master William Hamilton, my master's father-in-law, always gave his slaves enough to eat. I never left there hungry. Master Thomas at length said he would stand it no longer. I had lived with him nine months during which time he had given me a number of severe whippings all to no good purpose. He resolved to put me out, as he said, to be broken. For this purpose he let me for one year to a man named Edward Covey. Mr. Covey was a poor man, a farm renter. He rented the place upon which he lived and the hands with which he tilled it. Mr. Covey had acquired a very high reputation for breaking young slaves, and this reputation enabled him to get his farm tilled with much less expense than he could have otherwise. Some slaveholders thought it not much loss to allow Mr. Covey to have their slaves one year for the sake of training without any other compensation.

"I went to live with Mr. Covey on the first of January 1833. I was now for the first time in my life a field hand. I found myself more awkward than a country boy appeared in a large city. I had been at my new home but one week before Mr. Covey sent me very early in the morning of one of our coldest days in the month of January to the woods to get a load of wood. He gave me a team of unbroken oxen. He told me which was the in-hand ox and which the off-hand one. He then tied the end of a large rope around the horns of the in-hand ox and gave me the other end of it and told me if the oxen started to run that I must hold on to the rope. I had never driven oxen before and I had got a very few rods into the woods when the oxen took fright and started full tilt carrying the cart against trees and over stumps. They finally upset the cart, dashing it against a tree, and threw themselves into a dense thicket. How I escaped death I do not know. There I was alone in a thick wood, my cart upset and shattered, my oxen entangled among the young trees. After a long spell I succeeded in getting my cart righted, my oxen disentangled and yoked to the cart. I now proceeded with my team to the place where I had the day before been chopping wood and loaded my cart pretty heavily, thinking in this way to tame my oxen. I then proceeded on my way home. I had consumed half of the day. I got out of the woods safely and felt out of danger. I stopped my oxen to open the woods gate. Just as I did so, the oxen again started, rushed through the gate, catching it between the wheel and the body of the cart, tearing it to pieces and coming within a few inches of crushing me against the gate post. On my return I told Mr. Covey what had happened. He ordered me to return to the woods again immediately. I did so, and he followed on after me. Just as I got into the woods, he came up and told me to stop my cart and that he would teach me how to trifle away my time and break gates. He went to a large gum tree and with his axe cut three large switches and, after trimming them up neatly with his pocket knife, ordered me to take off my clothes. I made him no answer but stood with my clothes on. He repeated his order. I still made no answer. Nor did I move. Upon this he rushed at me with the fierceness of a tiger, tore off my clothes and lashed me till he had worn out his switches and cutting me so deeply as to leave the marks visible for a long time after. This whipping was the first of a number just like it and for similar offences.

"I lived with Mr. Covey one year. During the first six months I was seldom free from a sore back. Mr. Covey gave us enough to eat but scarce time to eat it. We were often less than five minutes taking our meals. We were often in the field from the first approach of day till its last lingering ray, and at saving-fodder time midnight often caught us in the field binding blades.

"Covey would be out with us. He would spend the most of his afternoons in bed. He would then come out fresh in the evening ready to urge us on. Mr. Covey was a hard-working man. He knew by himself just what a man or boy could do. There was no deceiving him. His work went on in his absence almost as well as in his presence. He had the faculty of making us feel that he was ever present with us. This he did by surprising us. He seldom approached the spot where we were at work openly if he could do it secretly. We used to call him The Snake. When were were at work in the cornfield, he would sometimes crawl on his hands and knees and all at once rise in our midst and scream, 'Ha, ha! Come, come! Dash on, dash on!' " Douglass had a rare gift for this kind of mimicry. Many of his hearers thought that he could have become a great actor had he chosen the stage. It helped to relieve the somberness of his theme, to break the tension and set up the next episode.

"Covey appeared to us as being ever at hand. He was under every tree, behind every stump, in every bush and at every window on the plantation. He would sometimes mount his horse as if bound to St. Michael's, a distance of seven miles, and in half an hour we would see him coiled up on the corner of the wood-fence watching every motion of the slaves, his horse having been left tied-up in the woods. His life was devoted to planning and perpetrating deceptions. He seemed to think himself equal to deceiving the Almighty. He would make a short prayer in the morning and a long prayer at night. Few men would at times appear more devotional than he. The exercises of his family devotions were always commenced with singing. As he was a very poor singer, the duty of raising the hymn generally came upon me. He would read his hymn and nod at me to commence. At times I would do so. At others I would not. My non-compliance would always produce much confusion. To show himself independent of me he would start and stagger through with his hymn in the most discordant manner."

Douglass found himself lapsing into a natural habit of mimicing. The audience relaxed with laughter as the speaker paused. He began again in a changed tone.

"Poor man! I do believe he sometimes deceived himself ito believing he was a sincere worshiper of God.

"Mr. Covey was just commencing in life. He was only able to buy one slave and he bought her, as he said, for a breeder. This woman was named Caroline. Mr. Covey bought her from Mr. Thomas Lowe about six miles from St. Michael's. She was a large, able-bodied woman about twenty years old. She had already given birth to one child which proved her to be just what he wanted. After buying her he hired a married man of Mr. Samuel Harrison to live with him one year and him he used to fasten up with her every night. At the end of the year the miserable woman gave birth to twins. At this Mr. Covey seemed highly pleased both with the man and the woman. The children were regarded as quite an addition to his wealth.

"During the first six months of my stay with Mr. Covey we were worked in all weathers. It was never too hot or cold. It could never gain, blow, hail or snow too hard for us to work in the field. The longest days were too short for him and the shortest nights too long. I was sometimes unmanageable when I went there, but a few months of this discipline tamed me. Mr. Covey succeeded in breaking me. I was broken in body, soul and spirit. My natural elasticity was crushed, my intellect languished. The disposition to read departed. The cheerful spark that lingered about my eye died. The dark night of slavery closed in upon me. Behold a man transformed into a brute!

"Sunday was my only leisure time. I spent this in a sort of beast-like stupor between sleep and wake under some large tree. At times I would rise up. A flash of energetic freedom would dart through my soul accompanied with a faint beam of hope that flickered for a moment and then vanished. I sank down again mourning over my condition. I was sometimes prompted to take my life and that of Covey but was prevented by a combination of hope and fear.

"Our house stood within a few rods of the Chesapeake Bay whose broad bosom was ever white with sails from every quarter of the globe. Those beautiful vessels robed in purest white so delightful to the eye of freeman were to me so many shrouded ghosts to terrify and torment me with thoughts of my wretched condition. I have often in the deep stillness of a summer's Sabbath stood all alone upon the lofty banks of that noble bay and traced with saddened heart and tearful eye the countless number of sails moving off to the mighty ocean. The sight of these always affected me powerfully. With no audience but the Almighty I would pour out my complaint in my rude way with an apostrophe to the moving ships.

" 'You are loosed from your moorings and are free,' I would say. 'I am fast in my chains and am a slave. You move merrily before the gentle gale, and I sadly before the bloody whip. You are freedom's swift-winged angels that fly round the world. I am confined in bands of iron. O that I were free! O, that I were on one of your gallant decks and under your protecting wing! Alas, between me and you the turbid waters roll. Go on, go on. O that I could also go! Could I but swim! If I could fly! O, why was I born a man of whom to make a brute? The glad ship is gone. She hides in the dim distance. I am left in the hottest hell of unending slavery. God, save me. God, deliver me. Let me be free. Is there a God? Why am I a slave? I will run away. I will not stand it. Get caught or get clear, I'll try it. I had as well die with ague as the fever. I have only one life to lose. I had as well be killed running as die standing. Think of it. One hundred miles straight north and I am free! Try it? Yes. God helping me, I will. There is a better day coming.'

"On one of the hottest days of the month of August, 1833, Bill Smith, William Hughes, a slave named Eli and myself were fanning wheat. Hughes was clearing the fanned wheat from before the fan. Eli was turning, Smith was feeding and I was carrying wheat to the fan. About three o'clock of that day I broke down. I was seized with a violent aching of the head and extreme dizziness. When I could stand no longer, I fell and felt as if held down by an immense weight. The fan stopped. Every one had his own work to do and none could do the work of the other.

"Mr. Covey was at the house. On hearing the fan stop, he came to where we were, inquired what the matter was. Bill explained. I had by this time crawled away under the side of the post and rail fence hoping to find relief out of the sun. He came to the spot and asked me what was the matter. I told him as well as I could. He then gave me a kick in the side and told me to get up. I tried but fell back. He gave me another kick. Again I tried to rise. I again staggered and fell. Mr. Covey took up the hickory slat with which Hughes had been striking off the half-bushel measure and with it gave me a blow upon the head. Again he told me to get up. I made no effort, but in a short time after receiving this blow my head grew better. I resolved to go to my master and enter a complaint. I watched my chance while Covey was looking in an opposite direction and started for St. Michael's. I was on my way to the woods when Covey called me. I disregarded both his calls and his threats and made my way to the woods as fast as my feeble state would allow. I walked through the woods to avoid detection. I had not gone far before I fell down and lay for a considerable time, the blood oozing from the wound on my head. After about three quarters of an hour I started on my way through bogs and briers barefooted and bareheaded and after a journey of a about seven miles I arrived at master's store. I was covered with blood. My hair was all

clotted with dust and blood. My shirt was stiff with blood.
My legs and feet were torn with briers and thorns and were
also covered with blood. I suppose I looked like a man
who had escaped a den of beasts. In this state I appeared
before my master entreating him to interpose for my protection. Master Thomas ridiculed the idea that there was
any danger of Mr. Covey's killing me. I belonged to Mr.
Covey for one year and I must go back to him. I might
remain in St. Michael's that night but I must be off early
in the morning. According to his orders, I started off to
Covey's in the morning. I was getting over the fence that
divided Mrs. Kemp's fields from ours [when] out ran
Covey with his cowskin. The corn was very high. It afforded
me the means of hiding. He gave up the chase. I spent that
day in the woods [considering whether] to go home and be
whipped to death or stay in the woods and be starved to
death.

"That night I fell in with Sandy Jenkins a slave. Sandy
had a free wife who lived about four miles from Mr.
Covey's, and he was on his way to see her. I told him my
circumstances and he invited me to go home with him. I
found Sandy an old adviser. He told me with great solemnity I must go back to Covey but that before I went I must
go with him into another part of the woods where there
was a certain root which would make it impossible for Mr.
Covey or any other white man to whip me. He said he had
carried it for years. Since he had done so, he had never
received a blow. To please him I took the root and carried
it upon my right side. This was Sunday morning. I started
for home. Upon entering the yard gate, out came Covey
on his way to meeting. He spoke to me very kindly, bade
me drive the pigs from a lot nearby and passed on towards
the church. This singular conduct of Mr. Covey made me
begin to think that there was something in the root Sandy
had given me.

"All went well till Monday morning. On this morning the virtue of the root was fully tested. Long before daylight I was called to go and rub, curry and feed the horses. I obeyed. I was throwing down some blades from the loft when Mr. Covey entered the stable with a long rope. As I was half out of the loft, he caught my legs and was about tying me. As soon as I found what he was up to, I gave a sudden spring and was brought sprawling on the stable floor. Mr. Covey seemed now to think he had me, but at this moment I resolved to fight and seized Covey hard by the throat. As I did so, I rose. My resistance was so unexpected Covey seemed taken aback. He trembled like a leaf. This gave me assurance and I held him. Mr. Covey called out to Hughes for help. Hughes came and while Covey held me attempted to tie my right hand. While he was in the act of doing so, I gave him a heavy kick close under the ribs. This kick fairly sickened Hughes so that he left me in the hands of Mr. Covey. When Mr. Covey asked me if I meant to persist in my resistance, I told him I did, that he had used me like a brute for six months and that I was determined to be used so no longer. He was leaning over to get a stick when I seized him with both hands by his collar and brought him to the ground. By this time Bill came. Covey called for assistance. Bill said his master hired him out to work and not to help whip me. He left Covey and myself to fight our own battle. We were at it for nearly two hours. Covey at length let me go, puffing and blowing and saying that if I had not resisted, he would not have whipped me so much. The truth was that he had not whipped me at all. He had drawn no blood from me but I had from him.

"This battle with Mr. Covey was the turning point in my career as a slave. It rekindled the embers of freedom and revived a sense fo my own manhood. It was a glorious resurrection. My long-crushed spirit rose, cowardice departed, bold defiance took its place. I now resolved that however long I might remain a slave in form the day had passed forever when I could be a slave in fact. The white man who expected to succeed in whipping must also succeed in killing me.

"From this time I was never again whipped though I remained a slave four years afterwards. I had several fights but was never whipped. My term of service to Edward Covey ended on Christmas day, 1833. On the first of January, 1834, I went to live with Mr. William Freeland. Mr. Freeland was a very different man from Mr. Covey. Mr. Freeland was himself the owner of but two slaves. The rest of his hands he hired. These consisted of myself, Sandy Jenkins who had given me the root to prevent whippings and Handy Caldwell. Henry and John, his two slaves, were quite intelligent and in a very little while after I went there I succeeded in creating in them a strong desire to learn to read. This desire soon sprang up in the others also. They very soon mustered up some old spelling books and nothing would do but that I must keep a Sabbath school. I agreed to do so and accordingly devoted my Sundays to teaching these my fellow slaves how to read.

"Some of the slaves of the neighboring farms found what was going on and also availed themselves of this little opportunity to learn to read. It was understood among all who came that there must be as little display about it as possible. I had at one time over forty scholars. And I have the happiness to know that several of those who came to Sabbath school learned how to read and that one at least is now free through my agency.

"At the close of the year 1834 Mr. Freeland again hired me of my master for the year 1835. But by this time I began to want to live upon free land as well as with Freeland. But I was not willing to cherish this determination alone. My fellow slaves were dear to me. I was anxious to have them participate with me. I bent myself to devising ways and means for our escape. I went first to one and then another. Our company consisted of Henry, John, Henry Bailey, Charles and myself. Sandy, one of our number, gave up the notion but still encouraged us. Henry Bailey was my uncle and belonged to my master. Charles married my aunt. He belonged to my master's father-in-law, Mr. William Hamilton.

"The plan we finally concluded was to get a large canoe belonging to Mr. Hamilton and upon the Saturday night before Easter paddle directly up the Chesapeake Bay. On our arrival at the head of the bay, a distance of seventy or eighty miles from where we lived, it was our purpose to turn our canoe adrift and follow the north star till we got beyond the limits of Maryland. We hoped to be regarded as fishermen. The week before our intended start I wrote several protections, one for each of us. Saturday morning came. We went as usual to the field. We were spreading manure. [Suddenly] I was overwhelmed with an indescribable feeling. I turned to Sandy and said, 'We are betrayed!'

" 'That [same] thought has this moment struck me,' he said. We said no more but I was never more certain of anything.

"The horn was blown as usual and we went up from the field to the house for breakfast. I was in the house looking out when I saw four white men with two colored men in the lane. The white men were on horseback. The colored ones were walking behind. I watched them a few moments till they halted and tied the colored men to the gate post. In a few moments Mr. Hamilton rode in with great excitement. He came to the door and inquired for Master William. He was told he was at the barn. Without dismounting, he rode to the barn with extraordinary speed. In a few moments he and Mr. Freeland returned to the house. I stepped to the door and they at once seized me.

"In a few moments they succeeded in tying John. They then turned to Henry and commanded him to cross his hands. 'I won't,' said Henry. With this two of the constables pulled out their shining pistols and swore by their Creator that they would make him cross his hands or kill him. Each cocked his pistol and with fingers on the trigger walked up to Henry. 'Shoot me, shoot me,' Henry said. 'You can't kill me but once. Shoot—shoot and be damned. I won't be tied.' At the same time, with a motion as quick as lightening, he dashed the pistols from the hand of each constable. As he did this, all hands fell upon him and after beating him some time they finally overpowered him and got him tied.

"During the scuffle I managed to get my pass out and put it into the fire. We were all now tied and just as we were to leave for Easton jail Betsy Freeland, mother of William Freeland, came to the door with her hands full of biscuits and divided them between Henry and John. She then addressed herself to me. 'You devil! You yellow devil,' she said. 'It was you that put it into the heads of Henry and John to run away. But for you, you long legged mulatto devil. Henry nor John would never have thought of such a thing!' I was immediately hurried off towards St. Michael's.

"About half way to St. Michael's Henry inquired of me what he should do with his pass. I told him to eat it with his biscuit and own nothing. We passed the word around, 'Own nothing.' At St. Michael's we all denied that we ever intended to run away. We found the evidence against us to be the testimony of one person. Our master would not tell who it was. We were sent off to Easton. We were delivered up to the sheriff and by him placed in jail.

"We had been in jail scarcely twenty minutes when a swarm of slave traders and agents for slave traders flocked into jail to look at us and to ascertain if we were for sale. I was kept about one week at the end of which Captain

Auld, my master, came up and took me out with the intention of sending me into Alabama. From some cause or other he did not send me to Alabama however but concluded to send me back to Baltimore to live again with his brother Hugh and to learn a trade. In a few weeks after I went to Baltimore, Master Hugh hired me to a shipbuilder on Fell's Point. I was put there to learn how to calk. There it was that I planned and finally succeeded in making my escape from slavery."

Garrison sprang to his feet as Douglass finished talking. It was some time before he could make himself heard above the tumult in the hall. No Negro had ever before received such an ovation in the United States for any cause. "Patrick Henry," Garrison asserted loudly, "never made a speech more eloquent in the cause of liberty than the one we . . . just listened to from the lips of that hunted fugitive." He then reminded the audience of the perils a self-emancipated young man faced in the North—"even in Massachusetts, on the soil of the Pilgrim Fathers, among the descendants of revolutionary sires." At the proper moment he put the question to them very directly. Would they allow Fred Douglass to be carried back into slavery? Law or no law, constitution or no constitution—would they? In his own words, "the response was unanimous and in thunder-tones—NO!"

"Will you succor and protect him as a brother-man?" Garrison cried out. "As a resident of the old Bay State?"

Again the thunder. "YES!" It was shouted with "an energy so startling" Garrison imagined "that the ruthless tyrants south of Mason and Dixon's line might almost have heard the mighty burst of feeling and recognized it as the pledge of an invincible determination on the part of those who gave it never to betray him that wanders but to hide the outcast and firmly to abide the consequences."

Douglass's power over an antislavery audience was close

to hypnotic. Hearing him plead the cause of the black man in bondage was an experience which few people ever forgot. But was the brutality of slavery the full explanation of Douglass's passion? Was the anguish of his eyes, the disturbing malaise which he awakened adequately accounted for by his recollections of bloody punishments? Or was it in part at least something he was trying to find—something he wanted to know?

III

100 CONVENTIONS

THE ABOLITIONISTS WAITED on him after the Nantucket meeting. He was their man, and no doubt about it. John A. Collins, general agent of the Massachusetts Anti-Slavery Society, made the offer. How would Douglass like to quit his job at Richmond's brass foundry in New Bedford and become an agent of the Society?

Douglass wasn't sure. Less than three years out of bondage, he doubted his capacity to serve the antislavery movement as a paid speaker. But Collins argued, and while he urged, he was joined by Garrison and James N. Buffum, both of whom later claimed credit for bringing Douglass around. Since the three men's memories of the incident were not quite identical, perhaps it is safest to recall it as Douglass himself did, and the man he named was Collins.

When Collins pinned him down, Douglass revealed another reason for his hesitation. As Garrison had intimated in his remarks on the platform, a runaway slave was in danger of being recaptured and returned. Wouldn't their notion of putting him on public platforms to tell his story to audiences in various parts of the country make him an easy mark for slave catchers? Douglass also pointed out that he had a family in New Bedford; he would have to continue to support them.

All this Collins swept aside. The Massachusetts Anti-Slavery Society would pay him at least as much as he earned in the foundry. And as for the risks to his person—those people he saw in the audience were dependable friends. Others would come to his side once they heard his story. Lines were now forming for an all-out struggle between freedom and slavery. Douglass had too much to contribute to that fight to be content to save his own skin.

What could he say to that? Douglass sighed as he accepted their proposal, but he made one condition: he would try it for only three months—three months at most. If by that time people were not tired of listening to his story, he was sure he would be tired of telling it. Having committed himself, however, he began to turn the plan over in his mind more carefully, and the more he pondered the more exciting it began to seem. A crusade was getting underway. One of the important moral issues of human life was involved. The men leading it were men of brave and noble spirit. To be associated with them in the fight was reward enough, but there was greater glory ahead. God was for them; they were sure to win.

Douglass hurried back to New Bedford to tell Anna and their friends what had happened to him at Nantucket. His first duty would be to travel through the eastern counties of Massachusetts with a white abolitionist in the interest of the *Anti-Slavery Standard* and the *Liberator*, he explained. The two of them would hold meetings at which both would speak, Douglass telling the story of his bondage and escape as he had told it at Nantucket. Then they would solicit subscriptions to the papers.

The Johnson family and their free Negro friends in New Bedford raised their eyebrows. Some of them began to wonder if the young fugitive was as bright as they had taken him to be. It wasn't sane for a colored man to ac-knowledge that he was a runaway slave. Apart from the danger of recapture to which it exposed him, there was the more pointed question of status. Slave birth was nothing to crow about in colored society. Freeborn Negroes were always ready to make the most of their advantage.

Anna did not oppose him, however, and there was no time to answer the other objectors. Douglass had given his word to Collins, Garrison, Buffum, George Foster and their associates at Nantucket, and now appointments were waiting.

A few days later he was in the field, assigned to start out with Foster, and the *Liberator* picked up his trail at the Middlessex County Anti-Slavery Society convention on August 31.

Fugitives from slavery were rare enough at that time to awaken curiosity. The prospect of hearing one speak in his own defense was a brand new experience to most people in this section. Usually, in the towns visited, Douglass and his companion were joined by local abolitionists who made arrangements for the public meeting, brought out the crowd and then sat with the visiting speakers on the platform.

Where Douglass went the cause of abolition perked up. Old crusaders for the unpopular cause were aroused to fight again. New converts were added to the ranks. As the confidence of the speakers increased, their act improved. Within a few weeks Collins himself replaced Foster, leaving no doubt that Douglass had already come to be regarded as a solid attraction. The public meetings grew livelier and livelier.

The speakers even ventured a note of satirical humor. Pointing to the handsome and dignified young Douglass, the chairman would grinningly refer to him as a "thing," "a piece of Southern property," a "chattel." When that had registered, he would slyly assure the audience that "*it* could speak." Even in the more remote villages this was good for laughs.

Nor was it long before the fugitive himself was clowning for the folk. He began to introduce playful asides into his story. Within three months he was doing a take-off on a slaveholder's sermon with a gift of mimicry that left his audiences in stitches. In this little monologue, which he varied from time to time, Douglass would have his minister take a text such as, "Do unto others as you would have others do unto you." He would have him begin by assuring the downstairs audience that this meant, "Slaveholders do unto *slaveholders* what you would have them do unto you." He would pause piously before actually putting his teeth into the impersonation. Then looking impudently up to the slaves' gallery and spreading his arms gracefully, he would let go. "You, too, my friends, have souls of infinite value—souls that will live through endless happiness or misery in eternity. Oh, *labor diligently* to make your calling and election sure. Oh, receive into your souls these words of the holy apostle, 'Servants, be obedient unto your masters.'" This was the point, according to the Tenth Annual Report of the Massachusetts Anti-Slavery Society, for shouts of laughter and applause. Presently Douglass, who never had to be taught not to step on his laughs, continued, still in character, "Oh, consider the wonderful goodness of God! Look at your hard, horny hands, your strong muscular frames, and see how mercifully he has adapted you to the duties you are to fulfill! While to your masters, who have slender frames and long, delicate fingers, he has given brilliant intellects, that they may do the thinking while you do the working." The abolitionists and their friends cheered wildly.

The tour was going fine. A typical local reaction was given by an editor who heard Douglass at Providence. To him the ex-slave was remarkable for his "wit, argument, sarcasm, pathos" and his "highly melodious and rich" voice. He it was who thought that Douglass's fine head would be of interest to phrenologists. Only one questionable note had been struck. A few times Douglass had to be reminded to stick to his script. "Give us the facts," Collins whispered, "we will take care of the philosophy."

But the fugitive had sampled the high air. He wanted to stretch his wings. The bald recital of his personal adventure was inhibiting him. Douglass had been reading constantly since he settled in New Bedford. He had talked with intelligent men, and he had been thinking. Ideas were popping in his mind. He was not content to narrate wrongs. He wanted to analyze and to denounce them. Frederick Douglass was growing before their eyes, and something about this growth disturbed his companions.

"People won't believe you ever were a slave, Frederick, if you keep on this way," one cautioned.

Another advised, "Better have a little of the plantation speech than not; it is not best that you seem too learned."

Douglass could see sincerity in their eyes, and he recognized a certain logic in the warnings, but he refused to take them seriously. Two months after the abolitionists hired him at Nantucket he was on a platform talking about the "progress of the cause." A week later he put his own escape story aside long enough to make an appeal for Lunsford Lane who, having purchased his own freedom, was trying to raise money to buy his wife and children.

Seeing they could not keep him in check, his fellow abolitionists decided to make the best use they could of his expanding interests and pent up energies. They added him to a team composed of Stephen S. Foster, Parker Pillsbury, Abby Kelley and James Monroe and delegated to go into Rhode Island and fight the adoption of a proposed new state constitution which would have denied suffrage to black people. The whirlwind campaign which these five made in the two weeks they were together saw meetings broken up by mobs in Woonsocket Falls and North Scituate and foul eggs and foul words hurled at the comely Miss Kelley as well as her companions, but it resulted in the raising of $1,000 to continue opposition to the Dorr Constitution and, as it seemed to Douglass, in influencing the eventual adoption of a state constitution without the unwanted feature.

The effort did something for Douglass too. As a result of his work in the campaign, the state Anti-Slavery Society of Rhode Island appointed him to a committee to go before the suffrage convention and canvass the ballots. It was a gesture of approval which he could not fail to recognize. Meanwhile Rhode Island Anti-Slavery people showed him a warmth of friendship that seemed even more remarkable because of the rough treatment occasionally met on trains, steamboats and in public buildings. Several times he was dragged from cars in which Negroes were not permitted to ride. On the Sound between New York and Stonington he was obliged to sleep on the freight topside one January night because he was denied a cabin. It was on occasions like these that he tested the friendship of men like Wendell Phillips and James Monroe who would never enter the first class quarters while he rode Jim Crow.

Douglass himself resolved never to accept segregation without protest. Segregation, he said, was the spirit of slavery, and he vowed to fight it wherever he found it. He refused to enter voluntarily cars marked for colored. If the officials of the road wanted him there, they had to conduct him to the places while listening to his denunciations and protests.

Nor was he always able to find halls in which to speak. In one town which he visited alone, finding neither hall, church, nor public square in which to hold a meeting, he entered a hotel and borrowed a dinner bell. With this in hand he passed through the main streets ringing it and shouting, "Notice! Frederick Douglass, recently a slave, will lecture on American slavery on Grafton Common this evening at seven o'clock. Those who would like to hear of the workings of slavery by one of the slaves are respectfully invited to attend." The audience which came in response was so large, and presumably so respectable, the pastor of the largest church in town reconsidered and invited Douglass to bring the crowd into his church.

Toward the end of January, 1842, Douglass returned to Boston to attend the annual meeting of the Massachusetts Society. A feature of this gathering was the report of the general agent. Collins assured the leaders of abolitionism that Douglass had proven his worth to the cause. Together the two of them had visited more than sixty towns and villages, and Douglass had displayed a free and forcible manner of speaking, given unforgettable descriptions of slavery and flavored his discourse with humor and satire. The Society on its part had paid him $170.34 for his first three months services. Since then, of course, Douglass had worked nearly two months for the Rhode Island Society. But the question before Douglass and the Massachusetts Society now was wether or not he would continue in their employ.

An offer was made, and Douglass turned it over in his mind. After all, this was far more exciting work than the unskilled labor he had found in New Bedford. If the earnings thus far had been about the same, the chances for a raise looked favorable. Besides, he was in this thing now. He was up to his neck in it, and there was actually no way to back out. The fight against slavery had already gone too far to be called off. The mobs at the meetings in Rhode Island, the bullies on the railroad platforms and hecklers in public squares—they left no doubt. The Massachusetts Society could count on him.

Presently he was off on another round of speeches.

The high points of abolitionist agitation, of course, were the conventions. Here the hard-bitten friends of freedom let themselves go. Perhaps it was just a coincidence that so many of the individuals resembled characters out of Dickens, but a whole gallery of arresting figures is embalmed in the reminiscent literature that followed the campaign. In the twilight of their careers, after the fight against slavery was won, most of the veteran abolitionist leaders wrote their memoirs. By then even the most unsmiling of them seemed to recall a certain colorfulness about their gatherings, though little enough of this is suggested by such sober titles as *Boston Anti-Slavery Days, Reminiscenses of the Great Agitation, Some Recollections of Our Anti-Slavery Conflict, Acts of the Anti-Slavery Apostles* or the *Story of the Hutchinsons.*

Crackpots were always present. One who kept showing up at abolitionist conventions insisted that slavery could be destroyed quite simply by means of habeas corpus. It isn't yet clear how that was to be managed, but this zealous man frequently got the floor for the purpose of expounding his theory. Often a gloomy young preacher rose to complain against the hostile attitudes the antislavery leaders expressed toward the churches.

No doubt he had in mind resolutions like one Douglass heard read at the Boston meeting: "That the religion of the United States of America is one vast system of atheism and idolatry, which, in atrocity and vileness, equals that of any system in the heathen countries of Asia or Africa, or the islands of the Pacific ocean—that the sectarian churches and the ministry of this country are combinations of thieves, adulterers and pirates, and not the churches and ministers of Jesus Christ; and should be treated as brothels and banditti by all who would exculpate themselves from the guilt of slaveholding." The condemnation of this resolution by those present, including Garrison, Wendell Phillips, Douglass, Collins and the rest, as "not likely to gain friends to the Anti-Slavery enterprise" may have seemed to the fledgling minister too tame.

Some persons, it was suspected, attended the conventions mainly to exercise their lungs or perhaps practice oratory. If so, they found the test severe. In addition to a horse-laugh element that hung around the edges, large boys bent on devilment and adult pranksters who delighted in disturbing the carryings-on, the audiences also included more serious hecklers. Confirmed antiabolitionists attended, too, together with individuals who did not favor slavery but despised the tactics of the agitators. From these elements would come questions, taunts, sometimes sneers.

Naturally the firebrands of the movement were prepared to answer all challenges. If such a set-up did not make for peace and quiet, neither did it make for dullness. Sparks always flew at abolitionist conventions, and the young Frederick Douglass, experiencing his first two or three gatherings, found himself almost giddy with excitement. In later years when people marveled at his fund of knowledge, his well-trained mind, it was to these conventions that he pointed. These had been his university.

The order of the meetings did not vary much. There was always an opening prayer, and sometimes Douglass would be called on for this. If the Hutchinsons or some other abolitionist singers were available, there would be songs which expressed antislavery sentiments. There were times, in the absence of more distinguished singers, when Douglass came on with "an abolitionist solo." The reading of reports and greetings followed. Sometimes these included words of encouragement from well-known antislavery people abroad such as Daniel O'Connell of Ireland or Harriet Martineau of England. Then resolutions were offered and discussed, a specimen of which is the following, adopted by the Boston meeting in January of 1842:

> *Resolved,* That the Anti-Slavery enterprise is strictly a moral enterprise, and not one of physical violence; that the revolution it seeks to accomplish is moral and peaceful, and not a revolution of force and arms; that, therefore, all its measures and instrumentalities are spiritual, appealing to the conscience and heart of an inhuman, slaveholding people.
>
> *Resolved,* That though political action is commonly regarded as peaceful, and favoring rather of moral than of physical force, yet, as regards the abolition of slavery, it is essentially military and compulsory, and therefore abolitionists cannot legitimately employ its agency in the prosecution of their enterprise.

This was a complex matter which had in it the seeds of confusion and internal strife for the antislavery effort. But nothing dismayed the young Douglass. He is on record as speaking for the proposition, little dreaming of the bloody noses and broken arms he would presently suffer in its defense. Nor did the twenty-four-year-old recruit anticipate that before he was thirty a change in his thinking on this subject would lead him to part company, amid hard feelings and recriminations, with the revered men with whom he shared the platform at that meeting.

The leaders of the movement tried to practice what they preached about democracy and freedom of speech. At least one of their number wondered whether or not a presiding officer was necessary. Anybody was free to talk and express any view. This atmosphere was fine for Frederick Douglass. Favored with a heroic figure, a remarkable voice, a ready wit, a quick grasp of issues and a flair for drama—he had everything it took to make a great convention man. This was the show in which he was soon to become a headliner.

Naturally abolitionists were not taken seriously by Northerners as a whole. The number of their adherents remained relatively small. They were tolerated as a sort of lunatic fringe of their day, an absurd crowd working a bit too closely with a kindred outfit in the British Empire where slavery had already been abolished. The North didn't fear abolitionists; it scoffed at them.

The South went into a spitting rage at the mention of their names, however. Time and again its spokesmen rose in their state legislatures to pay Garrison and later Douglass an others the compliment of frothing denunciation. They shouted their threats against these leaders. Presently they began posting large rewards for their arrest.

Above all, the antislavery North was convinced that the abolitionist agitation was a lot of sound and fury signifying nothing. Anyone could see that it did not change the situation one way or the other. If these fanatics insisted on continuing their useless hullabaloo, they could only blame themselves when respectable people became irritated and refused to let them hold meetings in public auditoriums or when the police failed to protect them from ruffians who hurled eggs and overripe fruit at their speakers.

In the eyes of the South the number of abolitionists was not insignificant. To the slave power they were neither quaint nor misguided nor lunatic. They were criminal. The South ignored the pious words renouncing violence. It wanted to hang Garrison and all his cronies. For the abolitionists, alone among the advocates of freedom, had found the slaveholder's exposed nerve: the moral issue. By touching it over and over again they had begun to drive the South crazy.

The South was winning the constitutional argument hands down. It seemed also to be getting the better of the North in the political tug of war. And it certainly did not fear a solution by violence. But that question of conscience

—the Gag Rule helped to silence those who raised it in Congress, but how could you stop those loud-mouthed abolitionists from ranting *without* hanging them?

For the rest of 1842 Douglass stumped Massachusetts and western New York. By April his schedule of engagements rated publication in the abolitionist press, and throughout the remainder of the year his speeches made news in Concord's *Herald of Freedom,* New York's *Anti-Slavery Standard* and Boston's *Liberator.* In a kind of all-star pick of the convention figures who did most to bring "fear to freedom's foes" that year the *Herald* named Douglass as one of its selections. His "heroic figure," the editors said, "was dilating in antislavery debate." He had "made color not only honorable but enviable." A reader of the *Liberator* wrote in to say how impressed he had been by a Douglass address at Northbridge. Another, attending a meeting at Nantucket and hearing Douglass for the first time, offered a confession. He hadn't cared much for abolitionism or abolitionists in the past, and what he had heard about this runaway slave called Douglass had left him cold. He had been totally unprepared to find the young man "chaste in language, brilliant in thought, truly eloquent in delivery."

That Douglass was coming on as an orator can scarcely be questioned. Collins continued to arrange his itinerary, but he shared rostrums and rubbed elbows with more and more abolitionist headliners. Wendell Phillips was of course the outstanding orator of the movement, and Garrison was its most strident editorial voice, but they were by no means the only ones who commanded attention. Samuel J. May, frequently a lecture companion of Douglass's, was Bronson Alcott's conception of "the Lord's chore boy." A Unitarian minister of a rather odd stripe, May's personality was perhaps reflected in his refusal to preach at funerals unless allowed complete freedom in dealing with the deceased's sins and shortcomings. He reserved the right to dwell on these and to draw such warnings as he could from them. In the fight against slavery he was a free-swinging and rugged campaigner and one of the first to bring out his memoirs of the struggle.

Charles Lenox Remond was a Negro who had visited England in 1840 as a delegate to the first World's Anti-Slavery Convention. He had been the first of his race to be employed in the United States as an antislavery lecturer. He and Douglass gravitated together several times that year and a sharp contrast in their personalities was noted. Remond was free-born and proud, perhaps too proud of his status. Dark, lean and sharp-faced, he seemed to bear "about him like a ceaseless neuralgic pain, the consciousness that he was the object of hateful race prejudice." Statements of this kind were never made of Douglass by his associates, despite his preoccupation with the "cause." Nevertheless the two did a turn together toward the end of the year when the case of George Latimer flared up.

Douglass did not stop to ask irrelevant questions when he heard that Latimer had been arrested in Boston merely on the strength of a letter from one James B. Gray of Norfolk, Virginia, who professed to be the fugitive's owner. He did not have to be told that if this could happen to George Latimer, anybody in the South could lay claim to *him* in the same way and have him thrown into jail in Boston. Naturally he went into a frenzy.

He wrote his first published item for the *Liberator* in behalf of the "outraged brother" who had been "hunted down like a wild beast and dragged through the streets of Boston." Within a month he and Remond were standing on platforms together night after night appealing with clinched fists and trembling voices to Massachusetts audiences to consider the meaning of this action.

John Greenleaf Whittier promptly supported them with a poem.

No slave-hunt in our borders,—no pirate on our strand!
No fetters in the Bay State,—no slave upon our land.

Given this clear case, the abolitionists quickly rallied
public sympathy for Latimer, and within a few weeks the
ex-slave was at liberty again, his former owner having
accepted $400 in payment for his lost property. This called
for antislavery rejoicing. A meeting was held in Salem to
allow sympathizers to see the object of their protests and to
express the hurt they felt in turn for his suffering. To the
dismay of everyone, however, Latimer turned out to be
almost white and not distinguishable as a Negro. Worse
still, he was wretchedly uncomfortable before the audience.
When they hailed him as a free man he was so embarrassed
he could scarcely mumble a reply.

Fortunately Douglass was on hand. He and Remond had
made the Latimer case a pet project of theirs, and Douglass
had no intention of letting the victory celebration flop
because the squirming victim was unable to hold up his
head. According to the *Liberator* Douglass "moved the
audience at will" in a "most wonderful performance."

Two major consequences of this effort were of course
unguessed at that moment, and the extent to which their
irony registered in Douglass's maturing thought can only
be imagined. Following the Latimer case the abolitionists
circulated a petition to which they received 65,000 signa-
tures. This was sent to the Massachusetts legislature and
resulted in a law which forbade state officers to help capture
runaway slaves and denied the use of the state's jails for
their detention. The other result followed much later when
Latimer, like the saved of so many ages and nations, proved
himself unworthy. He was arrested in Boston as a pick-
pocket.

But now it was time for the annual meeting of the New
England Anti-Slavery Society. Always lively affairs, the

session of 1843 was for Douglass and others present a land-
mark, for General Agent John A. Collins sprang one of
the boldest and most venturesome proposals in the Society's
history: a series of One Hundred Conventions in the Western States. This called for a band of brave men, tried and
true campaigners in the cause of freedom, to sweep through
the towns of New Hampshire, Vermont, western New York,
Ohio, Indiana and Pennsylvania, awakening a drowsy people to the iniquities of slavery and enlisting new recruits to
the thin ranks of active abolitionists.

Collins's proposal galvanized the meeting. Douglass
could not sit still. All that the American people needed, he
reasoned, was light. If Americans as a whole could just
know slavery as he knew it, they would rush into the fight
for its extinction. His heart pounded as the discussion
proceeded. In no time at all the Society was on record as
favoring the plan. The principals to play leading roles in
the drama were being named.

Of course Douglass was an obvious choice. He was already credited with giving a new impulse to the antislavery
fight in towns where it had been preached before. If anyone in the abolitionist movement seemed naturally fitted
to carry the flaming doctrine into untouched new areas, it
was this gifted and personally impressive mulatto.

Charles L. Remond was another natural for the effort.
His free status, his hurt pride, his dark and gloomy presence
would heighten by contrast the effect of Douglass's personality. Besides, Remond was a veteran of the struggle.
He had been tested. He could stand the rigors of a hard
campaign.

In addition to these two Negroes the speakers would include George Bradburn, a Unitarian minister who had
served four years in the Massachusetts legislature during
which time he had advocated measures favoring the rights
of Negroes. Jacob Ferris and James Monroe, both hard-

ened abolitionists and Garrisonians, were named, and William A. White of Watertown and Sidney Howard Gay, editor of the *Anti-Slavery Standard* volunteered to complete the corps. All were to work under the direction of Collins, strategist and mastermind of the campaign.

After the meeting broke up, circulars soliciting financial aid for the operation were issued and wheels began to turn all along the line. Douglass's heart singing, he hurried home to spend a little time with his family and pick up a fresh supply of clean linen for the journey. Collins had calculated that the tour would last six months, and the plan agreed upon was that the agents would work singly or in pairs in small villages and outlying districts, regrouping periodically in the larger towns for mass meetings which would consolidate interest thus awakened. Naturally the speakers would avail themselves of any abolitionist sentiment they might run across in the communities.

The stage was set.

The first town they hit was Middlebury, Vermont. To their surprise, Middlebury had prepared for their arrival. The town was placarded with signs describing Douglass as a convict recently escaped from the State prison. Other speakers in the company were branded in terms equally picturesque and with equal indifference to the truth. Edward Barber, a local man of some standing, spoke up for the antislavery cause and worked with the visitors to counteract the bad publicity, but little happened. The Vermonters, despite their long and tested fondness for freedom, stayed away in force. The first convention of the One Hundred was a sorry failure.

Other attempts were made in Vermont, but only the one in Ferrisburgh was mildly encouraging, and that was due to preliminary work by a handful of zealous and sympathetic townfolk led by Orson S. Murphy, Charles C. Burleigh and Rowland T. Robinson. Douglass and his companions grimly turned their backs on the Green Mountains and headed for New York. There, it was expected, their company would be joined by Collins who had not been in good health and was not actually participating in the campaign he had planned.

He did not meet them at once however. Douglass and Remond and the other companions of the unsuccessful Vermont attempt started the New York state series in Albany and worked along the Erie Canal. The responses they received ranged from apathy to aversion. Once or twice Douglass thought he detected a mob spirit, but hostility failed to reach a point of physical violence, and the conventions continued—voices in the wilderness. Even in Syracuse, later a center of abolitionist ferment, the speakers found difficulties.

The main trouble there was that nobody would let them have a church, a house, a market or a hall for their meetings. While they canvassed the city, some of the company lost heart and decided to move on to the next stop. Douglass refused to go with them. His back was definitely up now, and he angrily quoted the scripture commanding the disciples to go into the hedges and highways and compel men to come. Perhaps his nerves were fraying as a result of continuing reverses.

In this decision he was supported by his host, a hardened antislavery man named Stephen Smith, whose house stood on the southwest corner of a park in the center of town. Smith agreed that the fight against slavery would soon end if opponents discovered they could silence abolitionists by the simple means of closing halls and churches to them. With this backing, Douglass resolved to carry on in his own way in Syracuse. The next morning he selected a spot in the park and began speaking to an audience of five people. When he adjourned his meeting that afternoon, he had five hundred listeners, and officers of the Congregational church had followed him to his room and offered him the use of a building they suddenly remembered they owned. It turned out to be an old wooden structure which they had abandoned when they moved into their present church, but it was a great improvement over the out-of-doors and Douglass promptly arranged a three-day schedule of meetings.

In the midst of these Collins showed up. To Douglass's dismay, however, he was accompanied not by fellow abolitionists but by several well-known advocates of another doctrine in which Collins was also interested: communism. This fact in itself might not have been too disconcerting had not Collins risen in the midst of one of Douglass's sessions and proposed that the meeting adjourn discussion of antislavery and take up the subject of utopian communism.

This angered Douglass, but it also put him on a spot. As general agent of the Massachusetts Anti-Slavery Society, Collins was his superior and boss. Moreover the campaign of 100 Conventions was Collins' idea. He had proposed it to the Society and secured its approval, and he had been charged with its overall direction. On the other hand this gathering was strictly Douglass's meeting. He had worked it up after his companions had pulled out. Did he have a right to object to Collins's move to take it over? It was a delicate question and a tense moment, but Douglass did not hesitate long. After the tribulations of the past weeks he was ready for almost anything. He pounded on the speakers' table.

It was not only bad for the cause of antislavery to yoke it with the antiproperty fight, which was even more unpopular, but it was not playing the game with an audience which had come out to listen to the gospel of abolition, and it was certainly not fair to the Society that was paying

Collins's salary and that was sponsoring these conventions. That's what he thought of the proposal.

He was too young to realize he had touched off dynamite, but he learned quickly. The blast came in a reprimand from Mrs. Maria Weston Chapman, an important member of the board of managers of the Massachusetts Anti-Slavery Society. Mrs. Chapman charged Douglass with insubordination and pointed out the harmful uses rival groups might make of this act of rebellion against the recognized antislavery leadership. Douglass was simply stunned.

The more he thought about the incident the more convinced he became that he had done no wrong and hence had not deserved this rebuke. The Syracuse sojourn ended on this unpleasant note. With no intimation that the episode foreshadowed Collins's desertion of the antislavery cause later that year to devote himself to an experiment in communistic living at Skaneateles, New York, or his own subsequent clash with Garrison, Douglass moved on to the next convention.

It may not have been an accident that in Rochester he enjoyed remarkably cordial relations with several families who belonged to the rival abolitionist faction led by Gerrit Smith, Myron Holly and William Goodell. Garrisonians regarded slavery as a "creature of public opinion." They pressed the moral issue and avoided political activity as a means to end slavery. Their rivals saw slavery as a "creature of law" and looked to a political solution. The cleavage was sharp and made for spirited debates, but Douglass noted with surprise that these western folk did not seem to hate him for being a Garrisonian. He was attracted by their broadmindedness in helping him and his colleagues set up the Rochester convention, and he admired the "manly way" they disputed the main issues with the proponents of "moral suasion."

The public effort went better here too. Douglass sang

a solo at a session held in the open square, and all was love and harmony. The convention, participated in also by Ferris, Bradburn and Remond, was a success. But it was the kindliness and warmth of Samuel D. Porter, the Avery family and Isaac and Amy Post that impressed Douglass most. To what extent he also began to find their approach to the slavery question less objectionable at this time is not easy to measure.

Nevertheless he went on to Buffalo with fresh courage. He and Bradburn had ben assigned to work this bustling young city of steamboats and business. They discovered that the friend who had been designated to make arrangements for their convention had secured only a deserted and most dilapidated room formerly used as a postoffice. The first meeting had been announced however, and Douglass and Bradburn appeared on schedule. But the waiting audience consisted only of a few cabmen in work clothes who had left their teams standing on a nearby street while they used this means of filling in the time between jobs. Bradburn took one good look, turned to Douglass and announced that he had no intention of speaking to "such a set of ragamuffins." He boarded the first steamer to Cleveland where his brother lived.

Douglass remained nearly a week, speaking every day in this old room and watching the audiences grow in numbers and respectability till the usual thing happened. A church was offered to him. This time it was a Baptist church, but his audience increased so rapidly now he had to hold the Sunday meeting in the park.

While he was still in Buffalo, another convention came to town. It was one in a series of colored conventions begun in 1830 for the purpose of protesting the disadvantages suffered by free Negroes in the United States. Held intermittently in the thirteen years since they were started, these conventions had drawn together the most prominent

Negroes of the time and considered such questions as emigration to Liberia and vocational education for free Negro youth as solutions. The Buffalo convention had before it a proposal for endorsement of the Liberty party.

Remond, who had parted from Douglass at Rochester, made a point of coming to Buffalo for this. Amos Gerry Beman, a clergyman from New Haven, served as chairman. Henry Highland Garnet, a graduate of the Oneida Institute at Whitesboro, now pastor of a church in Troy, gave a startling address in which he urged slaves, none of whom could possibly be reached by his oratory, to rise in arms against their masters.

When resolutions were offered, including the one on the Liberty party, Douglass could not resist the temptation to speak. A newcomer in these circles, he was nevertheless heard respectfully, and the position he took was in line with the Garrisonian principles he had espoused. He stated the case against political action. The convention voted him down, most of the delegates recording themselves in favor of circulating petitions to Congress expressing their hostility to slavery in the territories and to the annexation of Texas.

This was obviously the position his white friends in Rochester would have taken, but Douglass did not have time to ponder the issue now. He and Remond were booked for a meeting in Clinton county, Ohio. They must hurry along. At the Clinton meeting, which was held under a great shed built specially for this purpose, the whole slate of convention speakers met again. Thousands of people were in the audience, all ablaze with abolitionist fire, and Douglass's faith in the ultimate success of their crusade took on a brighter glow.

Again the speakers separated.

Douglass's companions from that point were George Bradburn and William A. White. These three were appointed to carry the campaign into Indiana, and there is no indication that any of them expected a reception unlike the ones hitherto accorded. But at Richmond, scene of their first meeting in the state, it became evident that the Indiana air was charged. On the platform from which he addressed that gathering Douglass had his best clothes "spoiled by evil-smelling eggs," and he and his companions moved on to Pendleton with apprehension.

Of course no hall or meeting place was available. That was no surprise but the abolitionist campaigners also became aware of a measure of friendship for their cause. A number of Quakers had settled in this community. With the help of some of these well-wishers the speakers erected a platform in the woods outside the town and announced their first meeting.

This section of Indiana boasted even larger elements of proslavery migrants. Some of the more vigilant of these noted the preparations for the convention and rode to Andersonville to organize counter measures. Douglass and his colleagues appeared undaunted. They opened their first session with the usual formalities. Then the audience settled down and the orators went to work.

Before many words had been uttered a band of tough-looking characters swooped down on horseback, tied their mounts under the trees and began to space themselves around the edges of the crowd. Presently one of their leaders shouted at the speaker on the platform to shut up. Douglass, who was not unaccustomed to heckling, tried to continue.

The leader of the horsemen repeated his command. This time he threatened their abolitionist hides if they didn't obey. The other speakers rose to their feet now and all tried to reason with the intruders and to prevail on them not to disturb the meeting. But the riders from Andersonville were not prepared to argue. They had been selected for other than rhetorical qualifications, and they were adequately armed.

Presently, their patience exhausted, they converged on the platform and began tearing it down. Half a dozen rock-fisted frontiersmen began to give William A. White and George Bradburn a pummelling. Douglass saw White knocked to the ground where he rolled over and began spitting out his teeth. A moment later he saw a heavy club fall on the back of Bradburn's head cutting the scalp and topling the victim into an unconscious heap. How he himself managed to get his hands on a heavy piece of wood from the wreckage of the platform, he did not know. But in another second, surrounded by the fury of the mob, he was fighting back savagely.

How many he hit and how they fell he never learned, for in a moment or two the scene went black and his towering figure crumpled to the ground under a storm of angry clubs and fists.

SLAVE NARRATIVE

DOUGLASS OPENED his eyes to morning sunlight. Why was he bleeding? What was wrong? And his left arm —why could he not move it? He sank back on his pillow and began searching the little room for something familiar.

He tried to think. Who was he? What was he doing here? What did he want?

In his childhood he had been called Fred Bailey. But nobody in Tuckahoe, Maryland, was ever fooled by that name, least of all the light-brown-skinned boy and his velvet-dark mother. He dozed now, his wounds commencing to throb, and presently he was floating in a tortured zone between sleep and wakefulness.

His mother—he remembered her vividly. Back in that world from which he had been redeemed, the world of childhood and slavery and the Eastern Shore, she had slipped into the hut where he lay among the squirming offspring of the slave quarters. She had folded him in her arms and held him close till it was time for her to steal again to her cabin, miles away, in time to answer the bell that would send her into the fields at dawn. There had been only a few such nights, but Douglass lived them over and over again. She came to him dimly then, on the fringes of sleep, and so she returned now, touching his numbed left arm, soothing his bruises.

What she whispered back there was also vague. When he tried to recall the words, he became aware of uncertainties. Had she told him that his first master was his father, or had he dreamed it? Admittedly his father was a white man. But to think of him as the monster who stood his Aunt Hester on a stool, tied her hands to a hook in the joist overhead, stripped her naked above the waist and lashed her into bloody insensibility still filled Douglass with horror. The face of this brutal man, leering at him strangely, mouth soiled by chewing tobacco, scrubby whiskers bristling, was another image that reappeared now, and suddenly it seemed to Douglass that he had seen this disturbing likeness of his father more recently. The memory of it brought his eyes open again.

Yes, that was it. The flash had come in the midst of the melee at Pendleton. After the platform was destroyed, when Douglass had gotten his hands on a piece of timber and begun to take a certain toll of his attackers, just before the blow fell on his head and the sickening spectacle faded into darkness, the face had floated before his eyes, and there it was now, the confused image of a confused parent. What could such a man say to such a son? What could he say to himself? Captain Anthony's way was to let his whip speak.

In the clean and friendly bed in which he awakened, Frederick Douglass twisted to find an easy position for his left arm. Now the events of the previous day became clearer. The battle of words, the great battle for the souls of his brothers in slavery, had suddenly flamed into physical violence. Douglass tried to reconstruct the event in his mind—but no, what did those details matter? What he wanted now was to know his condition and to find out where he was and how he had come here. He tried to lift himself again. Well, never mind. He was too badly hurt. Let the questions pass.

The hoodlums had been afraid to challenge him publicly with words. Unable to dispute the issue on its merits, they had fallen back, like Captain Anthony, on the guilty alternative of force. If ever Douglass needed reassurance that right was on his side, he had it now. The cause for which he fought was more than right. It was holy.

Whether or not he would be able to rise up and fight again was another question. He was badly broken up. Perhaps he should not try to think any more. He needed sleep.

The white woman who finally opened the door looked familiar, and her first words revealed that she was a Quaker. Douglass sighed with relief, remembering the two Friends who had spoken to him and Anna on the landing at Newport. In another moment she was removing bandages and examining his wounds.

Dr. Neal Hardy, her husband, had lingered behind when the mob rode off toward Andersonville, leaving Douglass for dead. He had crept back for a closer look at the motionless body on the ground. When he discovered that there was still life in it, he had dragged the unconscious man into his wagon and carried him three miles to his home. Now he had returned to Pendleton to treat the other victims, leaving his wife to nurse their suffering guest.

Hearing the story, Douglass began to feel better, but he knew instinctively that it would be a good little while before he left Indiana. With people like the Hardys backing him up, he did not fear the mob's fury. His own big stick, while it was in action, had done more than just fan the air. Somebody had paid for the broken bones that now left his arm dead at his side. Perhaps at this very minute they were counting the cost. Well, they would pay again, and more dearly, before they put Frederick Douglass out of this struggle for keeps. He might be handicapped with one arm in a sling, but on second thought, perhaps not so handicapped either.

Violence was what the crowd from Andersonville wanted. What they feared was arguments, the argument of his personality as much as his words against the inhumanity of slavery. The blows that felled him in the grove had not impaired his voice, thank God. Soon, sooner than his enemies imagined, he would be standing before Indiana audiences again.

The one hundred conventions had only begun.

The Hardys sheltered Douglass a number of days, and in their home he recovered strength enough to resume the campaign, but the doctor set the broken bones hurriedly and failed to do a good job. The injured hand never quite regained its former dexterity.

Meanwhile the ringleader of the riot at Pendleton was arrested. He pleaded guilty and was jailed in Indianapolis. His cronies from Andersonville did not abandon him there, however. Three hundred of them, mounted and armed with rifles, galloped into the city and demanded his release. Governor Whitcomb promptly pardoned the man.

From that point onward the series of conventions seemed to run together in Douglass's consciousness. He spoke many more times in Indiana before leaving, and it is possible to follow the general direction of the return sweep through Ohio and western Pennsylvania in the antislavery press, but to Douglass the audiences began to look much alike. Tumult and threats began to form a kind of pattern. At the same time experience was adding to his own devices for dealing with hecklers and quieting bullies. When tension became great, he introduced humor and convulsed the crowd with laughter. When he had angered them with old testament denunciation till the lid seemed ready to blow, he cunningly struck a note of soft pathos.

Where it was that Douglass carried the banner alone and where he was joined by William A. White, Sidney Gay and James Monroe are details that were soon lost in the montage which those exciting homeward conventions left in his memory. He did retain however some of the questions that were thrown at him most frequently. Always someone wanted to know, often in a whining voice, if it was not true that slaves were better off in slavery. Were they not content and happy? An equal number of people in these western towns wondered if Negroes could take care of themselves, if given their freedom. Others asked if the masters were not generally kind. Wouldn't most slaves choose to remain in slavery if given the choice? Were not Negroes too lazy to work except in bondage? On the other hand, wasn't there danger that slaves, if emancipated, would all rush North and take work away from white men? Shouldn't they be returned to Africa?

Many of the questions that came up from the floor of these conventions surprised Douglass. He did not have all the answers, but he was learning fast. He was also becoming aware of some interesting contradictions in the pro-slavery argument. "You can never educate them," one heckler would assert. Another, supporting the same side, would add, "They now have the gospel preached to them. Isn't that better than heathendom?" For Douglass of course this was a good point at which to deliver himself of his Slaveholder's Sermon, indicating just how this preaching sounded to the black man in his chains.

Bit by bit the slaveholding mentality unfolded itself through its spokesmen and sympathizers, and the twenty-six-year-old youth whose own freedom had not been won till he was past twenty, began picking it apart systematically. The antislavery press grew lyrical in its reports of his platform effectiveness, his wit and his logic, his burning eloquence and his lack of bitterness. He was behaving like

a young champion, out to meet all Goliaths. But the opposition was not silenced. The voices droned on, a muttering debate between the slavery advocate and his conscience.
"They can't be improved, the Negroes, they need masters
to care for them. They made no progress in Africa. They
are not like white people. They are an inferior race. And
you—you are meddling with what does not concern you.
Mind your own business. You abolitionists are only making
the condition of the Negro worse by your infernal agitation. You have pushed the relations between the races back
fifty years. You will never in God's world put an end to
slavery. And there's another thing—if God wanted slavery
abolished, he would have done it long ago. The Bible
sanctions slavery. The Savior said nothing against it."

The pause was only for breath. In the next city and the
next the argument would continue in the same tone, even
though the words might vary. "What have we in the North
to do with slavery? The people of the South inherited slavery. The Negroes are their property, their wealth. You—
you would not give up *your* property, would you? Some
abolitionists are rich. We have not seen them disposing of
their wealth. What would you do with the Negroes if you
had them?"

That last one excited Douglass. Someday he would prepare a full-length address on that subject. But now his
answer had to be brief, and it was one word, "Nothing."
That was the seed of the whole trouble, he thought angrily,
people wanting to do this or that with the Negro. Who did
they think they were—God?

"But the North once held slaves," the opposition continued. "The North is no better than the South?" Finally,
ignoring Douglass for the moment, it addressed the crowning question to Sidney Gay or William White, "Would you
marry a Negro? Would you want your daughter—"

Douglass mused proudly. That was one he would someday answer at greater length too. But not now. In the heat and hurry of an abolitionist convention he could only point out that he was himself obviously not an unmixed descendant of Africa, though born in slavery, that such mixing was more common and more widespread under oppression. As an issue, he could say, it was also irrelevent to the moral question of depriving men of their freedom. Perhaps that took care of the matter where the conventions were concerned, but Douglass was by no means satisfied in his own mind. Maybe—maybe there *was* a certain relevance. He would think about that question of marrying a Negro—or the other way round. When there was less tension, when angry passions cooled, when time was less pressing, he would face that question along with the others. He would not dodge.

Douglass and his companions found a warm reception in Lisbon, Ohio. Friends of abolition made the meetings there a pleasant interlude. To cap it off, the Executive Committee of the Ohio Society urged Douglass to remain with them as a lecturer on regular appointment. Even though he did not accept it, the offer boosted Douglass's morale, and the crusade, now consisting of three men on horseback, moved across the hills into western Pennsylvania.

At New Brighton, the *Liberator* crooned, Douglass "preached the old antislavery of Massachusetts," meaning, of course, the Garrisonian doctrine of nonviolence, no political activity, and "No Union With Slaveholders." While the memory of Pendleton continued to haunt his dreams, while he was aware of the hazards to a fugitive like himself in venturing this near to the boundaries of slavery, he rode on boldly, flanked by his black and white companions, and in the first week of December the trio of weatherbeaten horsemen entered Philadelphia. They were just in time for the tenth anniversary of the founding of the American Anti-Slavery Society.

Robert Purvis greeted them. A light-skinned Negro educated at Edinburgh, Purvis lived in considerable comfort at Byberry, Pennsylvania. The unusual thing about him, considering the risks to a well-to-do Negro, was his association with the abolitionists. In the absence of Garrison, the Society's perennial president, Purvis was in charge of the anniversary celebration. Naturally Gay, editor of the New York *Anti-Slavery Standard,* with the well-known Remond and the new headliner Douglass, at once became central attractions, but by now this was just another convention to the road-weary trio. They moved on to New York and then to Massachusetts, where Douglass returned to his family in New Bedford.

He had been away from home six months, during which time he had heard little from Anna, and the babies, who now numbered three, had grown beyond recognition. He was relieved to discover that his free-born wife had fared well during this extended separation. Always a good housekeeper, she had found simple but effective ways of improving the appearance of their humble rooms—colorful rag rugs, curtains made of cheap remnants, chair frames restored to use by new bottoms, freshly painted tables and shelves. Everything was spotless. And in addition to caring for her babies, Anna had washed and ironed by the day and managed to save a little money. Good, dependable Anna! It was easy to see that she could get along without him, but she welcomed him home with a kind of homage usually reserved for visiting Princes. She was neither proud nor ashamed of her illiteracy, her lack of interest in intellectual subjects.

Her questions about his rugged and hazardous adventure all related to bodily comforts and safety. Had the distance been great? How about the food? Who ironed his shirts for him? Any interference from slave catchers and their kind? Douglass bounced the babies on his knees as he pieced his experiences together for her. But he did not talk about the questions hecklers had fired at him in the conventions, the questions he had been forced to answer without due consideration. Most of these had lodged in his mind, and he was determined to answer them all to his own satisfaction, but there was no point in troubling Anna with such matters. These were topics on which to mull as he sawed up a supply of stove wood, as he strolled the New Bedford streets at nightfall, as he lingered at his window after Anna and the babies had fallen asleep. "What would you do with the Negroes if you had your way?" "Would you marry a—"

December passed, and presently it was time for the annual meeting of the Massachusetts Anti-Slavery Society. Again Douglass packed his traveling bag. He arrived at Faneuil Hall in Boston on Wednesday morning, the twenty-fourth of January, and he had scarcely entered when he became aware of the pointed interest this session had in the one hundred conventions. The handshakes of Garrison and Phillips, Maria Chapman and Abby Kelley, James Buffum and Samuel May, the singing Hutchinsons and the rest were all accompanied by expectant smiles. "We've heard a little," they seemed to say. "We're waiting for the full report."

They did not have to wait long, and the report warmed their hearts. Though the amount of money collected in the actual conventions fell $70 short of the traveling expenses of the speakers, the total donations which followed their effort amounted to $56 more than total expenses. This operating balance had been made possible by the generous hospitality of sympathetic friends along the line, coupled with the fact that William A. White, who had his own resources, and Sidney H. Gay, the editor of the *Standard,* had asked no compensation for their services. The fact remained that the western conventions had actually yielded a small profit in the treasury. More important by far, however, were the intangible results. "Tens of thousands, perhaps hundreds of thousands of minds have been reached," said the report, "and consciences stirred, as to their duty to the slave. The seed has been flung broadcast over a magnificent field, and it cannot be but that much will take root and spring up unto the harvest."

It was enough to make a young fellow, just completing his first full year in the employ of the Society, burst his buttons. But Douglass did not let himself get too happy. There was still that matter of his "insubordination" to Collins in Syracuse. He had not forgotten the letter of reproof he had received from Maria W. Chapman, speaking as a member of the Board of Managers of the organization. He was not sure the issue would not bring on more talk.

His fears were soon put to rest, however. Collins resigned as general agent of the society and was replaced by Wendell Phillips. Instead, as the Thursday morning session of the meeting wound up its business, someone was reminded that Massachusetts had been neglected by the team of agents in their sweep through western New York, Ohio, Indiana and Pennsylvania. Feeling strong and revived, Douglass and White, supported by Buffum, Garrison and others, promptly stood up and proposed that they do it all over again in the Commonwealth of Massachusetts—a hundred more conventions!

On this note the meeting adjourned.

The second series of conventions was less eventful than the first. Douglas and White did this round with Parker Pillsbury, a rugged and thunderous young preacher whom James Russell Lowell called "a Theseus in cow-hide boots."

Attendance was generally good at their meetings, and the newspaper accounts mention no disorders. Their general tone appears to have been reflected in a note commenting on an address by Douglass at Concord. "No man," it said, "ever closed a speech with more dignity and respect." The same correspondent observed that "the house was crowded with the best of people—no clergy."

Before concluding the series Douglass doubled back to the seacoast towns at least twice. First it was to preside at a rally in Lynn where with Garrison, Remond, Stephen S. Foster and James Buffum he protested the public whipping of John L. Brown of South Carolina for attempting to help a slave girl escape. Next it was to stand beside Garrison and support his "No Union With Slaveholders" position at the May meeting of the New England Society. When the Massachusetts conventions were completed, he returned again to Anna and the young ones in New Bedford.

This time he had new experiences to ponder. Nowhere had he met physical violence on this tour. The defense of slavery as implied by questions raised in open meetings had been definitely weaker than that encountered nearer the borders of slave territory. Only one new twist had been given to the old arguments, but this twist was a sharp one, and it troubled him.

At these recent conventions people without personal prejudice had taken to buttonholing him after meetings and whispering. Did he really expect shrewd New Englanders to believe that he had been a slave, brutalized in the manner he described? The masquerade was too transparent. A more cultivated young speaker could scarcely have come out of Harvard. He might convince people in the West that only five years ago he had been in the debased condition of which he spoke so eloquently, but not citizens of the Bay State. They were attracted to him as a person and as a speaker, but if he offered himself as an example of the product of the slave system, he was actually helping the South.

They had also noticed, they pointed out, that he was never very clear about the place from which he had escaped, how he got away, who had been his owner, and the like. This vagueness, coupled with the fact that he was in his own person a contradiction of much that he said, left even open-minded people with questions. Mulling over these comments, Douglass began to feel strangely cornered. His mind went back to the words of Collins and George Foster when he toured with them in his first series of public appearances following Nantucket. Collins and Foster had sensed something of this sort. Come to think about it, so had Garrison.

"Let us have the facts," Foster had suggested tactfully, noting Douglass's first departure from the straight narrative of his bondage.

Collins had nodded strong agreement. "H'm. Give us the facts. We will take care of the philosophy."

Of course he had brushed them aside and thereafter they had not stood in his way. But he caught something of the same inference later when Garrison himself whispered to him as he stepped upon the platform. "Tell your story, Frederick." The words had puzzled him at the time, but eventually both Collins and Foster explained.

"People won't believe you ever were a slave, Frederick," Foster had entreated, "if you keep on this way."

Collins' suggestion was more specific—and more embarrassing. "Be yourself and tell your story. Better have a little of the plantation speech than not. It is not best that you seem too learned."

Had these indiscreet words by Collins been in the back of Douglass's consciousness during the meeting in Syracuse? Well, he had not accepted the suggestion when it was given and he had no intention of accepting it now that Collins was not longer working with the Society, but he had to admit that the thing which Collins, Foster, Garrison and others had feared from the first had happened. New Englanders were questioning his story. Some of the more outspoken ones, he suspected, were at the point of denouncing him as an imposter.

To adopt plantation speech was out of the question. His pride would not allow him to clown in that way. Another solution would have to be found, and it was for this that he sought as spring came to the waterfront and to the beaches beyond New Bedford. Swapping friendly talk at his doorstep, returning now and again to watch the calkers in the shipyards, learning to play the fiddle, he kept feeling around in the dark corners of his mind. By summer he had his answer.

It was a daring thing to attempt. Perhaps it was even reckless, but by now Douglass had considered and rejected every alternative. To answer those people who had begun to doubt his story, to silence the whispering that threatened to destroy his value as an abolitionist agent, he would throw caution away, he would put the full account in writing. That was it. He would write a *book*. In his book he would tell the whole world just who's slave he had been, how he had squirmed and plotted in his chains, where and when he had escaped. The only detail he would withhold would be the manner of his getaway. Even that would not be concealed for his own sake. He would reveal everything and take his chances as a fugitive in Massachusetts. But to disclose the maneuver by which he gave his owners the slip would be to close that particular gate to other slaves. That he would not do. As for the rest, the lid was off. Next time he undertook a series of lectures, he would have an answer for those who accused him of inventing personal history for the sake of winning antislavery sympathizers.

Yes, he knew the risks. For one thing, books don't let

just anybody write them. Authorship might present towering difficulties, considering the limitations of his learning,
the haphazard way in which he had taught himself. A year
spent in trying to put the record straight in this way might
be a year wasted. Could he afford it?

On the face of things he could not. Anna was with child
again. Soon the washing and ironing by which she had
supplemented the family income would have to be suspended again. Meanwhile Douglass had been thinking of
moving his family to Lynn, and moving meant extra expenses. A year without income from the head of the house
was not a pleasant prospect to a fugitive with a rapidly
growing family.

Nor was the problem of security less disturbing. Just
how safe would he be even in Lynn, a city known for its
abolitionist element, after he had revealed his past? What
would the results be for Anna and the young ones in the
event of his capture through the hocus-pocus of laws
favoring the slave catcher? Could he afford that? It was not
an easy decision, but the power to act decisively, even under
strain, was Frederick Douglass's peculiar trait, perhaps the
key to his rôle.

While Douglass was neither the first nor the last fledgling
writer to gamble his family's welfare on the fortunes of
a proposed book, his situation was perhaps more complicated than most.

Quietly, a little grimly, he went to work.

And authorlike, he stopped occasionally in the midst of
composition to fiddle around. Sometimes the fiddling was
on a violin, which he loved with an untutored love, but
more often it was just knocking about the house and wool-
gathering. England, he meditated, the home of his paternal
ancestors—what a place to visit that would be! Charles
Remond was always talking about experiences there. Every

issue of the abolitionist press told of the activities of British and Irish antislavery leaders. The names of William Wilberforce, Thomas Clarkson and Daniel O'Connell were familiar to all convention audiences, and the young Douglass had already noticed the odd deference Americans showed to opinions from this source.

Remond's admiration of the British was more personal, of course. The black men who had been abroad all assured Douglass that the freedom a Negro American enjoyed among the British was as different from that in New England as New England was different from the slave states. For a Negro there was as much freedom in one block of London as in the whole of Boston or New York. Certainly that would be something to see, something to feel.

Another attraction was the increase of prestige that resulted from European travel. Back from a sojourn in the British Isles, a speaker could always bear himself with extra assurance before American audiences. If he could somehow win the approval of the old world, his stature would be increased a full cubit. And this said nothing about the enormous advantage to the cause of abolition.

Think how he could point the finger of condemnation at the evils of American slavery from the safe but conspicuous distance of Britain! If the story of his bondage shocked Americans in the Northern states, what would it do to the British, the Irish and the Scots? What would the effect of sentiments thus aroused have on public opinion in the United States? The great agitation was bound to benefit. He would hold the idea firmly in mind. Right now, of course, there was this writing to finish.

Late in the autumn of 1844, the year in which a certain member of New Englanders prepared for the second coming of Christ, as announced by William Miller, Frederick Douglass took time from his first sustained writing effort to move his family from New Bedford to Lynn. Considering the preoccupation of many slaves with signs in the sun and moon, with falling stars and dark days, and the natural carry-over on the part of some who had followed the North Star to freedom, it is interesting that Douglass, who lectured in communities where the Millerite preaching was most intense, made no mention of it. He had his own excitements that fall and winter, under his own roof.

Wendell Phillips wrote to Elizabeth Pease, "Douglass who is now writing out his story thinks of relaxing by arranging a voyage." Evidently the abolitionists had knocked at his door to discover what was keeping him in. Not only had he been out of touch with them; in October he had turned down an assignment by the Executive Committee of the Massachusetts Society to campaign for the Cause in Pennsylvania. Now the news was out.

But what about this book writing? Was it safe? The officers of the Society began to wonder, as Douglass himself had wondered before deciding to try it, but they reserved judgment. And while they waited for the manuscript, that proposed trip abroad for their young headliner began to seem more and more like a good idea.

While Douglass sweated and squirmed at his writing table, Anna's labor began, and composition was interrupted by the crying of the writer's fourth child, his third son. Was it like this with the writing of all books? Did everything happen—everything possible—as soon as the pen touched the paper? Now he would have to stop and think up a name for a new baby. They had called the girl Rosetta, the first two boys Lewis and Fred junior. Thinking of England, no doubt, and remembering the friend and colleague who had told him most about the British Isles, he decided to call this one Charles Remond. Now he could return to his writing.

Early the following spring, 1845, he composed this passage:

While attending an anti-slavery convention at Nantucket, on the 11th of August, 1841, I felt strongly moved to speak, and was at the same time much urged to do so by Mr. William C. Coffin, a gentlemen who had heard me speak in the colored people's meeting at New Bedford. It was a severe cross, and I took it up reluctantly. The truth was, I felt myself a slave, and the idea of speaking to white people weighed me down. I spoke but a few moments, when I felt a degree of freedom, and said what I desired with considerable ease. From that time until now, I have been engaged in pleading the cause of my brethren—with what success, and with what devotion, I leave those acquainted with my labors to decide.

Having said that, he knew that the job was finished. The rest of his story was public knowledge. He had not written for his own amusement. He was still fighting slavery. In telling his personal experiences from lecture platforms, he had generally managed to leave his audiences convinced that the slave system was a savage violation of human personality. Had he succeeded in getting the same thing across in the 125 closely written pages on his table?

He would have to reread it to be sure. He would also want Phillips, Garrison and others to read the manuscript and comment. This meant an end of seclusion, of course. Now he must attend to the details of publication.

His own conclusion on rereading was that nothing of importance needed to be changed, but he did decide to add an appendix explaining his attitude toward the church's position on slavery. His sharp criticism of the way Christians had met this issue in the United States had nothing to do with basic christianity. That point clarified, he was ready to stand on what he had written. He was not ready, however, for Wendell Phillips's first reaction.

"In your place," Phillips's letter said, "I should throw the MS. into the fire." No lack of merit in the narrative was implied, for "we have known you long and can put the most entire confidence in your truth, candor, and sincerity." But frankly, it was a dangerous statement to publish, revealing as it did the persons from whom Douglass had escaped, while imputing to them the most disgusting characters and charging them with shameful crimes. Phillips calmly warned his Negro friend, "In all the broad lands which the Constitution of the United States overshadows, there is no single spot—however narrow or desolate—where a fugitive slave can plant himself and say, 'I am safe.' The whole armory of Northern Law has no shield for you."

But Douglass had considered all this in advance. If the little book was acceptable to the Massachusetts Society, he would be pleased to have them go to press with it. It was and they did. The book appeared in May, published at the Anti-Slavery Office in Boston under the title *Narrative of the Life of Frederick Douglass an American Slave,* written by himself. An exciting preface by William Lloyd Garrison recalled the Nantucket meeting at which the gifted young fugitive had been discovered by the Garrisonians, recounted his effectiveness in the movement since that time, and ended with the angry motto of their cause—*No Compromise With Slavery! No Union With Slaveholders!*

Phillips's letter was also included with the front matter, virtually tipping off the former owners that Douglass could be theirs for the taking, and immediately the little paperbound volume began to sell rapidly in abolitionist circles at fifty cents a copy. Of it the *New York Tribune* said, "It is an excellent piece of writing, and on that score to be prized as a specimen of the powers of the black race, which prejudice persists in disputing." The home-town paper, the *Lynn Pioneer,* went overboard: "It is the most thrilling work which the American press ever issued—*and the most important.*" And a woman reader wrote to Garrison, "Never before have I been brought so completely in sympathy with the slave. May the author become a mighty

instrument to the pulling down of the strongholds of iniquity, and the establishment of righteousness in our land!"

At the same time James N. Buffum, Maria W. Chapman,
Phillips and other friends of Douglass began taking pre-
cautions against an attempt by the slave power to capture
and return the daring writer to bondage. They quietly
started a fund to give him a trip abroad. But now Douglass
did not seem in a hurry to get away. Perhaps he enjoyed
the excitement of danger. Meanwhile the Massachusetts
Anti-Slavery Society gleefully saluted the *Narrative* as a
"new anti-slavery lecturer," and Phillips, who had advised
Douglass to burn the manuscript, now proposed a resolution urging that the book be placed in the hands of all
"who believe the slaves of the South to be either well
treated, or happy, or ignorant of their right to freedom, or
in need of preparation to make them fit for freedom."

So now it was summer, and in the company of abolitionist friends Douglass had new themes for conversation. No,
he wasn't planning to run away, now that he had provided
the slave authorities with the evidence they wanted, but
he had contemplated relaxing abroad after the ordeal of
authorship. Money? Well, the book was selling fast, and
this purse they talked about—he supposed he could count
on something from that quarter.

Tall, gold-spectacled James N. Buffum, an Old Hickory
abolitionist and known for his discriminating literary taste,
was quick to nod assurance. He had written letters to Gerrit Smith and other backers of their movement on the
subject, and he could assure Douglass that the gift would be
adequate. There was every reason why Frederick should
make this trip. An even better plan might be for Buffum
to accompany him. In fact, if Douglass wished it, Buffum
was prepared to make steamboat reservations for the two
right away.

Nothing could have pleased Douglass more, for James

Buffum, who had been one of Douglass's discoverers at
Nantucket, whose presence in Lynn had been one of the
influences attracting the Douglass family to that city, remained one of Frederick's favorite people, and during the
next month and a half he talked of nothing but plans for
the voyage. Everyone in Lynn soon knew what was afoot.
One of those who listened most intently was Jesse Hutchinson. Presently an idea flashed into Douglass's mind. Had
anyone ever considered taking the Hutchinson Quartet
abroad? Surely the British would appreciate the singing
Hutchinsons.

The Hutchinsons' grocery and stove stores were just a
few doors from the old house in which Douglass and his
family lived on Union Street. They provided ideal spots
for hard-bitten abolitionists to meet casually, draw up
boxes, and none was more welcome than the ebullient
Frederick whose anecdotes and entertaining small talk
were already being mentioned in the diaries of his Lynn
neighbors. On the subject of a British tour for the Hutchinsons, coinciding with his and James Buffum's trip, he soon
found himself choking up with his own enthusiasm. What
a delegation from the new world to the old!

The Hutchinsons would be a sensation anywhere. Douglass had heard them first at the annual meeting of the
Massachusetts Society in January of 1843, and he had been
deeply impresed by the willowy, long-haired appearance of
the brothers as well as by their perfect harmony and the
originality of their songs and arrangements. The Hutchinsons introduced something more than sweet voices and
rustic charm into the antislavery movement, however. As
background accompaniment to the oratory of Phillips, to
Douglass's disturbing account of suffering and escape, they
seemed to put the campaign itself on a lyrical plane.
Scarcely a session opened or closed without "a heart-stir-
ring song by the Hutchinsons," another song by the "New

Hampshire vocalists," or "a thrilling song by the Hutchinson brothers," according to the report of the secretary of the Society. But that was the annual meeting at which the membership was electrified by the daring proposal of 100 Conventions in the west, and this exciting adventure had momentarily snatched Douglass out of his musical reverie.

Since those Boston meetings of two years and a half ago Douglass had become a seasoned fighter and an important figure in the Garrisonian movement. In the same period a quartet of Hutchinsons, consisting of three younger brothers of the large tribe and one sister, the lovely and beloved Abbe, had become equally famous. With the young business man Jesse serving as manager and agent, doubling as arranger of songs and lyricist, and sometimes lending his own adequate voice to the group, they had appeared in recitals throughout New England and New York as well as at abolitionist conventions. By August of 1845 the Hutchinsons were an established musical attraction who, between quaint interludes during which they insisted on returning home to cultivate their farm at Milford, could even afford to snub attractive offers from P. T. Barnum.

Europe? Jesse beamed. Just the thing! He was sure that Judson and Asa and John and Abbe would be thrilled. They would be in Lynn presently, and if there was still time—if there was still available space, they might even sail with Douglass and Buffum on the *Cambria*. So now there really was excitement on Union Street.

The quartet arrived a few days later in a secondhand carryall drawn by a vividly unmatched team, a white and a bay. A big bull fiddle was strapped to the top of the carriage, and a hair trunk was tied on behind. Inside, this "nest of brothers with a sister in it" contained also two violins without cases, a guitar, and a bag of clothes. As usual, the charming company entered the town singing at the top of their lungs.

The high notes were produced by Judson, tallest of the four, a gentle and moody dreamer, who at twenty-eight was four years older than John, the sturdy and handsome baritone. Asa, who was just twenty-two and the smallest of the boys, possessed the bass voice. Sixteen-year-old Abbe sang alto. Round-faced and rosy, with big dark eyes, she was the darling of the whole Hutchinson family—a family which, incidentally, had included a total of sixteen attractive children.

The Hutchinsons had just completed another round of concerts and were hankering for a change, perhaps some hunting or fishing for the boys, possibly a visit here or there with older members of the family for Abbe. What did Jesse have in mind? His proposal of a voyage to the British Isles sounded perfect. Even the fact that the *Cambria* was scheduled to sail in just five days did not dismay them. That was enough time for troupers like themselves to put their things together, drive to Milford and say good-by to the family, return to Boston, buy tickets and get the baggage on board.

They would never be able to thank Frederick Douglass enough for suggesting such a wonderful idea. And Douglass, dreaming of bold adventures abroad but beginning now to worry more and more about the dangers to his person to which the growing popularity of his *Narrative* exposed him before the law, could scarcely wait till sailing time. Phillips had warned him in advance. Since he had insisted on going ahead with publication, however, abolitionists were themselves exploiting his peril. Douglass had publicly confessed himself to be a fugitive. In effect, he had challenged the slave power to return him to bondage. Could he depend on Massachusetts to shield him?

At first he had been ready to count on it. Now—now he wasn't sure. In fact, he had begun to tremble. By the eleventh of August he had begun to feel that he was no more than one jump ahead of the bloodhounds. If he escaped, it would be by the skin of his teeth. Fortunately that was sailing day.

The *Cambria* could not get up to the wharf, where crowds of abolitionists waited. While the Hutchinsons wept and laughed, their arms around relatives who had come to see them off, and finally burst into song in the prow of the tugboat that took them out to the big, ocean-going, sail-and-steam vessel, Douglass tried to make his good-bys as brief as possible. His feelings were definitely mixed.

V

SHADOW AND SUBSTANCE

OUGLASS WAS UNHAPPY in the steerage of the *Cambria*. He considered segregation a *part* of slavery, its extension, an underhanded device to nullify his hard-won freedom. In the first year of his association with the antislavery movement he had resolved never to respect a jim-crow sign. If railroad officials insisted on segregating him, they would have to take him by the collar. Never—never would he cooperate. Naturally he fretted in his below-deck cage, and the companionship of James Buffum, who had accepted the same conditions for himself when the steamship company refused to sell him a first-class ticket for his Negro friend, was limited consolation.

Seasickness put everything else out of mind for a few days, and when it began to wear off Douglass discovered that he had missed nothing of real interest on board. Nearly everybody else had been seasick too, including all the Hutchinsons. Now more and more of the passengers were beginning to feel steady again, and the lyrical Hutchinsons, who liked to be photographed with their heads close together, Judson's swanlike neck tilted toward the rest, were singing on deck and making friends right and left. Douglass listened uneasily, sniffed the fine ocean air and determined not to submit to restriction without protest. He began by sending messages to the captain.

The first concession he won was permission to come on the promenade deck when accompanied by Buffum. When the Hutchinsons realized what was going on, they responded like plucked strings. They invited Douglass to walk on deck with them. To those passengers who showed astonishment, Americans and Europeans, they passed out copies of their friend's little book, which they had brought along in quantity. Judson, who was near Frederick's age, was especially fond of Douglass; in addition to other mutual interests they shared a liking for the violin, which Judson had studied seriously and which Frederick was teaching himself to play for amusement.

The immediate problem, however, was the rather large number of wealthy slaveholders aboard the vessel. A party of them from Cuba had become particularly offensive after spilling wine on Abbe's silk dress at dinner. The responsible individual kept following the outraged girl around the deck and apologizing drunkenly. Being as strong for temperance as for abolition, the Hutchinsons resented him. Even the excitement of big icebergs, which appeared in surprising numbers, was marred by the intrusion of his unwelcome gallantry.

A group of the same species from Charleston presently contrived to bring to a head the issue which at that moment divided all Americans, whether at home, on the sea or abroad. The gentlemen from the South had read the *Narrative* by now and they were ready to be damned before they would put up with a "nigger" on the promenade deck any longer. The Hutchinsons' answer to this was an appeal to the captain, who had been captivated by their songs, to allow Douglass to address the passengers of the *Cambria* on the forward deck. They had seen hostile or divided audiences won over by Frederick's oratory before. They were sure—

But the mere announcement of this intention infuriated the slaveholders, and Douglass's heroic stature, his contempt for their sneers, his complete self-assurance, drove the men from Georgia, South Carolina and Louisiana crazy. By the time he began speaking, they were frothing and shouting, "Kill the nigger. Throw him overboard."

Naturally the blood froze in the veins of the gentle Hutchinsons, but presently one of them recovered enough to scamper breathlessly to Captain Judkins' cabin. This rugged old party did not enjoy being aroused so violently from his afternoon siesta, but the young Hutchinsons had become his special pets. He was a kind of singer himself, as it happened, who had not only sung with them evenings on deck but had more than once swapped them stories for songs until after midnight. He could not refuse to respond to their summons now. Just wait till he got his pants on. He'd show those rowdies who was captain of the *Cambria*.

A few moments later Captain Judkins was on deck bellowing to his bos'n to bring the irons. That did it, so far as the lynch mob was concerned. Quiet was promptly restored, and the old British lion turned to his young pets with a soft smile. "I was once the owner of two hundred slaves," he confessed, "but the government of Great Britain liberated them, and I am glad of it."

Gilbert-and-Sullivan-like, the Hutchinsons, aided and abetted by the captain's dubious singing voice, struck up "God Save the Queen" and followed it with "Yankee Doodle," "America" and "A Life on the Ocean Wave."

Douglass heard the singing from below. Before the arrival of Captain Judkins, when it had seemed certain that the planters from Charleston would make their pledges good, he had, with such dignity as he had been able to preserve under the circumstances, retired to the shelter of the deck awning and thence to the steerage, his coattails flying. The mob had been at the point of going down after him and dragging him out when the captain thundered his threat.

So peace was restored and Douglass returned to hobnob with his friends on the promenade deck. It was here that the captain joined them after dinner on August twenty-sixth and predicted that they should be able to see land before nightfall. This word ran through the vessel like electricity. Differences were forgotten as passengers of all persuasions crowded the rail to be the first to discern the shore, but it was 10:30 P.M. before the first light appeared and Captain Judkins informed them that they were looking at the southern tip of Ireland.

A quiet little man from Philadelphia who had been inconspicuous during the whole voyage suddenly cried out, "Oh, the dear spot where I was born!"

Not to be outdone, the Hutchinsons put their heads together, hummed a chord and began singing,

"The cold cheerless ocean in safety we've passed,
And the warm genial earth glads our vision at last."

The young slaveholders who had wanted to throw Douglass overboard rushed ashore at Liverpool and gave their version of the affair to the press, making much of their offended pride as gentlemen and Southerners. But Douglass soon discovered that this was the finest introduction he could possibly be given to the people of Ireland. Crowds of people from every level of society were instantly eager to see the dark stranger and hear what he might have to say. He did not even have to use the glowing letters of introduction with which Garrison, Phillips and other leaders of the American movement had provided him.

With no definite plan of sojourn, Douglass and Buffum spent three days in the Liverpool hotel at which the Hutchinsons were stopping and then took leave of their friends and moved on to Dublin, where they were received by Richard D. Webb, an agent for the *Anti-Slavery Standard*. Douglass began to look around and to take his bearings.

It was a comfort to realize that eleven days of tossing sea now separated him from those who claimed the right, backed by the power of the United States government, to enslave him. It was a deep comfort to know that now he was beyond their nastiest threats, that now he could say what he wanted to say about American institutions without fear of being mobbed, that while he did it he could travel as a man and give no more thought than was normal to the questions of where he would sit in a public carriage, whether or not he would be courteously served in the dining room of a hotel or how he would be met in museums, music halls or art galleries. It was a comfort just to be in such a place. But it was no comfort at all to remember that Anna and the children were on the other side of the water.

Of course he had provided for them as well as he could. All the money the American edition of the *Narrative* earned during his absence would go to their support. They were among abolitionist friends in Lynn. He had confidence in these friends. More important, Anna had found work in a shoe bindery. If necessary, she could still do laundry work on the side. Naturally he hoped—but what good could he do them by mooning? He was in Ireland now, and where they were concerned it was better to have him out of the reach of slave catchers than at their side. He must make the best of his time and his talents. Certainly Anna knew that this was the way in which he could do most for them.

Leaving Buffum to exchange experiences with their host, he went out alone to explore the streets of Dublin. Presently a swarm of beggars picked up his track. Soon they were all around him so that he was scarcely able to step.

"Will your honor please to give me a penny to buy some bread?"

"May the Lord bless you, give the poor old woman a little sixpence."

All were in rags, dreadful rags. Some who were without feet dragged themselves on the ground. Some had lost hands and arms and held up their stumps for Douglass to see. Others were so deformed their feet lapped around and laid against their backs. Among them were women shamefully exposed by their tatters. Some of these carried pale, emaciated infants whose sunken eyes horrified the former Maryland slave. All were barefooted, of course.

"For the love of God, leave us a few pennies—we will divide them amongst us."

"Oh my poor child, it must starve! For God's sake give me a penny. More power to you! I know your honor will leave the poor creature something. Ah, do! Ah, do! I will pray for you as long as I live."

Frederick Douglass began emptying his pockets. Later he decided he would have to restrain this impulse or be reduced to the same condition. Instead he would try to learn more about this wretchedness. In his experience hunger and filth and exposure and shame were associated with slavery. How could the same things be explained in Dublin?

The more he explored, the more degradation he found. The poor of the city lived in mud huts about ten feet square and six feet high. These were covered with straw. A mud chimney at one end reached about a foot above the roof. There were no partitions inside, and the hut was without floor or windows. Some huts even lacked chimneys. None was without its disposal hole in front of the doorway, however. In these shallow pits, ten or twelve feet in circomference and three or four feet deep, the filth of the hut was preserved. Douglass noticed a green scum on some of them, bubbles on others, and he observed that large families, including men, women and children, frequently shared these close, unsegregated quarters with a family pig.

But no Irish hut that he saw was without a picture of Christ's crucifixtion pasted conspicuously on the wall. The presence of these pictures reminded Douglass of a distinction between the condition of the suffering poor in Ireland and the slaves of Maryland. Actually there were several points of distinction. Slaves were not permitted the consolation of religion. They were deprived of Bibles. The poor of Dublin, on the other hand, were free. No one was waiting to pursue them with bloodhounds if they ran away. Freedom made a powerful difference. But this detracted nothing from his sympathy. "I know the cause of humanity is one the world over," he concluded. "He who thinks himself an abolitionist, yet cannot enter into the wrongs of others, has yet to find a true foundation for his anti-slavery faith."

While slavery was the enemy to be put down in America, in Ireland the demon was whiskey. "Most beggars drink whiskey," he observed. That was the thing they had in common. He had begun to check this hypothesis when a man approached him on a main street with a white cloth over his face, feeling his way with a cane.

By now Douglass was not stopping for every beggar's solicitation, but this one seemed different. He asked the man what was wrong. The poor fellow explained that he had been drunk and lying in the street when it happened. A hog had come along and torn off his nose and most of his face. Douglass lifted the white cloth and saw the living skeleton underneath. He began to feel a little sick.

Had the Roman church fallen down on this matter of temperance just as the Protestants had fallen down on slavery? He was inclined to believe that they had.

Meanwhile James Buffum had not been idle. While

Douglass probed and collected impressions, Buffum arranged speaking engagements. In the first two weeks of their stay in Dublin they held "four glorious anti-slavery meetings—two in the Royal Exchange and two in the Friends' meeting house—all crowded to overflowing," Douglass wrote to Garrison. To this he added a side comment on the Friends' meeting house in Lynn. "On this side of the Atlantic its spacious walls would probably at once welcome an anti-slavery meeting; but, as things now stand, it must be closed to humanity—lest Friends get into the mixture!" Another lecture had been arranged for the Dublin Music Hall, the seating capacity of which was three thousand. Meanwhile Douglass and Buffum had dropped in on several large temperance meetings, and Buffum had always managed to reach the chairman and let it be known that Frederick Douglass was in the audience. Sometimes this was unnecessary, for Douglass automatically headed for the first rows if he saw a vacant seat. One way or another, by spontaneous demand of the audience, by discovery of the chairman or by Buffum's tactful arrangement, he generally managed to wind up on the platform. But he alone was responsible for what usually followed.

Often this amounted to uproar. Twenty-eight years old, now seven years out of slavery, Douglass was a thrillingly romantic figure. The Irish fell head-over-heels in love with him. They loved his wit, the sharpness of his argument, his manly beauty. Even more, they loved him as a fresh new champion of all the downtrodden, including themselves. Daniel O'Connell, their own popular hero of the moment, was introduced to the young American orator on the speakers' platform in the course of a noisy meeting for the repeal of the Corn Laws, and O'Connell made it plain that Irish suffering under their oppressors was not unrelated to Negro suffering in America under slavery. Thereafter

Douglass was introduced to Irish audiences as the "Black O'Connell," and ovations followed.

This was the Ireland of the potato rot as well as the corn issue and the temperance campaign. The young Queen Victoria had begun her reign in England, and men like Disraeli, John Bright, Sir Robert Peel and Lord John Russell were the voices of the nation's conscience. Slavery had been abolished in the Empire, but Thomas Clarkson, George Thompson and other veterans of that struggle were eagerly awaiting the outcome in the United States. The spirit of reform was the dominant social force in British life, the obvious wave of the future.

"The cause is rolling on," Douglass exulted in his second published letter from abroad. "I glory in the battle as well as the victory."

In Ireland he had good reason to glory. The British edition of the *Narrative* was published while he was in Dublin and began at once to repeat the good sales it was enjoying in the United States. Soon it was apparent that he would be able to live comfortably in Britain on the income from this source alone. But it was not the limit of his earning power. After five weeks in Dublin, as he and Buffum packed their bags to move on, he checked up on his engagements and found that between Cork and Belfast he had enough lectures scheduled in Ireland to occupy him for another month.

Douglass was welcomed to Cork at a public breakfast given in his honor, and the mayor of the city served as chairman of the meeting at his first evening lecture. Perhaps this was to be expected in a city where the local anti-slavery society had resolved not to disband till slavery was abolished in the rest of the world as well as in the British Empire. In this atmosphere Douglass hammered violently on the theme which served him during the whole British sojourn: the attitude of the churches, both Protestant and

Catholic, toward the temperance movement and abolition. Since both were essentially moral issues, as he saw them, indifference or opposition or compromise by organized religion seemed to him not only inexcusable but monstrous. Naturally the objects of his attacks began to set themselves for counter blows.

But meanwhile he was handsomely dined and entertained by Father Mathew, a happy temperance warrior who had to his credit nearly five and one-half million signers of the temperance pledge. Charmed by his host's friendliness, Douglass signed one himself, apparently with adequate ceremony, and accepted an invitation to a rally in St. Patrick's Temperance Hall, where he was greeted by a song of welcome especially composed for his entrance. "All true reforms are kindred," he beamed in response.

Buffum left him in Cork to visit Manchester, but Douglass continued in triumph to Belfast, after sending to Webb in Dublin for another supply of copies of the *Narrative*. At Belfast the hostility of the offended clergy began to catch up with him, but it was not yet strong enough nor sufficiently organized to offer a real obstacle. The whisperers were beginning to ask who had given this exotic traveler authority to criticize American institutions, much less British. This only spurred Douglass's zeal. What perplexed him most in Belfast was the discovery that the people of that city "drink wine and pray."

With Belfast as a base for the next month, he returned to Liverpool and spent several happy hours with the everlilting Hutchinsons, visited Birmingham and spoke before an audience of seven thousand at the annual meeting of the Temperance Society in the Town Hall and made a staunch friend of Joseph Sturge, another powerful reformer of the time. Toward the end of December he was cheered by news that his family was getting along well at home. Then Buffum returned from Manchester and together they began making plans to carry the "noble agitation" into Scotland.

Meanwhile, marking time for a few weeks at the Victoria Hotel in Belfast, Douglass fell into a reflective mood and wrote a long letter to his "Dear Friend Garrison." "I am now about to take leave of the Emerald Isle for Glasgow," he said. Thus far he had not tried to summarize his impressions of the past four months, but now he was ready to take stock. "I have spent some of the happiest moments of my life since landing in this country. I seem to have undergone a transformation. . . . In the Southern part of the United States I was a slave . . . *held, taken reputed and adjudged to be a chattel in the hands of my owners and possessors, and their executors, administrators, and assigns, to all intents, constructions, and purposes whatsoever. . . .* In the Northern states, a fugitive slave, liable to be hunted at any moment like a felon . . . shut out from the cabins on steamboats—refused admission to respectable hotels—caricatured, scorned, scoffed, mocked." But in Ireland, "I breathe, and lo! the chattel becomes a man. . . . I employ a cab—I am seated beside white people—I reach the hotel—I enter the same door—I am shown into the same parlor—I dine at the same table—and no one is offended. No delicate nose grows deformed in my presence."

In addition to this strange sensation there was a record of actual work done. He had stood before more than fifty audiences in Ireland, most of them large. His *Narrative* continued to sell well. Mayors and members of parliament had introduced him from public platforms. He had dined with the Lord Mayor of Dublin and others of almost equal rank. Between engagements he had visited the residence of the Marquis of Westminister, a showplace of Liverpool, traveled from the "hill of 'Hawth' to the Giant's Causeway and from the Giant's Causeway to Cape Clear" and taken a peek into nearly everything he passed along the way.

What young man with poetic instincts would not have enjoyed such an exile! Even the disappointment of spending Christmas abroad, the pangs of homesickness induced by the message about his family and the soft melancholy of the hotel parlor could not spoil his mood. He corrected the letter carefully, knowing that it would probably find its way into the *Liberator,* and closed with a sort of prose poem based on the different times and places he had been told in the United States, "We don't allow niggers in here." Nearly all of them, from the keeper of a menagerie near Boston Common to an usher in the meeting house in New Bedford, could be set against contrasting experiences in Ireland.

On this note he took leave of the island that had been his home since the twenty-eighth of August.

Scotland promised exciting jousts to the two knights errant of American abolitionism. At that moment a stink filled the nostrils of British antislavery people following the Free Church's acceptance of a gift of "tainted" money from America. A newly formed communion, organized less than three years before by four hundred dissident Presbyterian clergymen, the Free Church was itself in danger of rupture on the issue of slavery. The fat had been tossed into the fire by members who wished to exclude slaveholders from fellowship. Thomas Chalmers struck back vigorously on behalf of the opposition, and deputies of the church sent to the United States to raise funds adopted a proslavery line and avoided the abolitionists completely. Their return with three thousand pounds from the States, most of it collected in South Carolina, brought the controversy to a flaming issue.

Sunday morning worshipers found the walls of the Free Churches decorated with huge black letters saying "The Slave's Blood" and "Send back the Slave Money." Presently posters bearing the same slogans appeared in the large cities of Scotland. The words were painted on pavements. And in Edinburgh a new popular song included the lines,

> "Where gat ye the bawbies, Tammy?
> I dinna think they're canny."

The uncompromising position taken by O'Connell in Ireland on the question of financial help from slave states for his country's cause stood in sharp contrast and spurred the antislavery element in Scotland. "I do not want your blood-stained money," the Irish orator had thundered.

Douglass and Buffum caught a whiff of the battle when they landed in Glasgow late in January. In Perth a few days later they met the rugged, eccentric and generally tactless old abolitionist Henry C. Wright, reputed to have been the only person anywhere who dared address Garrison as "William," and got a more detailed briefing on the nature of the debate. At Dundee, Douglass wrote Richard Webb excitedly, "All this region is in a ferment. The very boys in the street are singing out, 'Send back that money.'" And when he read in the Dundee *Courier* that the St. Peter's session had unanimously recommended the return of the money, he could hold his peace no longer.

"Old Scotland boils like a pot," he chuckled. In a speech at Arbroath on February 10 he stated the case as it appeared to him. "I am not here alone," he explained, alluding to recent newspaper charges that he was a meddling outsider "unknown to respectable people in this country." "I have with me the learned, wise and reverend heads of the church." Not only did he and his fellow abolitionists have strong clergy support, as he claimed, but their strategy at that time was to fight slavery on moral grounds, within the church if possible. They felt that the disfellowship of slaveholders, if it could be accomplished, would do their cause more good than any limited political gain. Indeed

Frederick Douglass as a young man

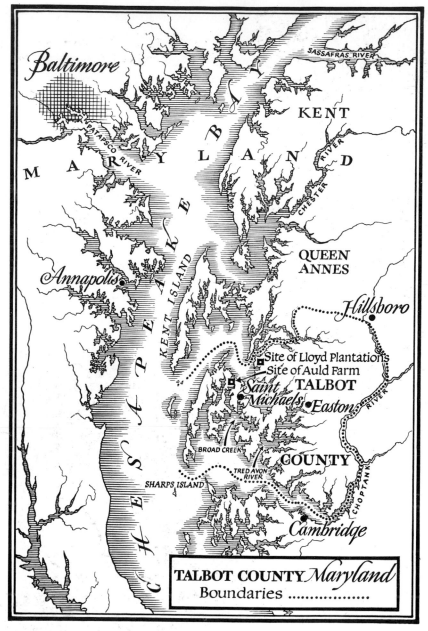

Talbot County, Maryland, where Douglass was born into slavery

"The last time he saw his mother." Drawing from 1882 edition of Douglass's autobiography.

Douglass in 1845

Douglass's first wife, Anna Murray Douglass

William Lloyd Garrison

Wendell Phillips

Charles Sumner

George Thompson

Douglass in 1855

Gerrit Smith

John Brown. From painting by Nahum B. Onthank
in the Boston Athenæum.

Harpers Ferry seen from Maryland Heights

GEORGE L. STEARNS

GERRIT SMITH

FRANK B. SANBORN

T. W. HIGGINSON

THEODORE PARKER

SAMUEL G. HOWE

John Brown's northern supporters

Theodore Parker

Theodore Tilton. From a portrait by Thomas LeClear, N.A.

John Mercer Langston

Douglass circa 1870

Douglass's home in Washington.

Douglass as marshal at inauguration of President Garfield. Both pictures on this page are from drawings in the 1882 edition of his autobiography.

Helen Pitts Douglass

Douglass circa 1890

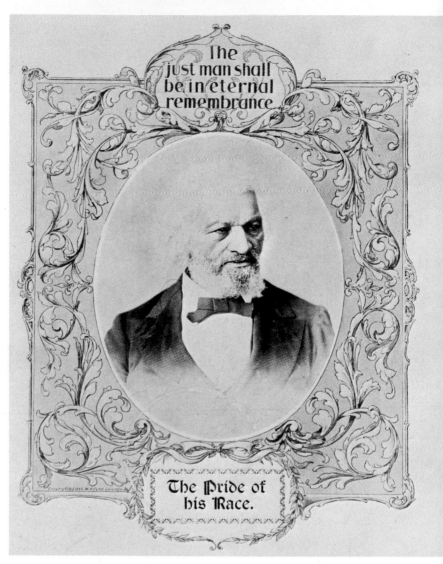

The
just man shall
be in eternal
remembrance

The Pride of
his Race.

Memorial tribute to Douglass following his death in 1895

moral issues *belonged* to the church. "But with or without their sanction," Douglas quickly added, "I should stand just where I do now, maintaining to the last that man-stealing is incompatable with Christianity; that slaveholding and true religion are at war with each other, and that a Free Church should have no fellowship with a slave church. . . . The Free Church in vindicating their fellowship of slaveholders have acted upon the damning heresy that a man may be a Christian, whatever may be his practice, so his creed is right. So he pays tithes of mint, anis and cummin, he may be a Christian, though he totally neglect judgement and mercy. It is this heresy that now holds in chains three million of men, women and children in the United States. The slaveholder's conscience is put at ease by those ministers and churches."

Two months later, invitations to speak on the subject having poured in rapidly since his first blast, he was still thundering away. "Not only did the Free Church Deputation not preach the Gospel or say a word in behalf of the slave," he shouted in Glasgow on April 21, "but they took care to preach such doctrines as would be palatable, as would be agreeably received and as would bring them slaveholders' money." That night he was followed on the platform by George Thompson, a member of Parliament whose name was perhaps as well-known in Boston as Glasgow.

Old but still terrible in battles of this kind, Thompson cried, "Oh that a thousand pounds should out-weigh the chains of these million slaves!" And as he spoke Douglass recalled the connection in which he had first heard this man's name. The mob that dragged Garrison through the streets of Boston in 1835 with a rope around his neck had actually assembled to manhandle Thompson who, as Lecturing Agent of London Anti-Slavery Society, had been described as a "paid agent of the enemies of republican institutions." A one-hundred-dollar purse had been offered to the first individual to lay violent hands on Thompson. The episode had not been forgotten in Boston.

But despite the abolitionist's best efforts in Glasgow, Edinburgh and other cities of Scotland, the money was not sent back. Douglass did not consider the effort wasted, however, and began at once to gird himself for new assaults on American slavery. Ireland and Scotland had provided stimulating skirmishes and trial engagements, but the real challenge awaited him in London. The success or failure of the British tour hung on that outcome. Douglass hoped he would be equal to it.

Meanwhile a news item from the United States gave him a jolt. It was contained in a December issue of the *Liberator* that reached him more than a month late. It was quoted by the *Liberator* from the *Delaware Republican,* and to Douglass, the subject of the article, it was no less shocking because it had been expected. He had certainly not guessed that the slave power's first public response to his *Narrative* would be a rather quibbling defense of the good names of some of the people accused by Douglass of almost unspeakable cruelty to him in slavery. The more he examined the item however, the less he resented it. By the time he sat down at his table to reply, he was ready to shake the hand of A. C. C. Thompson of 101 Market Street, Wilmington, Delaware.

"You, sir, have relieved me," he gushed in an expansive reply published in the *Liberator* of February 27, 1846. "I now stand before the American and British public endorsed by you as being just what I have represented myself to be—to wit, an *American slave.* You say, 'I knew this recreant slave by the name of Frederick Bailey' (instead of Douglass). Yes, that was my name; and leaving out the term recreant, which savors a little of bitterness, your testimony is direct and perfect—just what I have long wanted. But you are not yet satisfied. You seem determined to bear the most ample testimony in my favor. You say you knew me when I lived with Mr. Covey—'And with most of the persons' mentioned in my narrative, you are 'intimately acquainted.' This is excellent. Then Mr. Covey is not a creature of my imagination but really did, and may yet exist.

"You thus brush away the miserable insinuation of my Northern proslavery enemies."

Having paid his thanks to the writer for this unintentional good service, he took up the points of dispute and ended by giving the man in Wilmington a stern antislavery lecture. This disposed of, his thoughts turned homeward again.

His new friends in Scotland had almost crushed him with fondness. Many of them urged that he forget the land of his birth and make Britain his home. But to Garrison he wrote from Glasgow in the middle of April, "I long to be at home. . . . Nor is it merely to enjoy the pleasure of family and friends that I wish to be at home: it is to be in the field, at work, preaching to the best of my ability salvation from slavery to a million fast hastening to destruction. I know it will be hard to endure the kicks and cuffs of the pro-slavery multitude to which I shall be subjected, but then, I glory in the battle as well as in the victory."

He might have pointed out at that moment that the battle in which he was engaged involved also some unpublicized strife. Maria Weston Chapman, the Board member of the Massachusetts Anti-Slavery Society who had twitched Douglass's ear for insubordination following the Syracuse dispute with Collins, now wrote a letter to R. G. Webb of Dublin. The tone and contents of her missive are partly indicated no doubt by Douglass's reply. He had been deeply hurt, he said, to see that she betrayed "a want of confidence in me as a man and a abolitionist."

Her primary apprehension, one gathers, was that he might fall into the hands of the London committee, an abolitionist group not entirely in step with Garrisonians. Mrs. Chapman's sectarian exclusiveness did not of itself bother Douglass, though his own inclination was different, but her reasons for apprehension in his case were offensive. "In that letter you were pointing out to Mr. Webb the necessity of his keeping a watch on myself and friend Mr. Buffum, but as Mr. Buffum *was rich and I poor* while there was little danger but Mr. Buffum would stand firm, I might be bought up by the London committee. Now, dear Madam, you do me great injustice by such comparison. They are direct insinuations and when whispered in the ear of a stranger to whom I look up as a friend, they are very embarrassing. Up to the time of hearing Mr. Webb read that letter, I supposed I shared your confidence in common with that of other members of the committee at Boston. I am disappointed. I can assure you, Dear Madam, that you have mistaken me altogether if you suppose that the love of money or the hate of poverty will drive me from the ranks of the old Antislavery Society. . . . I have withstood the allurements of New Organization, Liberty party and no-organization at home. Why should I not withstand the London committee? . . . If you wish to drive me from the Antislavery Society, put me under overseership and the work is done. Set some one to watch over me for evil and let them be so simple minded as to inform me of their office, and the last blow is struck."

If she was wondering about his income, he could easily set her mind at rest. Buffum had offered to collect money for his passage on the *Cambria*. The sum raised amounted to $60, just two dollars short of the cost of steerage. He brought with him $350 saved from earnings of the *Narrative* in the United States prior to August 16, 1845. At home he had "managed to get on and keep in the field with very little means, lived in a small house, paid a small rent, indulged in no luxuries," happy to be fighting in the "thin but brave ranks" of the Garrisonians. Abroad he was able to live comfortably on income from the English edition of the *Narrative*.

"I have said what I now have because I wish you to know just how I feel toward you," he concluded. "I wish to be candid with my friends. It would have been quite easy to have passed the matter over had you not sent me the *Liberty Bell* and made it my duty to write to you." Despite these disarming sentences however, it was a reckless letter for a young fugitive in Douglass's situation to write to the wealthy and influential woman in whose house on Chauncy Place, Wendell Phillips and William Lloyd Garrison had first met.

But such personal grievances did not rankle in Douglass's mind overlong. Having given a piece of his mind to the most powerful woman in the antislavery movement in America, he could swing around, scarcely pausing to catch his breath, and resume the fight against the real enemy. His next published letter from Scotland was directed to Horace Greeley, and the occasion was merely the attention the New York *Tribune* had begun to give Douglass's denunciation of the slave power from the safe distance of the British Isles. When Greeley reprinted Douglass's bitter Belfast letter to the *Liberator,* in which he contrasted the respect shown him abroad with the insults to which he was accustomed at home, repeating over and over the old refrain, "We don't allow niggers in here," the New York *Express* had responded by calling the young Negro a "glib-tongued scoundrel, running amuck in greedy-eared Britain against America, its people, its institutions, and even against its peace." Even some of the *Tribune's* readers were angered to the point of writing harsh attacks on its editor for paying attention to a runaway slave and showing sympathy.

To Douglass the attitude of the *Tribune*'s editor was a hopeful sign. He thought he saw in it a small indication of change in the position of the general press, which in the past had seldom shown anything but scorn for abolitionists and all their works. He thanked Greeley profusely, poked fun at the letter writer and then proceeded to the point of issue. "The wisdom of exposing the sins of one nation in the ear of another has been seriously questioned by good and clear-sighted people, both on this and on your side of the Atlantic," he admitted. He had himself been troubled by the same thought. Now that words were flying, however, he had begun to see things more clearly. "I am satisfied that there are many evils which can be best removed by confining our efforts to the immediate locality where such evils exist. This, however, is by no means the case with the system of slavery. It is such a giant sin—such a monstrous aggregation of iniquity, so hardening to the human heart, so destructive to the moral sense, and so well calculated to beget a character in every one around it favorable to its own continuance, that I feel not only at liberty, but abundantly justified in appealing to the whole world to aid in its removal. Slavery exists in the United States because it is reputable, and it is reputable in the United States because it is not *dis*reputable out of the United States as it ought to be, and it is not so disreputable out of the United States as it ought to be because its character is not so well known as it ought to be. . . . I would attract to it the attention of the world. I would fix upon it the piercing eye of insulted Liberty. I would arraign it at the bar of Eternal Justice and summon the Universe to witness against it."

The following day, still bubbling in anticipation of the campaign in London, Douglass made a personal decision of the greatest importance. "I have been frequently counselled to leave America altogether and make Britain my home," he reported to Garrison from Glasgow. "This I cannot do, unless it shall be absolutely necessary for my personal freedom. I doubt not that my old master is in a state of mind quite favorable to an attempt at re-capture. Not that he wishes to make money by selling me or by holding me himself, but to feed his revenge. . . . Nothing would afford him more pleasure than to have me in his power . . . or he would not have broken the silence of seven years to exculpate himself from the charges I have brought against him, by telling a positive lie. He says he can put his hand upon the Bible and with a clear conscience swear he never struck me or told any one else to do so! The same conscientious man could put his hand into my pocket and rob me of my hard earnings. . . . 'He that will steal will lie'—especially when by lying he may hope to throw a veil over his stealing. . . . I had no idea the gentleman would tell a right down untruth. He has certainly forgotten when a lamp was lost from the carriage without my knowledge that he came to the stable with the cart-whip and with its heavy lash beat me over the head and shoulders to make me tell how it was lost until his brother Edward, who was at St. Michael's on a visit at the time, came forward and besought him to desist, and that he beat me until he wearied himself. My memory in such matters is better than his. . . . He finds fault with me for not mentioning his promising to set me free at 25. I did not tell many things which I might have told. Had I told of that promise, I should have also told that he had never set one of his slaves free, and I had not reason to believe he would treat me with any more justice and humanity than any one of his slaves."

The implication that Douglass dreamed of returning home legally free could easily be drawn. Whether or not he had discussed such an idea with his British friends is not suggested, but he was certainly in a fine bucolic mood, if that's an indication, when he arrived in Ayr the following week.

He had come to speak in a church, but it was veneration for the countryside so intimately described by Robert Burns that made this visit to the poet's birthplace memorable. Douglass had a special fondness for the highland singer, a fondness shared by many American Negroes. The sweet longings of the unschooled country boy, his gay moments, his dark hours fitted their experience perfectly. Burns's personal tragedy was theirs over and over again. In a dozen ways he was kin to them, and Douglass thought of them all as he was received by a little pink-cheeked woman nearly eighty years old, the surviving younger sister of the immortal Bobby.

With the poet's sister were her two handsome daughters. In a letter to Greeley's *Tribune* in which he commented on the visit Douglass described the two daughters as "truly fine looking women. Coal black hair, full, high foreheads and jet black eyes sparkling with the poetic fire which illumined the breast of their brilliant uncle. Their deportment was warm and free, yet dignified and ladylike." They brought in letters in their uncle's handwriting for Douglass to read and showed him an original portrait which evoked family memories and comments. So quickly and so completely did they put Douglass at ease, in fact, that when he said good-by, he felt "as if leaving old and dear friends."

"Burns lived in the midst of a bigoted and besotted clergy," he reflected afterward, "a pious, but corrupt generation—a proud, ambitious and contemptuous aristocracy who . . . looked down upon the plowman, such as was the noble Burns, as being little better than a brute. . . . He broke loose from the moorings which society had thrown around him."

Was it necessary to point the analogy? Douglass reread

"Tam O'Shanter," "The Cotter's Saturday Night," "Man Was Made to Mourn," and "To My Mary in Heaven," and his own heart began to sing in the highlands.

He was ready for London.

It was May and time for the annual meeting of the British and Foreign Anti-Slavery Society. While in Edinburgh, Douglass had received a note from a Committee of the Society asking him to be the speaker on this occasion. A letter from George Thompson followed, an invitation to make Thompson's house at 5 Whitehead's Grove his home during the London sojourn. To Douglass in Scotland the stage seemed well set. He timed his arrival for the day of the meeting.

When he reached Freemason's Hall on Great Queen Street, however, his heart sank. The meeting had been properly called. He had been loudly announced. But the audience was definitely thin. There were no more people present than Douglass was accustomed to seeing at business sessions of the American Anti-Slavery Society. Douglass could not refrain from mentioning his disappointment.

The secretary attributed the poor turn out to counter-attractions in London that evening. Several other philanthropic meetings were being held, and the friends of emancipation were no doubt scattered among these. If this did not soothe Douglass's feelings, it did forestall complaint, and the program went ahead as planned. At the close of Douglass's talk someone came forward and proposed that the Society undertake to give him a better meeting toward the end of the week. Would Douglass consent?

He would. In the meantime he need not be idle. Reform was in the air. All kinds of issues were being publicly debated and advocated in London, and most of them seemed in some way related to the cause for which he was fighting. In any case, their supporters welcomed his help, and he was seldom reluctant. The night following the Anti-Slavery meeting he found himself on the platform before a large meeting of the Peace Society, a pacifist group. Following that, he put in a word for the Suffrage Association, predicting that after the Anti-Corn Law movement complete suffrage would become the next great reform to sweep the country. An evening later he spoke at the National Temperance Society's rally in Exeter Hall. Wherever he appeared, slavery bobbed up as an issue, even when he himself refrained from mentioning it. His presence was enough to arouse the ever-ready abolitionists in the audience.

His own meeting was held at Finsbury Chapel on Friday night, May 22, and the place was "crowded to suffocation." Evidently his appearances before the societies for peace, complete suffrage and temperance had turned the tide. He had arrived in London on Monday expecting to win the city to his crusade that same night. He had miscalculated. It had taken till the following Friday.

The measure of his success may possibly be indicated by the fact that he spoke for three hours that night without any apparent loss of favor. Before the applause subsided, Thompson had a bright flash. A few moments later, after another speaker had expressed the wish that Douglass might be induced to cast his lot with the antislavery movement in Britain rather than return to the United States, he bounced to his feet and put his idea to the audience. The speaker under whose spell they had lost the sense of time that evening was actually a sad young man, Thompson revealed. He violated no confidence, he hoped, by disclosing references Douglass had recently made to his family in Massachusetts and the great longing that had come into his voice as he spoke of his wife and children. What time could be better than this glowing moment to pass the plates and raise money to bring the family to Britain?

The thing was quickly done, but it left Douglass more

confused than happy. He was pleased to have five hundred unexpected dollars suddenly put at his disposal, but he was embarrased by the inference his British friends had drawn from his expressions of homesickness. True, he had said that he couldn't think of staying away from his family more than a year, and perhaps to more than one of them he had remarked that he must go home in August *unless* he decided to bring the household over to join him, but he had never decided to do that. Indeed his thought was now running rather strongly in the opposite direction. The fight was hotter in the United States. That's where he preferred to be—provided he could stay out of the hands of Hugh Auld, his erstwhile master.

Even August was a good many weeks away, however, and there was no rest in the cause of freedom. A week in London had guaranteed that there would certainly be none for Douglass in the England of 1846. At the rate that invitations to speak were coming in he could carry on for months, possibly years—or as long as his vocal chords held up. But there were also other activities to fill his time. He had no intention of missing London's Botanic and Zoological gardens, its museums and panoramas, its halls of statuary and galleries of paintings. His natural appetite for such delights was doubly keen as a result of having been deprived of them in the United States on account of his color. In London he saw a chance to make up for what he had missed. But he would have to keep moving.

A visit to a session of Parliament came under the same heading. Accompanied by Thompson, he was not only admitted courteously but was shown into the Speaker's Gallery, which seemed to Douglass a rather special consideration. He sat entranced as Sir Robert Peel, Lord John Russell, Mr. John Bright and their fellows debated a bill for restricting the hours of factory labor. But the thought that kept flashing into his mind during the proceedings related to his native land, and he went out, as the galleries were cleared preparatory to voting, muttering bitterly. "If I should presume to enter Congress as I have done the House of Parliament, the ardent defenders of democratic liberty would at once put me into prison." His laughter was sardonic. "Hail, Columbia, happy land! Liberty in Hyde Park is better than democracy in a slave prison— monarchical freedom is better than republican slavery— things are better than names. I prefer the substance to the shadow." But growing fury against injustice at home only made him more impatient to get back. He returned to his room in Thompson's house and wrote a fighting letter to the *Liberator*. Let the haters of abolition chew on that while he stretched his wings in the British Isles!

A month later he was in Liverpool again waving good-by to the departing *Cambria*. At its rail stood the singing Hutchinsons, their arms around each other, their voices blending sweetly. With them again, his eyes moist behind his octagonal spectacles, was Douglass's faithful friend James Buffum.

Alone now, Douglass started another round of lectures and sight-seeing jaunts through Ireland and Scotland. Meanwhile the word was that Garrison had accepted invitations to come over and lend his fire to the Free Church fight and other British reforms related to Emancipation. This was exciting news. Even abroad the name of the editor of the *Liberator* caused a stir among the die-hards of entrenched reaction, and the thought of teaming up with him in Britain was flattering to the waxing Douglass.

Anticipation of Garrison's arrival turned Douglass's thoughts backwards again, and on the night of July 29 in Edinburgh he was awakened by a bad dream. He thought he was in Pendleton, Indiana, where the mob had broken up the meeting and left him bleeding on the ground. The dream brought back William A. White, the young white

man who had been his companion in that western adventure. A true friend was William, a brother in the cause
of freedom and as willing to risk his life for it as was
Frederick. Joining the fight for emancipation against the
wishes of his family and friends, William White had proven
himself at Pendleton.

Douglass decided to write him a letter. "How you looked
bleeding," he recalled, "I shall always remember. Such
noble blood—so warm and generous—was too holy to be
poured out by the rough hand of that infernal mob. Dear
William, from that hour you have been loved by Frederick
Douglass." As he wrote he began to be angry at Old Massachusetts for letting itself fall into the "piratical grasp of
Texas" and being thus drawn with the rest of the American
Union into the sinful business of robbing Mexico. Finally
he came to the personal matter that probably inspired all
this. "William," he asked, "do you think it would be safe
for me to come home this fall? Would master Hugh stand
much chance in Mass.? Think he could take me from the
old Bay State? The old fellow is evidently anxious to get
hold of me. Staying in this country will not be apt to increase his love for me. I am playing the mischief with the
character of slaveholders in this land."

Garrison landed at Liverpool the following day, and a
day later Douglass headed back to London. There they met
and greeted each other with great warmth of feeling. From
Douglass's point of view there was a double reason. The
pride of campaigning with Garrison in Britain was scarcely
less stimulating than the letters Garrison brought from
home, the news that Douglass's family was getting along
well and the report of the impressive send-off given Garrison by the colored people of Boston the night before he
sailed. "Come as the waves come," they had invited their
friends, and the friends had responded in that way, both

colored and white, crowding the Baptist Church in Belknap Street.

One of the letters Garrison brought was from Maria Western Chapman, to whom Douglass had written so sharply on account of her statements to Webb about him. As it turned out, Mrs. Chapman was conciliatory now. She had meant no offense and hoped Douglass was not implying a break in their friendship. Like other Garrisonians she looked upon the British antislavery groups as deviationists. And she convinced Douglass that her zeal was pure. He answered in a soft tone and assured her that he hadn't even flirted with the rival movements in London.

His rapproachement with Garrisonianism may have lacked depth, but certainly the next two months showed nothing but solidarity. Together Douglass and Garrison began attending the big gatherings of the various groups drumming for reforms. At the World Temperance Convention they took a punch at jim-crowism in the American temperance movement, thus provoking a leading American delegate, who happened also to be an apostate abolitionist, to strike back through the columns of the New York *Evangelist,* charging that Douglass was "supposed to have been well paid for this abomination." Two weeks later they were side-by-side at the Crown and Anchor Tavern at the first public meeting of the newly organized "Anti-Slavery League for all England," which was Garrison's answer to the existing abolitionist groups in London, and Douglass's speech was called by Garrison "one of his very best efforts."

Toward the end of the month the two were welcomed to Bristol by Dr. J. B. Estlin, a celebrated ophthalmic surgeon as well as a Unitarian minister and a leader of reform. Douglass still carried in his pocket a letter of introduction to Estlin from Samuel May, Jr., of Syracuse, brother-in-law of Bronson Alcott, but Estlin's letters to May following the visit indicate that the introduction was unnecessary. On the morning of their arrival Douglass was carried to a blind asylum where sixty of Estlin's patients, who had heard the *Narrative* read, huddled about the tall visitor, running their fingers over him and plying him with questions. A public meeting had been arranged for the next evening, and despite an admission charge the hall bulged. The mayor of the city served as chairman. At the close of the meeting Douglass was overwhelmed by a host of handshakers.

Among those who lingered longest and held his hand tightest was a certain Mary Carpenter. A month later she was still sighing. "Such a union of powerful reasoning, facts impressively brought out, touching appeals, keen sarcasm and graphic description" she had never before heard. In what other ways she conveyed this to Douglass himself is not too clear, but the sixty-one-year-old Estlin, fellow of the College of Surgeons of England, warmhearted humanitarian, man of the world and one of Bristol's most beloved citizens, detected a nuance he thought worth mentioning to his friend in Syracuse. Some of Douglass's female fans in Britain, he confided, went beyond the "bounds of propriety." Douglass, however, remained "most guardedly correct, judicious and decorous." But Estlin knew too much about human nature to feel completely at ease thereafter. "My fear is that after having associated so much with women of education Douglass will feel a void when he returns to his own family."

Londonward the American agitators turned again. The following Sunday afternoon they baited Mrs. Grundy and the Sabbatarians by bowling on the greensward in company with a like-minded Unitarian minister. This little gesture of defiance turned out to be the prelude to a very rough fight against a federation of Methodists and Free Churches known as the "International Evangelical Alliance" later in September. Thanks to the prodding of London abolitionists, a committee of the Alliance was already debating the question of allowing slaveholders to retain membership. When this committee brought back a weasly recommendation, making a distinction between selfish and unselfish slaveholders, the two Americans and their friend Thompson took the platform. Hissing and heckling of the speakers turned the meeting into a British counterpart of the old rough and tumble antislavery meetings in which Douglass and Garrison had both been schooled.

Nothing came of the demonstration except a further highlighting of the issue as it related to the churches and slavery in the United States, from which more than sixty delegates had come to the London Conference, and without waiting for the dust to settle, the two agitators were off on another fast tour of Scotland, appearing on some platforms together, separating at other times to cover more territory. By November they were in Liverpool to say good-bys. Garrison was going home.

Standing on the dock between Webb and Thompson, the new friends, Douglass proposed three cheers for the old one departing, and somehow or other the moment was embalmed for all of them. Homesick for his family, wondering when it would be safe for him to return to Massachusetts, Douglass turned his eyes slowly from the moving ship. Should he remain abroad six more months as Garrison and Thompson had advised? Should he reconsider the proposal to bring his wife and children to British soil? Should he—but what was the use asking? The questions multiplied.

Within another month, however, he had an answer to some of them.

While he traveled from city to city seeking to awaken in the British a moral and religious distaste for American slavery, a woman of Newcastle had begun a quiet campaign of her own, presumably with Douglass's consent. Her name was Ellen Richardson and she was a member of the Society of Friends. Associated with her in the project was Mrs. Henry Richardson, her sister-in-law, and their first move was to correspond with Walter Forward of Pennsylvania and through him to make contact with Hugh Auld, to whom Thomas Auld, Douglass's erstwhile master, had transferred legal ownership of the now famous runaway. In this way they learned that the holder of the papers, which had only a nuisance value now, could be bought off for $700. With almost no fanfare they raised $710.96, paid the ransom through their representative in Pennsylvania and soon thereafter placed in Douglass's hands a document which read: "To all whom it may concern: Be it known, that I, Hugh Auld, of the city of Baltimore, in Baltimore county, in the State of Maryland, for divers good causes and considerations, me thereunto moving, have released from slavery, liberate, manumit, and set free, *My Negro Man*, named Frederick Bailey, otherwise called Douglass, being of the age of twenty-eight years, or thereabouts, and able to work and gain a sufficient livelihood and maintenance; and him the said Negro man, named Frederick Bailey, otherwise called Frederick Douglass, I do declare to be henceforth free, manumitted and discharged from all manner of servitude to me, my executors, and administrators forever.

"In witness whereof, I the said Hugh Auld, have hereunto set my hand and seal, the fifth of December, in the year one thousand eight hundred and forty-six.

"Hugh Auld."

The bill of sale was attached.

So that was that. Now he could go back to the United States, roll up his sleeves and start fighting the forces of slavery on more nearly even terms. Now he could walk like a man in his native land. Now he could play the fiddle

and sing. Now—now—but his rejoicing was quickly choked.
A strange thing happened. He began to realize that he was
laughing alone. His abolitionist friends, his fellow Garrisonians, wrinkled their brows. Some of them shook their
heads.

A letter from Henry C. Wright put it bluntly. He was
positive that Douglass would make a grave mistake if he
accepted the manumission papers, and this might mark a
change in their personal relations. Seeing in this advice
an abolitionist attitude which was likely to grow, Douglass
sat down at his desk in a room in St. Ann's Square in Manchester and wrote a careful defense of his intention to keep
the papers and the legal status which they symbolized.

On abolitionist premises, his reasoning was not strong.
Over and over again Garrisonians had made the point that
slavery was a sin against mankind. Traffic in human beings
was a ghastly business which could not and must not be
recognized. Law or no law, constitution or no constitution,
government or no government to the contrary, slavery was
against nature and against God. Contracts and legal instru-
ments binding human beings to the relationship of master
and slave were null and void. Any man who held another
in bondage and paid him no wages for his labor was a thief.
Those who bought and sold slaves were pirates, kidnappers
and thugs. It was a righteous thing for a free man to help
a slave escape. It was no crime for a slave to attack and
destroy his enslaver if he got a chance. The purchase of the
slave was the first crime. And no one had argued these
matters more effectively in America or Britain than the
young runaway Frederick Douglass. How then could he
turn around and meet the villainous breed on their own
grounds? How could he let himself be a party to a legal
transaction which recognized the whole wicked machinery?
How could he approve the bloody deal even though it involved him?

Douglass argued expediency. He wished to go home and take an active part in the fight for freedom of all slaves. After pointing out that the sacrifice of theory in occasional dilemmas of this kind was not unprecedented in the experience of abolitionists, he added, "I agree with you that the contest which I have to wage is against the government of the United States. But the representative of that government is the slaveholder, *Thomas Auld*. He is commander-in-chief of the army and navy. The whole civil and naval forces of the nation are at his disposal. He may command all these to his assistance and bring them all to bear upon me until I made entirely subject to his will, or submit to be robbed myself, or allow my friends to be robbed, of seven hundred and fifty dollars. And rather than be subject to his will, I have submitted to be robbed, or allowed my friends to be robbed, of the seven hundred and fifty dollars."

When the long letter was printed in the *Liberator* at the end of January 1847, it brewed a storm among Garrisonians in the United States as well as abroad. Garrison himself, reluctantly it seems, and perhaps swallowing hard, went along with Douglass on the issue, however, and in a few months the worst of the murmuring began to subside.

Meanwhile there was another round of speaking engagements to be filled in the British Isles before he could get away. As he went through this series, appearing every night most of the time, Douglass began to show the physical effects of his exertions. He looked tired and thin to audiences who heard him in March. His voice showed strain. But now his thoughts were flying homeward. He couldn't stop. Early in the month he bought a ticket at the London office of the Cunard Line for passage to Boston on the *Cambria*. It was a first-class ticket, and the sailing was to be from Liverpool about a month hence. Despite all he could do, the days and weeks dragged.

On the 30 of March his British friends gave Douglass a farewell reception at London Tavern. Present that night were "400 persons of great respectability," including Douglass Jerrold, popular playwright and humorist, according to the *London Morning Advertiser* of the following day, and after every few sentences of Douglass's long and occasionally sentimental speech, aimed at the British people as a whole, they broke in with laughter, cheers, applause and shouts of "Hear, hear."

Still glowing from the warmth of this leave-taking Douglass set out for Liverpool where the *Cambria* lay at anchor. When he attempted to go aboard, however, he found himself suddenly yanked down from the cloud on which he had been walking since the night in London Tavern. As an agitator against slavery Douglass had succeeded too well for his own comfort. He was known in Liverpool and remembered by the agent on the Cunard Line at that port. It was this individual who informed him that there would still be conditions attached to his boarding of the *Cambria*. He would have to agree to take all his meals alone. He would have to promise not to mix with the saloon company. The agent and his associates remembered Douglass's former voyage on their vessel.

As always on such occasions, Douglass spoke his piece. He argued. He denounced. And he made sure that spectators, including newspaper reporters, heard what he said. But he went aboard and proceeded to the stateroom to which he had been assigned to ponder a secret he had not even disclosed to his most confidential friends in the abolitionist movement.

VI

THE NORTH STAR

THE ACT of discrimination which marred Douglass's sailing was reported in British newspapers. His abolitionist friends saw to it that by releasing notes to the press, notes which quoted him as saying, "I have traveled in this country nineteen months, and have always enjoyed equal rights with other passengers; and it was not until I turned my face toward America, that I met with anything like proscription on account of my color." The desired result followed.

Editorials censuring the Cunard steamship line appeared in the *London Times* and a dozen or more other papers. Readers replied with sharp letters, and a fine old-fashioned controversy began. One letter writer, representing himself as a Virginian and a proprietor of the Company, defended the action on economic grounds. The Cunard lines would lose money by following any other course, he asserted. But this statement got a rise from Mr. Cunard himself. He had never heard of the alleged Virginian. Moreover he was ready to assure the British public that nothing of the sort would happen again aboard a Cunard ship.

If this brief tempest was actually inspired agitation, the same can not be said of at least two other expressions that

followed the *Cambria*'s departure. Elizabeth Pease, great
friend of Wendell Phillips, warmly respected by reformers
on both sides of the Atlantic, echoed a sincere and widespread attitude when she wrote: "Much had I longed to see
this remarkable man, and highly raised were my expectations, but they were more than realized. A living contradiction is he, truly, to that base opinion, which is so abhorrent
to every humane and Christian feeling, that the blacks are
an inferior race." And a Manchester poet, signing himself
F. N. D., seemed also to be speaking from his heart in lines
"On the Embarcation of Mr. Frederick Douglass Upon His
Return to America:"

> Brother, farewell. Although unknown to thee,
> Familiar am I with thy wrongs and woes;
> Thou brave opponent of base slavery,
> Which o'er our brethren still its fetters throws.
> At mention of thy name my bosom glows,
> And, in the spirit, do I grasp thy hand.
> Oh, Fred'rick, doubt not, what though power oppose,
> Justice shall triumph in thy fatherland!
> And thou shalt burst, as straw, thy fellows' clanking band.

In his present situation, unfortunately, such cozy sentiments could not reach the one who had awakened them.
Douglass lolled in a stateroom big enough to seat a score of
people, a room which had been occupied on a previous
sailing of the *Cambria* by the Governor-General of Canada.
Treated as a kind of prisoner of state, he was not permitted
to leave these swank quarters. His meals were brought to
him. Even attendance at religious services held on shipboard was denied. Douglass fretted and paced the floor.

But perhaps he was less unhappy than he seemed. He
could not fail to notice the difference between his status
on the *Cambria* now and on the earlier crossing. The steerage, with cattle mooing and jostling nearby, though allevi-
ated by the witty and intelligent companionship of James

Buffum, a true friend by any measure, was not to be compared with the deluxe banishment of this voyage. Moreover he was tired, dog tired, and needed nothing so much as a couple of weeks of complete rest. Again and again, during the final months of his stay in England, Douglass's friends had reported that "he appeared thoroughly worn out" or "was too ill from long continued exertion to do himself justice." His throat bothered him, and he had lost weight. Still, they agreed, he "pleaded powerfully" for the cause to which he was dedicated.

Now the curtain had fallen on that act. Yes, a plush curtain, and behind it Othello mused in royal custody. In his last weeks abroad he had been much too busy for reveries. On the long voyage home there was time, ample time, and his mood was right for reflection. Douglass was in love with freedom as some men are in love with love. He was launched on a romantic enterprise, and at this moment, suspended on the waters between the two worlds, there was certainly much to sigh about in addition to the secret which he would have to find a way to divulge. His thoughts ran all the way back to the farewell meeting his friends had held for him in Lynn on the eve of his departure.

The ordeal aboard the *Cambria* then followed. Douglass would never forget the characters who made up Captain Judkins' passenger list on that earlier sailing. A doctor, a lawyer, a soldier and a sailor stood out clearly. There had been a clockmaker from Connecticut, a scheming fellow. This individual's companion had been large and surly, a New York lion tamer, and these two had sometimes found themselves in the presence of a Roman Catholic bishop. Other clergy aboard had included an Orthodox Quaker, a minister of the Free Church of Scotland and a Church of England rector. Christian and Jew, Whig and Democrat had been represented, and Douglass retained a clear recollection of a man from Spain, another from Montreal and still another from Mexico moving among the assorted slave-holders from Cuba and the states of Georgia, South Carolina and Louisiana. He cherished from his shipboard experience of the former crossing an impression of a small world, perhaps a microcosm, sharply divided between those who wanted to lynch him and those who wanted to join him in the fight against the lynchers. But the thing that bothered him most about this line-up was the evidence that Christians were not unanimously on his side.

He and his fellow Garrisonians were committed to a moral struggle, and everyone agreed that the church was the place to expose moral issues. He had naturally lost no time when he saw a chance to get into the church fight in Scotland. But the England of Charles Dickens's stories, the England of Punch-and-Judy Shows, of debtors' prisons and the Romantic movement, of humanitarian reform and equalitarian philosophy had suggested another point of view to the young Douglass, a point of view sharply opposed to Garrisonian principles, but one which Douglass was now ready to explore, privately at least, despite the danger to his personal relationship with the venerated Garrison, the admired Phillips and the respected friends who had nurtured him in the antislavery struggle.

Despite all their efforts in Scotland, the Free Church had never sent the money back to South Carolina. Moral suasion had simply not been a strong enough force, and would not be powerful enough to abolish slavery in the United States, human nature being what it is. Whether or not the cause of the slave had been advanced in any significant way by his activities abroad was open to serious question. On the other hand, of course, there could be no doubt whatever that the status of one particular slave, a runaway known as Frederick Douglass, had changed almost unbelievably.

On the whole the British had greeted him as a brother, a richly pigmented symbol of man's will to rise. A body of romantic literature about the "noble savage" had helped to prepare them for him, and the fact that he came as a slave in danger of being returned to hideous bondage in his native land surrounded him with a sort of glamour. One result of their approbation was his overworked voice. The gift of money which had been offered quietly was another. Both of these posed problems to Douglass in his stateroom.

The change in circumstances while abroad was not merely that Douglass had left home a slave and returned a freedman. His rôle in abolitionist circles before leaving had been in the nature of a prize exhibit. "It can talk," Collins and the others used to say to the villagers who gathered at their meetings, and Douglass would smile and go along with the joke. Very soon he had begun to step out of the rôle, of course, but to the general public he remained only an unusually articulate fugitive, an attraction in the road companies of the abolitionist shows.

Abroad he made news in America. The church and slavery issue was picked up by *The Evangelist* as well as more secular periodicals. The New York *Sun*, the *Tribune* and the *Express* reacted briskly to his criticisms of American institutions before British audiences, while the antislavery papers followed him step by step and applauded nearly every word he uttered. Eventually this uncritical chorus turned to wrangling when he allowed his British friends to buy off his legal owner, but the name of the man at the center of the discord lost nothing as a symbol. The brash fugitive had become a celebrity, a returning champion of antislavery agitation.

The *Cambria* made harbor on April 20 after a voyage of sixteen days, and Douglass proceeded to his home in Lynn.

The indirect reports he had received from Anna and the children while abroad had not been unfavorable, but he was not inclined to take them too literally. He assumed that the messages referred only to the health of his family. A fear that they might have suffered want lurked in the back of his mind there. No comment had ever been made about the money he sent them from time to time, and he suspected that it had been insufficient. While friendly neighbors in Lynn had promised him that they would not let them down in his absence, he knew that Anna had her pride. How much she had been able to earn herself while keeping her little house and attending to the three youngest children was a question. Likely very little. At least he was glad to be solvent himself and to have with him money to pay the debts that would probably be waiting.

Surprisingly, however, the sturdy, plain woman who greeted him showed no signs of suffering. The little house was spic and span, the unrecognizable youngsters clean and well behaved. Without waiting for him to ask the question that was in his mind, Anna went to a bureau drawer and brought out a bank book. In it Douglass found a record of every sum he had sent from abroad. Other deposits were also noted. He could not believe his eyes. Anna explained.

She had been employed by a shoe bindery to do piecework. This left her hours flexible, an essential for a woman worker trying to keep a house and look after three small boys, all under seven, but the earnings had been adequate. Indeed, with income from the continuing sale of the American edition of the *Narrative* and at least one gift of $20 from the Massachusetts Anti-Slavery Society, she had not only been able to support the family and put aside small savings but had systematically allotted the earnings from a certain number of shoes as her donation to the antislavery cause through the sewing circle at Lynn and the annual fair in Faneuil Hall, Boston.

Douglass's heart melted. This was his woman all right, dark, harsh-featured Anna, her hands hardened by cobbling and laundry work. The disparity of more than four years in their ages was more noticeable now than it had seemed two years ago, but that did not matter. Compared to the cultivated women in whose company he had spent so much time in the British Isles, she was another creation. But a certain nuance in this reunion did not escape the Douglass children. It was at this time that they began to observe that "Father was always the honored guest. He was home so seldom . . ."

Nor did he talk about the propriety of criticizing American institutions before foreign audiences, the dialectical confusion which followed his acceptance of manumission papers purchased by British friends, the theological point raised by churches which fellowshipped slaveholders, the connection between segregation and slavery or any of the other topics which were the themes of his public life. He was at home now. Those matters were shop talk in which Anna was unable to participate. Clean linen, warm food, well-behaved children who honored their dignified and serious-minded father—these were her concerns.

His legs still wobbly from the sixteen-day voyage, Douglass settled down with a sigh and tried to get used to a floor that did not rock. Before he could make the adjustment, however, abolitionist groups began to clamor for him. In Lynn they organized a welcome-home reception in the Lyceum Hall at which he recounted his travel experiences but begged to be excused from discussing the heavy issues. He could still feel the tossing of the *Cambria* as he stood before them, and it wasn't good. He succeeded in holding off the colored people of Boston, who wanted to honor him, for ten days, but even then he was not well. Though escorted to the platform triumphantly by Garrison and Phillips and given every incentive to a soaring oratorical performance, he again confined himself to a recital of the high points of his journey abroad. By this time it was clear even to Douglass that more was wrong with his health than just the aftermath of seasickness.

He had not recovered from the bronchial infection which plagued him during his final months abroad, and he was far from well when he set out for New York City the following week to be feted by Negroes in Zion's Church. Anna went with him. She was eager to visit Rosetta, their oldest child, who was still living with the Mott sisters in Albany, and whom neither she nor her husband had seen in two years. Suffering from hoarseness and other cold symptoms, Douglass had to push himself hard to keep moving. Nevertheless he found energy enough to attend a session of the state legislature with a young white woman who happened to be visiting in Albany and then caught the night boat for New York City. A stateroom had been secured to enable him to rest up for a scheduled address before the anniversary meeting of the American Anti-Slavery Society, but this had required connivance. Jim crow was still the rule on these steamers. Douglass's ticket had been purchased for him. Nothing happened that evening, and he thought no more about the maneuver till the next morning when he left the boat.

The captain was muttering as Douglass passed him. The language was shocking, and it was punctuated with *niggers*. The monologue ended with a threat. The captain wanted it understood that he had no respect for the sneaky trick by which the colored passenger had secured the stateroom nor for the white collaborator. They had better not try it again. Douglass did not stop to answer, but he fumed inside and when he reached the Tabernacle in which the Society was meeting, his hurt feelings expressed themselves in an extremely bold, Garrison-style address on "The Right to Criticize American Institutions." The *National Anti-Slavery Standard,* reporting the speech in full, asserted that the audience cheered as the hoarse-voiced crusader thundered, "How can I love a country thus cursed, thus bedewed with the blood of my brethren? A country, the Church of which, and the Government of which, and the Constitution of which, is in favour of supporting and perpetuating this monstrous system of injustice and blood? . . . I desire to see its overthrow as speedily as possible, and its Constitution shivered in a thousand fragments, rather than this foul curse should continue to remain as now."

Perhaps it is no wonder that after another such homecoming welcome, arranged by his friends in New Bedford for the following week, Douglass had to return to Lynn and go to bed again. There may also have been some connection between his ill health and the series of angry letters that issued from his home during the next month. While Anna nursed his weakened body, he licked his spiritual wounds. "I have before me the New York *Sun* of 13th May," he wrote to Thomas Van Rensselaer, editor of a brave little antislavery sheet called *The Ram's Horn.* "It contains a weak, puerile, and characteristic attack upon me, on account of my speech in the Tabernacle." The editor of the *Sun* had accused Douglass of abusing the right of freedom of speech. Douglass was deeply hurt. How could he speak differently, he wanted to know, of a government which failed to protect him in his person?

After this outburst he sank back among his pillows again. More than two weeks passed before he felt like writing again, and then it was to lash back at a particularly underhanded attack growing out of the Albany visit and the Hudson River boat ride that followed it. A thing which called itself *The Switch* and purported to be published in Albany carried its own unsigned version and commentary on Douglass's activities on that trip. "A depraved portion of the people, and of the press," it grumbled, "have for some time past been gratifying their morbid tastes in lionizing a disgusting, impertinent Negro, who styles himself Frederick Douglass." There was something suspicious, it thought, about the fact that Douglass's companion on the occasion of his visit to the legislature had been a white woman. Worse still, this same woman had ocupied a stateroom adjoining his on the steamer that night. *The Switch* paused only to spit. "Disgusting!"

Douglass was not too sick to answer that. "It is perfectly true," he sneered, "that I was accompanied to the Assembly Chamber by a lady—*a white lady* (very criminal!)." And it was also true that this white friend had secured his stateroom reservation for him and occupied the adjoining one. Moreover, Douglass had found the door between the rooms open when he entered, and it had remained open for a while as they conversed. Finally his friend retired to her stateroom and closed the door, and he remained in his. The next morning, when the *Hendrick Hudson* landed, he knocked at his friend's door and offered to help her with her luggage. That that experience, resulting from the humane desire of a friend to spare him a night's exposure on deck in his illness, should be cited as a lewd episode seemed to Douglass sheer wickedness. He thought its final sentence was especially revealing, for *The Switch* concluded with the suggestion that "this thunder-cloud . . . be kicked into his *proper place, and kept there.*"

The fight was getting dirty.

Even a tonsillectomy that summer failed to put Douglass on his feet immediately. The bronchial trouble was not cleared up for several months, and its recurrence at two-year intervals can be followed over a long stretch of his subsequent career. But more disturbing than the problem of his health during those first months after the return from abroad was the question of his future work with the anti-slavery movement. That he had outgrown his former rôle could scarcely be questioned. Where did he go from here?

Friends in England, led by Ellen Richardson of New-castle, the Quaker woman who had been mainly responsi-ble for his legal freedom, had foreseen this crisis. To help him meet it without loss of pride or usefulness they had proposed a subscription of money large enough to support him and his family when he returned to his home. Doug-lass had unhesitatingly rejected this offer. He was sure he could have no influence in the cause of abolition if it were known that he was living on money from abroad. Neither his fellow abolitionists nor their opponents could be ex-pected to stomach that.

On second thought the British friends agreed. There was certainly wisdom in Douglass's point, but was there not something else they could do to express their good-will and interest and to strengthen his own efforts upon his return to his native land? Douglass pondered. Finally he revealed to them a secret ambition. He had often felt that he would like to edit a newspaper. The public attention given to his frequent letters to the *Liberator,* the *Tribune* and other widely read papers, no doubt, had helped to convince him that he was capable of such an undertaking. At the same time, he pointed out, he felt shamed by the fact that no newspaper, edited or published by a Negro, was to be found at the moment anywhere in the United States.

Of course attempts had been made. The first, known as *Freedom's Journal,* had run for a few months in 1827, a joint effort by Samuel E. Cornish, a Presbyterian minister, and John B. Russwurm, a young Jamaican who a year be-fore had earned a special niche for himself at Bowdoin by becoming the first Negro to graduate from a college in the

United States. The *Albany Sentinel,* issued sometime in 1832, was a fly-by-night affair which disappeared so quickly that *The Weekly Advocate,* edited by Cornish and others in New York City between 1837 to 1841, was generally considered the second Negro newspaper. Early in its career the *Advocate* had changed its name to *The Colored American,* and under this masthead had been a contemporary of David Ruggles's quarterly and later monthly magazine *The Mirror of Liberty,* 1838 to 1841.

Douglass had firsthand knowledge of the more recent journalistic efforts by Negroes, for they had all begun and expired since he joined the abolitionist movement. *The Elevator* was published briefly in Albany in 1842, *The Clarion* in Troy, and *The People's Press* and *The Mystery* had had equally short careers in New York City and Pittsburgh the following year. Only *The National Watchman,* launched in Troy toward the end of 1842, and *The Ram's Horn* of New York City, which Douglass mistakenly thought was dead too, had survived more than a year. Altogether these fledgling attempts caused Douglass to blush. He was sure he could do better if given a chance.

The British friends were pleased with the suggestion, and it was agreed that they would provide the wherewithal to launch a Douglass-edited-and-published newspaper in the United States whenever he gave the word. That was the way he had preferred to leave matters as he boarded the *Cambria,* for there was a delicate side to the project. He must first consult with Garrison and other leaders of the American antislavery movement. He was obligated to them in a thousand ways, and he certainly had no desire to duplicate, much less interfere with, the objectives of the *Liberator,* or even the *Anti-Slavery Standard.* Indeed there was a chance that he had already gone too far on his own. Perhaps he should not have mentioned his journalistic ambitions without first speaking to Garrison, but Garrison had not been available for conference at the proper moment, and now there was a danger of misunderstanding.

Days were slipping by, and already his English friends were asking in their letters if he was still interested in publishing the paper. From his sick bed in Lynn he assured them that his intention remained the same but said nothing about the problem that gave him pause. When the issue could be postponed no longer, Douglass went to Garrison and to Phillips and put his cards down. What did they think of the plan?

Separately they gave essentially the same answer. It was no good. Garrison based his objection, he said, on the fact that *The Ram's Horn* was still being published in New York to dispute the argument that there was no newspaper in the country edited by a Negro, that one or two others were about to be started, and that moreover Douglass was born to the platform and should not take on the responsibilities of editorship lest it draw him away from his primary calling. Phillips was afraid a newspaper would make a pauper of Douglass, as had sometimes happened to men with far greater resources. Neither left any ground for haggling. It was their judgment that Douglass should give up the idea.

Douglass's heart sank. He remembered a previous statement by Garrison that the *Liberator* had once had four hundred colored subscribers in New York City and an equal number in Philadelphia, while now there were fewer than a half dozen in either place, and he wondered whether or not this fact was in any wise related. He wondered if Garrison had forgotten that the editor of the *Liberator* had managed to keep up a full schedule of lectures while getting his newspaper out regularly. And the hazard of going broke in a publishing enterprise seemed amusing in his circumstances. What had he to lose?

A trace of bitterness may have shown in his voice and his

expression as he went the rounds of conventions and abolitionist rallies that summer. At the same time the question
on which he had been, in effect, overruled by his superiors
trickled down to the rank and file. Even the general press
caught wind of it and passed comments. The gossips represented Douglass as having had his wings clipped by the
Boston Board. Most of the comment was slyly favorable
to Douglass, so much so, in fact, that he had to write a letter
to the *Liberator* about the middle of July to deny that he
was pouting or that his decision not to publish had been
made for him by others. The arguments presented had
simply caused him to change his mind—for the present.

Even so, two things apparently designed to soothe Douglass's feelings were arranged by unseen hands in the weeks
that followed. First he was asked to contribute a weekly
column to Sidney Howard Gay's *National Anti-Slavery
Standard*. Perhaps this would take care of his hankering to
write. At the same time, and without fanfare, the Garrisonians quietly offered him the greatest honor they could
bestow: a joint lecture tour with the leader of their movement. Naturally he could resist neither of these tempta-
tions, even though his throat was only partially healed.

The lectures went well in Norristown, Pennsylvania,
with hundreds of Philadelphians coming up in cars for the
meetings, but in Harrisburg the speakers found the air
charged, and Douglass's initial column in the *Standard* of
August 19 reported, "We were last night confronted by a
most brutal and disgraceful mob—the first fruits of our
Western tour, a sort of foretaste of what may await us
further West. To the everlasting shame and infamy of the
people of Harrisburg, I record the fact that they are at this
moment under the domination of mob law."

It happened in the Harrisburg courthouse on a Saturday
night, Douglass explained (and the account of the incident
found in Garrison's letters is essentially the same). A large

crowd had gathered. This was unusual, for antislavery meetings had not previously drawn well in Harrisburg, and it was noted by Garrison that "some of the most respectable citizens" of the city were included. Garrison spoke first and argued for an active interest in the issues of slavery by the people of the North. He wanted them to know that they were involved whether they wanted to be or not. After about an hour in this vein he introduced Frederick Douglass.

Up to now the audience had been attentive, the women sitting on one side of the hall, the men on the other, with perfect propriety. Nor did the tone of the meeting change immediately when Douglass took the floor, even though this marked the first time, according to later comment, that a Negro had undertaken to address a public meeting in Harrisburg. In the back of the room sat a row or two of colored people. A few others were among the standees. Douglass studied his audience as he warmed up. Before he could make a single telling point, however, "a volly of unmerchantable eggs" poured through the window. They spattered the desk at which he stood and the wall behind him. Presently an evil stench blossomed in the hall. The audience showed alarm but no one moved toward the door. Douglass pulled himself together and began again.

A few moments later a pack of firecrackers began to pop on the ladies' side of the auditorium. Considerable movement and confusion followed, accompanied by frightened outbursts and squeals, before it was discovered under whose skirts the pack was exploding, and Douglass was obliged to interrupt his speech again. The firecrackers disposed of finally, however, he made another attempt. This time he was interrupted by a second volley of "addled eggs . . . slavery's choice incense." In addition, Cayenne pepper and Scotch snuff were blown into the air in several parts of the room, with the usual results.

Still he was not ready to quit. Once more he began talking after the hiatus. And once more the barrage of foul eggs poured through the window. Only now a general confusion broke. People in the audience rose and made for the doors. The passages were instantly jammed. Then it was that Douglass heard the voice of the mob, clear and distinct above the tumult in the hall of the courthouse, "Throw out the nigger. Throw out the nigger." He stepped away from the desk as the angry shouts continued.

The courageous, unshaken Garrison rose from his chair, a study in serenity despite the evidence that one of the eggs had struck his back and spattered his head. With almost frightening dignity he announced, "Our mission to Harrisburg is ended." If there was not enough love of liberty in the city, he added, to protect the right of assembling and the freedom of speech, he would not degrade himself by attempting to speak under such circumstances. The second meeting, already announced to follow on Sunday night, was hereby canceled.

Oddly enough, these remarks disturbed the audience considerably. A little wizened man who said he was a private secretary to the governor of the state rose and assured Garrison and the audience that he for one wanted very much to hear the two speakers, but he must defend the people of Harrisburg from the implied and stated charges. There was nothing he or they could do about the blackguards responsible for this disorder and disrespect. Nothing. He hoped Garrison did not plan to give his city a bad name.

Another member of the audience thought otherwise. He gave his name as Rawen and announced that he wished to defend Harrisburg from the charge of the secretary that it was incapable of quelling a mob. They could certainly do it, and if they did not, it was because they did not want to. These remarks touched off a warm exchange on the floor which Garrison prudently attempted to compose, implying that there was still a chance he might be persuaded not to call down fire on the city. But his effort was answered by another volley of overripe eggs through the window and a repetition of the cries, "Throw out the nigger, throw out the nigger."

Garrison promptly declared the meeting adjourned, and a surge toward the doors began again. A good part of the audience would not venture outside however, and while they waited, stones banged against the building. The friendly element within suddenly became seriously alarmed for Douglass's safety. This mob wanted blood. It was not a mere crowd of boys and pranksters. Amid the confusion, while Douglass hesitated, a white woman stepped into the aisle and dramatically offered to walk into the street with the Negro speaker. He would be safe, she thought, leaving the courthouse arm in arm with her.

As tactfully as he could, Douglass declined. The lady's disinterested gesture, he thought, would further arouse the angry mob. At the moment he did not wish to test the better natures of his attackers in this way. Instead he made his way to a group of Negroes huddled in the rear. Without speaking, he took one of the men by the arm. The others quietly formed a tight, wedgelike phalanx around him, and the wedge moved toward the door. Unfortunately he towered above his companions.

"There he goes! There he goes," a voice shouted as he reached the steps. Again stones began to fly. One whistled past his ear. Another struck him in the back, but it failed to knock him down.

"Give it to him," the mob cried. "Let the damned nigger have it."

Two of the colored men behind Douglass caught heavy blows. One was so stunned he staggered, but he kept his feet till he recovered and the wedge remained unbroken. When they turned a corner into a darker street, they broke ranks and scattered, running. Safely out of range, Douglass sighed and blessed his colored friends. They had stopped the blows intended for him. No doubt they had saved his life. Garrison slipped out of the courthouse undetected in the crowd.

As church bells rang the next morning Douglass wrote his column for the *Standard,* an angry report of this grim incident, and on Monday the two men left town together on a stagecoach bound for Chambersburg, a distance of fifty-four miles.

Actually they were headed for Pittsburgh, and Douglass's ticket called for through passage, but Garrison was obliged to lay over in Chambersburg from 2 o'clock that afternoon till 8 in the evening for the next stage, a circumstance which did nothing to cheer either of the travelers. The crowded stage in which Douglass continued the journey lumbered slowly over the beautiful but difficult Alleghany Mountains in the melting heat of the August afternoon. Sometimes the dust was almost stifling, and the long pull, two days and two nights of it, seemed to Douglass nearly as interminable as an Atlantic crossing. To make it worse, he was barred from the tables at which the other passengers had their meals en route, but this he bore without complaint.

Withdrawn from the companions of the journey, his stomach empty, his dignity unruffled, he was in an excellent situation to mull over the darker side of the struggle in which he was engaged. While Garrison had all the dedication a man could possibly have to a cause, while he was sensitive to the very shadow of injustice and had proved more than once that he would not hesitate to give his life in the fight for freedom, the fact remained that the Harrisburg mob had not objected to his speaking while it had objected to Douglass's. The fact remained that Garrison had left the courthouse unnoticed and unmolested while Douglass had been saved only because his Negro friends shielded him with their bodies. Eventually he and they had been forced to scurry into the darkness like rabbits chased by dogs.

No, it had not been the same with his friend Garrison. And it would not be the same with him as he journeyed by stage to Pittsburgh. He would miss no meals at watering places along the way on account of his abolitionist sentiments. Clearly there was a difference. White men were converted to the principle of abolition. Negroes were the natural abolitionists. There was a certain dark section of the forest into which the hunted black man fled alone, into which his white antislavery friend could not follow. Accordingly there was an area of his thought not shared by Garrison and the other white abolitionists. The idea of his publishing a newspaper, for example—what about their thinking on that subject?

Even so wretched a journey as the one from Chambersburg to Pittsburgh by stage in the middle of August in 1847 eventually ended, of course, and in Douglass's case it came to a rousing conclusion, despite a 3 A.M. arrival. A committee of twenty people was on hand, supported by a colored band. They had waited up all night, and despite the hour they gave him an enthusiastic musical welcome which warmed his heart. Negroes were well represented on the committee of twenty, and a growing interest of blacks themselves in the activities and achievements of the young orator was beginning to show.

He ate and rested and by afternoon he was whole again, for the report of the meeting he addressed in the Temperance Hall that day was that he gave a good account of himself. Of course Garrison had been expected too, and his absence was a disappointment, but by evening he arrived and the two speakers looked out on an overflow audience.

More big meetings followed in the remaining days of that week, two of them in the open air, and Garrison wrote his wife, "The place seems to be electrified, and the hearts of many are leaping for joy." From Pittsburgh they went by river steamer to New Brighton, accompanied by a crowd of Negro and white followers who went along as much for the boat ride as for the company of their heroes, and from New Brighton the speakers continued to Youngstown by way of the Beaver and Warren Canal.

"The "great Oberlin tent," famous throughout antislavery circles for its capacity of from four to five thousand people, was flapping in the rain when they reached New Lynne, Ohio, but the zeal of the Western Anti-Slavery Society, there in session, had not been dampened. Acres of carts and carriages and wagons and horses surrounded the tent. Community folk with an eye to business had set up booths, tents and covered wagons in a carnival spirit. Their auctioneering provided a kind of raucous background music. Some in the audience had come distances as great as one hundred miles. One black man had ridden three hundred miles on horseback to shake the hands of Frederick Douglass and William Lloyd Garrison.

Two tingling sessions were held the first day, the visiting headliners occupying most of the time, and both noted the heavy attendance and friendly spirit of Liberty party members. Unlike members of this party in the East, this western group showed little personal animus toward Garrison and Douglass because of the disunion and no-political-action tenets of Garrisonianism. They seemed to feel that fundamentally the two antislavery groups were not enemies. Douglass had noted this attitude with pleasure on his visit to Rochester more than four years earlier, but refrained from comment now as Garrison himself observed it. In his heart Douglass had renounced sectarianism in the struggle against slavery, but apparently he had made up his mind to have no more spats with Maria Weston Chapman or other members of the Boston Board on the fine point at issue.

But if Liberty party members in the immediate area were friendly, the same could not be said for other elements of the community. That night abolitionists of all stripes stood by in the shadows to guard the great Oberlin tent and make sure that threats to damage it were not carried out. As usual tension of this kind heightened interest in the conference, and the next day, the rain having subsided, crowds were even larger. By Friday evening the series was over, and Garrison became almost lyrical as he and Douglass watched the long lines of vehicles disappearing in the darkness in each direction. Douglass, however, had little to say.

Perhaps the reason was that his voice had given out on him again. He seemed to be catching cold too, and a tooth had begun to throb. At Painsville, their next stop, he was forced to retire from the meeting to have the troublesome molar extracted. He could say only a few words when he came before the crowd, which Garrison estimated as larger even than the one at New Lynne. He went to his room from the afternoon session and tied a wet bandage around his throat. By the next evening he was sufficiently improved to entertain the audience with his Slaveholder's Sermon, and the approval of the people was so marked the chairman suggested six cheers to the two visitors, and Garrison observed in his letter to his wife that it was "the most interesting meeting I have ever attended in this country."

Joined first by Stephen S. Foster and later by James and Lucretia Mott, the touring advocates of radical Eastern abolitionism and disunion continued to stir up small Ohio towns for another month. In Oberlin they debated the college president on the question of whether or not the Constitution of the United States was opposed to slavery.

President Asa Mahan thought it was. Garrison and Douglass held that it favored slavery and therefore could not stand. More important than the debate at Oberlin, however, was the impression Douglass made on one of the students in the graduating class. Her name was Lucy Stone, and it may have been at this time that she began to notice how closely the Negro's condition, with respect to freedom and citizenship, paralleled the condition of women in American society.

The meetings in Twinsbury, Richfield, Munson, Medina and Massillon repeated a pattern that had by then grown familiar. In Salem the rain caught them again but, according to Garrison, "the people would not disperse; and we looked the storm out of countenance and wound up gloriously." But when they headed into Cleveland, hell broke loose. The *Plain Dealer,* an organ of the Liberty party, announced loudly, "The Menagerie Coming." "Garrison, Douglass, Foster, (and, we expect, Satan also)," it chortled, "are to be here on Saturday next, and open at 7 o'clock in the evening in their big tent, and continue their harangues over the Sabbath. The trio have made sale for a great many unmerchantable eggs in other places."

Of course that was no way to dissuade Clevelanders or anybody else from attending a public event, and the crowds came as expected. For some reason or other the big Oberlin tent did not arrive, and the meeting, scheduled for a church which could not begin to accommodate it, had to be moved into an open grove. The unmerchantable eggs failed to materialize too, but a far more serious misfortune struck the company on the day following the Sabbath. Garrison came down with a high fever.

For five weeks the editor of the *Liberator,* the man whose name was already a synonym for moral indignation and hatred of oppression, the voice of conscience itself for hosts of Americans, lay dangerously ill in Cleveland. During those weeks Frederick Douglass, the emancipated, the symbol of the Negro's upward glance, decided to part company with his revered friend and go his own way in the quest for the freedom of his people.

The whys and wherefores became muddled immediately. A kind of mystery clouded the break between the two men, though several explanations or levels of explanation are handy enough, and it may now be too late to catch all the nuances, but on the surface the events are not confused. Nor was the rupture completed all at once.

When it became apparent that Garrison would not be on his feet again soon, the striken crusader urged Douglass to go on alone. Douglass insisted afterwards that he hesitated—hesitated to leave his friend on a sick bed and hesitated to substitute for him before audiences that had been drawn by the magic name of Garrison. But Garrison had his way as usual, in Douglass's account, and the young Negro reluctantly boarded a lake steamer for Buffalo. There are indications that as he did so he was in a blue mood, and the winds and tossing waves of Lake Erie did nothing to improve it. He came to his first speaking engagement a day late and emotionally spent.

Charles Remond, companion of the 100 Conventions, whose namesake was Douglass's third son, the bitter black man whose work and example helped to make possible Douglass's own association with the Eastern antislavery group, showed up again in Buffalo. There to greet his friends, the featured speakers, Remond had undertaken to hold the group together when the two failed to arrive on time. To Douglass, who was not ungrateful, the effort scarcely seemed worthwhile. After the huge audiences in Ohio the little crowd Remond was holding looked insignificant. In his piece in the *Standard* that week he blamed the lack of interest in Buffalo on the American Board of

Commissioners for Foreign Missions who had succeeded in drawing the sympathies of the people to "the heathen of the South Sea Islands" at the expense of "the heathen of our own Southern States."

On the lake steamer, in Buffalo with Remond, or aboard the stage to Rochester, the next appointment—somewhere within this span, it would seem—Douglass revived his plan to edit and publish a newspaper. Naturally he would have to do it without Garrison's approval or the approval of the Boston Board. But in his present mood and surroundings this approval began to seem less and less decisive. Within a month after leaving Garrison in Cleveland he announced his intention to go ahead with the project.

Details remained to be filled in, and meanwhile there was the Rochester meeting, other stops at Waterloo and Auburn, and still another engagement pending in Syracuse. At each of these he had been billed to share the platform with Garrison, so he would have to pull himself together and carry on the fight alone as agreed. At Rochester he received word that Garrison's condition had taken a turn for the worse and recovery was by no means assured, so he headed toward Syracuse, after a fair meeting, tortured by self-reproach and hoping that somehow Garrison would surprise him by showing up there. Perhaps he should not have allowed his sick colleague to talk him into going ahead alone. What if Garrison should die?

All this Douglass expressed to Samuel J. May, his host in Syracuse. May in turn wrote a letter to Garrison on October 8 telling how disturbed Douglass was about leaving him and how concerned about his condition. But the Syracuse meetings, arranged and promoted with great enthusiasm by May, went on as scheduled, with favorable public results. Despite disappointment over Garrison's failure to appear as announced, the *Daily Star* noted something "fascinating in the oratorical efforts of an earnest, talented, eloquent man, who feels deeply, and speaks out fearlessly and boldly what he feels."

Back in Cleveland, however, his fever subsiding finally, the whole business looked different to Garrison. Forgetting, or brushing aside May's letter, forgetting, or remembering very differently the circumstances of Douglass's leave-taking, On October 20 he wrote his wife a hurt, disappointed letter saying that Douglass had let him down. "Is it not strange," he asked, "that Douglass has not written a single line to me, or to anyone in this place, inquiring after my health, since he left me on a bed of illness?" What grieved him to the heart, however, was Douglass's "impulsive, inconsiderate, and highly inconsistent" decision about the paper. "I am sorry that friend Quincy (who was running the *Liberator* in Garrison's absence) did not express himself more strongly against this project in the *Liberator*. It is a delicate matter, I know, but it must be met with firmness."

Possibly neither party had been utterly candid in his handling of this "delicate matter." The lack of feeling on Douglass's part, charged by Garrison, had no basis. May's letter of October 8 does not jibe with Garrison's of the 20. Douglass, on the other hand, wrote to a British friend, "I had not decided against the publication of a paper one month before I became satisfied that I had made a mistake and each subsequent month's experience has confirmed me in the conviction." Evidently he kept it to himself most of the time, however, though he later insisted that he had mentioned it to Garrison in Cleveland. Garrison had no such recollection. It may also be relevant that one of the men associated with Douglass in the undertaking was a resident of Pittsburgh whom he had probably met during the lectures in that city. In any case, Garrison's feelings were badly wounded, and the extent to which his recent illness or Douglass's own ailments contributed to the situation is perhaps beside the point.

To avoid further offense to his antislavery friends in New England and to remove his paper as far as possible from competition with the *Liberator* and the *Anti-Slavery Standard,* Douglass decided that his effort would be made in the West. Although the brand of abolitionism that flourished there was out of line with the Garrisonianism which had nourished his own growth, he was drawn to Rochester where an active Female Anti-Slavery Society had existed since 1835—a society which included in its membership Susan B. Anthony, Elizabeth Cady Stanton, Amy Post, Salley Holley, Mrs. Samuel D. Porter, and Sojourner Truth, some of them among the outstanding women in America. Cleveland interested him as a possible site too, but he finally picked Rochester, and on November 1, 1847 the following announcement appeared in the *Ram's Horn:*

PROSPECTUS FOR AN ANTI-SLAVERY PAPER TO BE ENTITLED—*THE NORTH STAR*

Frederick Douglass proposes to publish in Rochester, New York, a weekly anti-slavery paper with the above title. The object of *The North Star* will be to attack slavery in all its forms and aspects; advocate Universal Emancipation; exact the standard of public morality; promote the moral and intellectual improvement of the colored people; and to hasten the day of freedom to our three million enslaved fellow-countrymen.

The paper will be printed on a double medium sheet, at $2.00 per annum, paid in advance, and $2.50 if payment be delayed over six months.

A month later the first copy came from the press, and with it a new life began for Frederick Douglass, age thirty.

It may also be fair to say that publication of *The North Star* brought a new day for Negroes generally in the United

States. Certainly it marked the beginning of another phase
of their struggle for freedom and citizenship. The lead
article in the first edition of the paper suggested the new
strategy. It reported a National Convention of Colored
People held on October 6 at the Liberty Street Church in
Troy, New York, a meeting attended by Douglass after he
left May in Syracuse. Carrying the byline of William C.
Nell of Boston, listed elsewhere in the paper as "publisher"
of *The North Star* under the editors Frederick Douglass
and Martin R. Delaney, the item dealt at length with a
speech made by Douglass before the Convention.

Nell reported that Douglass had urged "the colored people to come out from their proslavery churches; exclaiming
that his right arm should wither before he would worship
at their blood-stained altars; they were not the places for
colored men. This sentiment," he added wryly, "created
some excitement, for colored men, like others, don't care
to be reminded of their inconsistencies." How significant it
was that the president of the Convention was Nathan Johnson, the man who had befriended Anna and Frederick on
their arrival in New Bedford and given them the name
of Douglass, Johnson's literary hero of the moment, Nell
had no occasion to mention. Nor was it relevant to his account to point out that James W. C. Pennington, one of
the three vice presidents, was the same escaped slave, school-
master and clergyman who had married Anna and Frederick in the home of David Ruggles after Frederick's dash
for freedom. The fact that William C. Nell himself was one
of the three secretaries assigned to cover the deliberations
was also a small matter, but like the others it hinted at a
line-up among these representative Negroes which could
hardly be unfavorable to Douglass in the event of a bid by
him for leadership of the Convention—and beyond the
Convention of leadership of all race-conscious Negroes in
the United States.

No such aspiration was voiced at the Convention or in

the first issue of *The North Star*, of course, but Douglass's editorial was plainly aimed at the sixty-six colored delegates he had addressed in Troy and at the vague, free Negro constituencies behind them. "Brethren," he purred confidently, "the first number of the paper is before you. It is dedicated to your cause. Through the kindness of our friends in England, we are in possession of an excellent printing press, types and all other materials necessary for printing a paper. Shall this gift be blest to our good, or shall it result in our injury? It is for you to say."

Naturally all of them knew how closely he had been identified with Garrison's movement and had heard rumblings of a split. They had read the weekly columns in the *Standard* in which Douglass had provided a running account of his recent tour with Garrison, and they had not forgotten his midsummer decision to drop the idea of editing his own paper. It was no secret to them that the weekly articles as well as the speaking were part of an internal settlement of a conflict. A clarifying statement was needed.

Yes, he could explain, Douglass felt. He had no dissatisfaction with the present abolitionist press. The appearance of *The North Star* was not to be taken as such. But the conviction persisted in his mind and heart that somewhere in the nation the *victims* of slavery should be attacking the institution in a press of their own. "The man who has suffered the wrong is the man to demand redress."

Apparently that was enough. Though Garrison's personal wounds showed no signs of healing, one of his first acts on returning to the management of his own newspaper on the seventh of January, 1848, was to print without comment a salute to Douglass in his new rôle written by the occasionally irritating Maria Weston Chapman. Nobly, as always, she extended her hand:

Let him be, as heretofore, proof against every form of temptation, and a long and glorious career, like that of

Clarkson (whose past is already sealed) and Garrison (whom God preserve to a like late and faithful ending) lies before him. More fortunately circumstanced than Toussaint . . . may his success be made proportionate to his ability by his devotedness and perseverance to the end.

The *Liberator* also reported that a subscription list for *The North Star* had been hung up by Mrs. Chapman in her famous annual Anti-Slavery Bazar. The Eastern abolitionists had evidently decided not to be unpleasant about it.

Exactly what her allusion to the various guises of temptation implied was better known to Douglass than to most readers of the *Liberator,* no doubt. Although he was not flaunting it, neither was he trying to hide anything. He had seen her again—the white woman with whom he made the trip from Albany to New York City last spring—and his Boston friends suspected that a battle for his soul had begun. In her own careful way Maria Chapman was urging dear Frederick to be a knight in armor and not to let a seductive voice or a clipped, British accent beguile him.

Certainly there was nothing he could say to that. Besides, life had become hectic in other ways. He was in New York City to fill a speaking engagement at Market Hall when he placed the announcement in *The Ram's Horn.* A few days later he was in Lynn again, parrying the warnings and entreaties of his good Garrisonian neighbors, and making preparations to dispose of the house he had built on Union Street and to move his family to Rochester. The die had been cast. There was no turning back now. Moreover a letter from J. D. Carr of London, enclosing a draft for £445 17s. 6d., the amount subscribed by his British friends, had arrived during his absence.

The move, with all it entailed, and the beginning of publication in the new location had been accomplished within the month. Back in Rochester a deed for forty acres of land awaited him in the mail. It was the gift of Gerrit Smith, a wealthy antislavery man of Peterboro, New York, who had decided to donate 100,000 acres of his holdings around North Elba to free or escaped Negroes. A like gift had been received by Nell. Independent of Garrison and his particular sect of abolitionists, Douglass was free now to consider with an open mind the merits of Smith's or anybody else's plan to help the Negro rise. This circumstance, evidently, had occurred to Smith too and prompted his gift.

Interestingly enough, at that same moment, two other people, equally zealous in the Negro American's behalf, each representing a different approach to the problem, were observing the career of Frederick Douglass with a view toward recruiting him to their own ranks. A heavy veil of mystery surrounded the activities of each. And one of them was a wool merchant in Springfield, Massachusetts, named John Brown.

The other was Julia Griffiths, a young Englishwoman who had been offended by Garrisonian tirades against the churches. She was convinced that the Christian ethic was not basically proslavery and that those who said so were not seeing things as a whole. She also favored political action in the cause of the Negro, thus indicating belief that the constitution was not a document favoring slavery as the South claimed and as the more rabid abolitionists agreed. She was a gentle girl, but she knew her own mind, and her quiet resolution, her obvious infatuation with Douglass and the thing he symbolized awakened a strange uneasiness in Eastern antislavery circles.

She and Douglass had been corresponding regularly for a year when he moved to Rochester, and guarded references to her had slipped into the public prints, but in none had her name appeared. Hers was a face that floated into view and out again, troubling one's dreams. When Julia Griffiths returned to England a few months after he started the paper, she and Douglass continued to exchange letters. Given the circumstances, and the talk their friendship had already occasioned, perhaps it is no wonder that not all the correspondence has survived.

Meanwhile just three months of publishing a weekly newspaper was enough to snatch the soaring dreamer down to reality again. By March 31 he was ready to concede at least one of Garrison's points: it was difficult indeed to combine editorship with a tight schedule of lectures. Yet the lectures were needed to help build circulation. Wendell Phillips's dire prediction that publication of a newspaper would make a pauper of Douglass began to haunt him. While he had no dread of losing the little money he had accumulated, he had made so much of the need to show the world that a successful paper could be operated entirely by Negroes that failure in his case could only be a crushing humiliation. Nevertheless the number of subscriptions continued to fall short of expectations, and by the fifth of May *The North Star* was fighting for its life. The first of a series of urgent requests for financial help appeared in that issue.

Publishing at 25 Buffalo Street, opposite the Arcade, Douglass found that it cost him about $80 dollars an issue to put out his paper. The circulation, on the other hand, fluctuated from the start, but apparently did not reach 3,000 in those months. The presswork was a headache too. Despite the handsome equipment of which he boasted, Douglass had to admit shamefacedly that early runs of the paper had to be printed in the shop of the *Rochester Democrat*. He hired two white apprentices and began to wonder if he could hold on till his own youngsters were old enough to set type and help address wrappers for the mailing.

Another incentive to keep *The North Star* going was the forthcoming Colored Convention. Scheduled to be held in Cleveland the first week of September, this convention promised to keep alive the spirit and objectives of the one recently held in Troy as well as of the one he had attended in Buffalo in the course of his work with the 100 Conventions. Douglass had not been taken too seriously by the leading Negroes gathered in Buffalo, but that was five years ago. At Troy he had made an impassioned speech which aroused the delegates and produced some dissention, and some of his close friends had filled conspicuous offices. Naturally he could not afford to miss Cleveland.

Actually the Convention Movement among free Negroes was considerably older than Douglass's association with it. A series of events, beginning soon after the War of 1812, had convinced free men of color, as they were called, of a studied plan in the nation to reduce them to inferior status, socially and politically. Segregation in Philadelphia churches, which led to the organization of independent Negro denominations in 1816 and 1820, was an example. The organization of the American Colonization Society was another. Though its stated purpose was to help free Negroes by repatriating them elsewhere in the world— Africa, Haiti, anyplace but here—Negro Americans thought they detected behind it a clearer objective: to bolster slavery by removing free Negroes. This started in 1816 too, and the Missouri Compromise which followed in 1820 struck them as part of the same pattern.

The trend was not favorable. When a new wave of slave insurrections broke in the South, notably South Carolina in 1822 and Virginia in 1831, hostility toward the free Negro increased in the North. In this charged atmosphere efforts toward concerted action by free men of color were suggested. Not counting a protest meeting in Philadelphia against the American Colonization Society in 1817, the first of these conventions was the one called in the same city in 1830 to consider action on the same question. Interestingly enough, the man behind this meeting was Hezekiah Grice, a Baltimorian and a protégé of Benjamin Lundy and William Lloyd Garirson during their publication of *The Genius of Universal Emancipation.*

The second convention, which Grice did not attend, having by then set his mind on emigrating to Haiti himself, it seems, was addressed by both Garrison and Lundy and was reported rather fully in the *Liberator* of September 1831. By then the aims of the Convention had shifted. The big question that year had to do with the establishment of a "collegiate school on the manual labor system" for free Negroes. New Haven was suggested as a good site, and Arthur Tappan, well-to-do New York abolitionist, offered land for the purpose. When opposition to the proposal was voiced by the Mayor of New Haven, his Aldermen, and the Common Council as well as freemen of the city, on the grounds that it would cause their community to be overrun with Negroes from all parts of the world, the idea was dropped. A more rewarding effort of the gathering was the setting up of a Convention Board to issue calls for subsequent meetings.

For five years thereafter the Conventions of free men of color met regularly, most often in Philadelphia, though not always, and considered such common problems as the purchase of lands for settlement in Canada, abolition of slavery in the District of Columbia, lending their support to Garrison's efforts and encouragement of local "Phoenix Societies" in their communities to promote improvement of "morals, literature and the mechanic arts." Thereafter some of the momentum was lost, so that the movement was without direction by 1843 when Douglass first attended. The session in Troy in 1847 was only slightly better, but by then Douglass appeared to be convinced of its importance in the struggle against slavery and toward first-class citizenship for Negroes.

In any case, his courage was good as he traveled to Cleveland in early September. Nor was he disappointed in the caliber of the men he met there: John Jones of Illinois, Charles H. Langston of Ohio, Thomas Johnson of Michigan, Abner Francis of New York and the like. The fact that they promptly selected Douglass as their president was also to their credit. They had only the assurance of their own judgment that under his guidance the colored convention movement would spring to new life, but that was the faith they pledged in the courthouse meetings in Cleveland, and Douglass returned to Rochester the following week with the fearful burden of leadership on his mind and conscience.

He also carried home from the meeting a whispered message that had been delivered in the darkness behind cupped hands. The mysterious John Brown, a man whom some of the delegates knew by sight, whose reputation all of them knew, who gave them shivers by advising free Negroes to carry guns to perk up their self-esteem, who buttonholed colored men on the streets and held them with his powerful eyes—this man, the whisper said, was inviting Frederick Douglass to visit him in Springfield, Ohio.

Gerrit Smith's magnificent offer of free lands to Negro settlers around North Elba, the disturbing break between Douglass and the Garrisonians, even the question of when or where another convention should be held, seemed pale and pointless beside this man's flaming vision. Some delegates trembled and lost their breath when they tried to speak of him in the seclusion of their rooms, but the convention as a whole was strangely impelled to set up committees to organize vigilant groups in several states to enable their people "to measure arms with assailants without and invaders within." Douglass, who had listened avidly, decided to reserve judgment till he could see and hear for himself.

VII

SOMEONE TO HIVE THE BEES

HIS FIRST MEETING with John Brown did not make news at the time it happened, but *The North Star* reported Douglass's lecture in the Town Hall of Springfield on October 29, 1848. Again on the eighteenth of the following month he spoke in the same place. Between these dates, one must conclude, occurred the first of a series of fateful conversations between these looming figures, conversations on which History itself waited impatiently.

Douglass called at his host's place of business. The firm of Perkins & Brown occupied a better than average brick building in the heart of the city. Here the tall Negro was cordially greeted by a man who seemed smallish by comparison. Lean, somewhat under six feet, the merchant nevertheless gave an immediate impression of sinewy strength. Mixed gray hair, close cropped, grew low on a gloomy forehead. He was cleanly shaved around his square mouth, his craglike chin. About fifty years old, Douglass guessed.

Lights came up in the man's blue gray eyes when he talked, and Douglas knew instantly that he was in an unusual presence. The wool merchant, wool grader and exporter was dressed in ordinary American woolens, including cravat of the same material. He wore rough cowhide boots. A New Englander of New Englanders, Douglass thought, but more than the rest this one was built for times of trouble. His straight symmetrical figure—it was like a mountain pine.

On the street, a little later, Douglass noticed his companion's stride and was reminded of the long, springing step of a race horse. Brown's intense absorption in his own thoughts also fascinated Douglass. He seemed neither to seek nor shun the observation of those they passed. Nor did he seem aware of the look of astonishment that came over the Negro's face as they left the main street and came into a working-class neighborhood. To Douglass it did not make sense that a partner of Perkins & Brown should live at 31 Franklin Street.

The house they entered was equally out of keeping. Plain as was the outside, the inside was plainer. Spartan was not the word; the appointments in John Brown's house suggested destitution. But the wife, the sons and the daughters of the host received the guest with great cordiality and began arranging the table for tea, as they called it. Everybody helped, but no cloth was laid on the unpainted, homemade table, and the meal they served consisted of beef soup, cabbage and potatoes. No excuses were made for the simplicity of the fare or the bleakness of the service. The Browns seemed to be doing what they were in the habit of doing, and they let it go at that.

Whenever John Brown spoke in the course of the meal, his family listened gravely or sprang to obedience. His language was flavored with biblical phrases, and the attitude of his children toward his utterances was unfailingly reverent. Observing this, Douglass began to feel uneasy. When he questioned one of his host's remarks, ever so slightly, he became aware of the family's astonishment. To them John Brown's words were gospel. He was indeed the master of his house, Douglass mused. And if he, Frederick Douglass, didn't get out of there soon, the man was likely to become his master too.

How John Brown had gotten that way, he could only guess, of course, but Douglass could tell when a man had been through torment. He remembered his own damnation, the twenty-one years in hell, and in this strange house as in the eyes of its master there was more than a suggestion of trial by fire.

His house in Springfield was still full of children, but John Brown had not forgotten the ones who were dead. He had not forgotten Dianthe, the wife of his youth, nor the four-year old boy she had had snatched out of her arms by death. Dianthe, insane with grief, had clasped another dead baby as she herself died two years later. Mary had given him more children, many more, the number was finally to reach thirteen, but tragedy had dogged his life with her as with Dianthe. A shattering blow fell in 1843, and John Brown had wrung his hands in agony. "God has seen fit to visit us with pestilence and four of our number sleep in the dust; four of us that are still living have been more or less unwell. . . . This has been to us all a bitter cup indeed and we have drunk deeply; but still the Lord reigneth and blessed be His holy name forever." Then just two years prior to Douglass's visit, following still another infant death in the family, the hurt man had meditated, "I have sailed over a somewhat stormy sea for nearly half a century, and have experienced enough to teach me thoroughly that I may most reasonably buckle up and be prepared for the tempest. Mary," he had sighed, addressing his wife, "let us try to maintain a cheerful self-command while we are tossing up and down, and let our motto still be action, action—as we have but one life to live."

The death of his children had been only one side of John Brown's suffering, however. He had suffered for all living things. When he was a shepherd, he had once gone two weeks without taking off his clothes while caring for ewes disowned by their mothers. A disease called grub-in-the-head had caused it, and Brown had spent the nights with a lantern in his hands finding the little ones and holding the mothers to make them let the young suck. His only rest during that period had been cat naps in a chair.

The enslavement of Negroes had been a crushing hurt to him since his childhood, and one of the things that impoverished him now was gifts to fugitive slaves. But he had also lost money in the panic of 1837 and gone into bankruptcy in 1842. Always he had been on the move. From Connecticut to Ohio, from Ohio to Massachusetts, from Massachusetts to Ohio, from Ohio to Pennsylvania, from Pennsylvania, back to Ohio, from Ohio to Virginia, from Virginia—always on the move. And only the details of his tortured odyssey escaped the half-bewitched guest with whom Brown sat at the table after the dishes were cleared away.

Brown spoke with caution at first. He had followed Douglass's career in the abolition movement. He knew Garrison's doctrine, which Douglass had advocated, and he knew about the split and the founding of *The North Star*. He did not know whether any fundamental difference as to the means of ending slavery was implied, and there was reason to suspect that Douglass might oppose his views. But this was no time for guess work.

Slaveholders had forfeited the right to live, John Brown blurted suddenly.

Douglass's eyes must have brightened, for John Brown began talking freely. Enforced slavery was a state of war. A slave had a right to free himself by any means whatever. Garrison and the preachers of moral suasion were getting nowhere. Nor would the political action advocated by Ger-

rit Smith and the western abolitionists ever put an end to
slavery.

That was strong talk. What did Brown propose?

It was to answer that question, Brown confided, that he
had invited Douglass to his home. He had a plan—a most
secret plan.

No people can have self-respect or be respected by others
who will not fight for their freedom, the wool merchant
intoned ominously. He paused as if to let the broad implications of his remark sink into Douglass's consciousness.

When Douglass urged him to continue, the strangely
tortured man unfolded a map of the United States. With
his finger he pointed to the Alleghany mountain range and
traced it back and forth from the borders of New York to
the Southern States.

"These mountains," said John Brown, "are the basis of
my plan. God has given the strength of the hills to freedom." With growing intensity, he added, "They were
placed here for the emancipation of the Negro race. They
are full of natural forts, where one man for defense will be
equal to a hundred for attack. They are full also of good
hiding places, where large numbers of brave men could
be concealed and baffle and elude pursuit for a long time.
I know these mountains well," he mused, remembering, no
doubt, the Blue Ridge lands he had surveyed for Oberlin
College, the mountain town in Pennsylvania in which he
had once served as postmaster, the slopes on which he had
kept flocks of sheep at another period of his life, the
numerous trips he had made across the whole range by
stage or wagon. "I know these mountains well and could
take a body of men into them and keep them there despite
all efforts of Virginia to dislodge them."

Having crossed the Alleghanies a few times himself,
Douglass was not inclined to dispute this statement, but

something in his eyes and on his face wanted to know the purpose of this guerilla warfare John Brown was dreaming, this brave stand by desperate antislavery men in the sanctuary of hills.

John Brown's answer was ready. "The true object to be sought is first of all to destroy the money value of slave property. That can only be done by rendering such property insecure."

A man who could arrive at that conclusion was certainly worth hearing to the end, and Douglass made no effort to conceal his interest.

"My plan," Brown went on, encouraged, "is to take at first about twenty-five picked men and begin on a small scale, supply them with arms and ammunition and post them in squads of of five on a line of twenty-five miles. The most persuasive and judicious of these shall go down to the fields from time to time, as opportunity offers, and induce the slaves to join them, seeking and selecting the most restless and daring."

Douglass wondered if Brown had considered the danger of treachery and disclosure, recalling his own first effort to escape from slavery with his companions in Maryland.

Brown had. He knew that the utmost care would have to be used in selecting men for his force and that of those selected only the most conscientious and skillful should be sent to plant the seeds of discontent among slaves and induce them to join the hazardous adventure of freedom. He proposed to pick his men wisely and to drill and train them till each had found the place for which he was best suited. Then and only then would they start on their mission. They would run off slaves in large numbers, sending the weak and timid ones northward via the Underground Railroad and retaining the brave and strong ones to reinforce the guerillas in the mountains. As his forces grew, Brown proposed to expand his operations.

But how did he expect to supply these fighting men, Douglass wanted to know?

Very simply. He would subsist them upon the enemy. Remember, Brown repeated, slavery was war. The slave had had a right to anything necessary to his freedom.

"But suppose you succeed in running off a few slaves and thus impress the Virginia slaveholders with a sense of insecurity in their slaves, the effect will be only to make them sell their slaves further South," Douglass commented.

To this Brown nodded. Exactly. "That will be what I want first to do. Then I will follow them up. If we can drive slavery out of *one county*, it will be a great gain. It will weaken the system throughout the state."

Again Douglass saw difficulties. "But they would employ bloodhounds to hunt you out of the mountains."

"They might attempt, but the chances are we should whip them, and when we should have whipped one squad, they would be careful how they pursued."

"But you might be surrounded and cut off from your provisions or means of subsistence."

Brown brushed that danger aside. Of course it was possible. Defeat was always possible in war, but he was convinced that forces sent to trap his trained men would find it extremely difficult to keep his bands from cutting their way out. If worse came to worst, he shrugged, the enemy could do no more than kill him, and he could think of no better use for his life than to lay it down in the cause of the slave.

A pained look twisted Douglass's countenance. Wouldn't it be better, he ventured, to try to convert the slaveholders? Before the words were out of his mouth, however, he knew he had said the wrong thing to the leathery, sun-tanned wool dealer. The angry man fairly left his chair.

Convert slaveholders! What nonsense. "I know their proud hearts," he exploded. "They will never be induced to give up their slaves until they feel a big stick about their heads." A moment later, in a calmer tone, he assured his dark visitor that his whole life was dedicated to the plan he had outlined. If Douglass had been puzzled by the austerity of Brown's home life, he now had the explanation. John Brown was saving money to carry out his great purpose.

Douglass was profoundly impressed, and the spell was not broken by a night's sleep in the clean, hard bed John Brown provided. Indeed, as he journeyed back to Rochester several days later, he began to be aware of a fundamental change in his whole attitude toward the controversy over slavery. It was not a complete or an immediate conversion, but somehow the hope of breaking the slave's chains by argument and appeals to the better natures of the men in power began to seem forlorn.

His speaking and writing meanwhile began to show a degree of hopelessness which disturbed and baffled his friends. So much so, in fact, that in Salem, Ohio, holding an antislavery meeting spellbound as usual, Douglass painted a picture so filled with despair and gloom that a quaint old black woman, gaunt and tall, her head tied in a white turban over which she wore a field hand's sunbonnet, rose in agony and cried out, "Frederick, is God dead?"

Remembering John Brown, the speaker paused, then answered positively, "No, dear sister, God is not dead, and because God it not dead slavery can only end in blood."

Sojourner Truth, as she was called, had no answer for that.

Remembering John Brown, he began to see the Free Soil movement in a different light too. A few months earlier he had attended their organizational meeting in Buffalo with mild curiosity. The presence of Remond and

several other Negro acquaintances there helped to put him
at ease in that gathering, but they all knew him as a political come-outer who didn't really belong. The slogan "Free
Soil, Free Speech, Free Labor and Free Men" had moved
him when it was proclaimed by spokesmen of the new
party, and when the meeting cheered the mention of his
name and invited him to the platform, he had accepted the
bid, apologized for an unwell throat that prevented him
from making a speech and wished the convention the best
of everything in their "noble undertaking." But his words
had been perfunctory. It was after his visit with John Brown
that he began to wrestle seriously with the idea of a political approach to the Negro's problems.

While it lacked the thunder and lightning of John
Brown's compulsion, it was not an incompatible line of
struggle like the Garrisonian moral suasion. Lacking the
mystery and shock of the earth's elements, to which the
old shepherd's purposes seemed atuned, the Free Soilers'
idea of a common front on which all antislavery people
could fight began to impress Douglass as good strategy as
he returned to Rochester. So promising did it appear, in
fact, that within another month he accepted an invitation
from Gerrit Smith, most zealous of the political action
abolitionists, to spend a week at Peterboro, Smith's home.
During that week, no doubt, Frederick Douglass's defection from the way marked by William Lloyd Garrison,
whose devoted protégé he had been since the early morning
of his freedom and intellectual awakening in New Bedford,
was completed.

The two courses before him now were not logically opposed. He could publicly urge his people to work with
political groups favorable to their cause while at the same
time encouraging John Brown more or less openly. Certainly Brown's faith rested on the constitution. He regarded it as a solid rock of freedom. And so that abused

document seemed to Douglass—now. The fog that had obscured his horizon began to break. Now he could see the landscape clearly again. Now he could go home and put himself to work in earnest.

But, no, not yet, not in such haste at any rate. The year of 1848 was at its end and Anna was very big. Would this one be a fourth boy or a second girl? Rosetta would be ten years old at her next birthday. While she had not yet been placed in a Rochester school, her mind was active and she was learning to play the piano. Lewis was eight. He and Fred Junior and Charles were growing fast. It had been several years since there was a new infant in the family, and up to now none at all born in this two-story brick house of nine rooms which Douglass had bought for them with his earnings as a lecturer. Back from important visits with John Brown and Gerrit Smith, Douglass could not escape the implications of this sturdy and comfortable house, a house which, he boasted to his slave master of a little more than a decade ago, was the equal of the one the latter occupied on his Maryland plantation.

A man in his situation was cheating himself if he did not play the violin sometime and sing old songs to his children. Soon, perhaps, he would be able to stand the boys on boxes and teach them to set type for *The North Star.* With healthy children coming on, a man could look ahead without fear, a man with his own brick house on the outskirts of Rochester, with forty acres near North Elba, with his own newspaper—a man lined up with wealthy Gerrit Smith of Peterboro and with John Brown of Springfield.

At little of this stretching of the legs in an easy chair was enough for the Douglass of that year, however. By February the Wendell Phillips prediction that publication of a newspaper would be his ruin was back to haunt him. Checking *The North Star*'s financial accounts, Douglass decided to turn the editorial work over to his associate Nell

while he took to the road again to win new subscribers—
and collect lecture stipends. Fortunately there were plenty
of these. At twenty-five dollars for each appearance he
could have had twenty lectures for every one he accepted,
but he preferred to keep it that way rather than increase
the fee. There would be a time for that. Besides, while his
voice held out and he averaged from four to six engagements a week, he could get along nicely. In the eyes of some
people he was already well-to-do.

Excitement always accompanied Douglass's lectures, but
on that tour things that happened away from the public
platforms eclipsed the lectures. Anna's baby came in March,
and it was a girl. In May the father of five was in New York
City to meet a boat. Julia Griffiths was returning to America accompanied by her sister Eliza. They had made reservations at the Franklin Hotel, but when they reached it,
escorted by the conspicuous Douglass, they were told that
Negroes were not admitted. They found lodging elsewhere
and proudly turned up their noses at all who snubbed their
handsome escort.

In company with Douglass they began to see the town.
The three were often together at public meetings. Douglass
took the young women to the annual gathering of the
American Anti-Slavery Society and introduced them, rather
stiffly, no doubt, to Garrison, for he continued to see his
former colleagues and to move in Eastern abolitionist
circles another two years before making an open issue of
his new convictions. Neither he nor they were inclined to
widen the breach more than necessary at the moment. Nor,
with the exception of the wounded Garrison himself, did
the prominent abolitionists to whom Douglass introduced
the Griffith sisters hint at any impropriety in the relationship, and Garrison's subsequent charge in the *Liberator*
was promptly retracted as a result of pressure by Harriet
Beecher Stowe and others of his own followers.

Julia listened critically to "a poor weak speech" by Henry Bibb, one of Douglass's colored friends, on a proposal to give Bibles to the slaves, but she sat entranced from three o'clock until five and again from half-past seven till eleven as the light-brown Douglass and the intensely black Samuel Ringgold Ward, next to Douglass the most highly regarded Negro speaker in the country, debated the consitutionality of slavery.

Arm in arm with Douglass on Broadway, the two British girls created a sensation. A woodcut of a cartoon showing the two fair sisters vying for the caresses of "Nigger Douglass" showed up in Boston, an indication of the kind of talk that was in the air and the distances it traveled. In New York insults from strangers became commonplace. The worst of these occurred near the Battery as Douglass strolled with the girls. A band of hoodlums sprang up suddenly and mixed punches with the Negro in an unequal skirmish in which he was "roughed up." This one got into the newspapers and Douglass, asked for a statement, told a reporter for the London *Times* that his offense, if you could call it that, was not that he walked with white people but that he walked with them "on terms of equality. Had I been with those persons simply as a servant," he went on, "I should have been regarded with complacency by the refined, and with respect by the vulgar class of white persons." The American "aristocracy of Skin," he suggested, allows the whites "the high privilege of insulting a colored man with the most perfect impunity."

If this behavior did anything for Julia's feelings toward Douglass, it was to strengthen her interest in him and in his work. Out of this fortnight of mingled pleasure and revilement a unique, sometimes puzzling, loyalty grew. Toward the middle of May the party of three sailed up the Hudson on the river steamer *Alida*. En route Douglass took his place between the young women in the dining room.

The steward ordered him to leave. As usual Douglass resisted, which made it necessary for the steward to call the mate. The mate, having no better success, called the captain. When Douglass was finally helped from the table and put out of the dining room, the sisters followed in protest. For the rest of the voyage to Albany they subsisted on lozenges.

They proceeded from Albany to Rochester, where the visitors, cordially received in the Douglass home, unpacked their bags and went out with Douglass and Rosetta to walk through the city and drive on its country roads. Conservative Rochester was not pleased, and soon Anna, patient, faithful Anna, nursing her fifth baby in the seclusion of her room, began to have misgivings about the guests her famous husband had brought into their home.

Eliza soon stepped out of the picture, but Julia continued to live at the Douglass residence. Before long she was an active figure in the antislavery circles of Rochester, hobnobbing with Susan B. Anthony, Elizabeth Cady Stanton and the rest. Her passionate interest, of course, was *The North Star,* the special project of her abolitionist associates back in England. To helping Douglass with the editorial and publishing chores she at once directed her sharp wits and boundless energy.

Within a month of her arrival, for some obscure reason, Martin R. Delaney, one of the two men linked with Douglass in the founding of the paper, decided he wanted out. The June twenty-ninth issue announced that Frederick Douglass had become sole editor and taken responsibility for all obligations. Whether this was a move instigated by Julia, whose judgment in business matters Douglass soon came to trust, to reduce the overhead, or one initiated by Delaney to avoid further contributions to a deficit or a squeeze based on pride of hierarchy was not stated, but Delaney's duties from the start had consisted mainly of drumming up subscriptions on the road. In retrospect the shake-up looks like Julia's work, but it was more than six months later that the first change in the format of the paper was made. By then her silent partnership in the Douglass enterprises was an open secret.

Between times, she and Douglass visited Niagara Falls and smiled at the consternation they caused on one side, the approbation he was shown on the other. Back in Rochester she formed the habit of reading to him at night and grew increasingly solicitous about his health. Meanwhile she became secretary of the local antislavery society, started compiling a little annual called "Autographs for Freedom," and made visits to the home of the Gerrit Smiths in Peterboro. Naturally the people of Rochester began talking a mile a minute, and presently Anna Douglass was spitting mad.

With the Smiths, Julia let her hair down. Anna was giving the unblemished Douglass a hard way to go. Poor man, only Julia knew what trials he suffered behind the brick walls of his home. Her fire was not to be quenched by the stupid suspicions and jealousy of an illiterate woman whose capacity for intellectual growth and new horizons was so limited. Certainly the mission of Frederick Douglass was too clear and bright to be allowed to bog down in that way. Certainly the crusade for freedom was the main thing, and the help that Julia Griffiths could give should not be withheld because of petty irritations. The Gerrit Smiths, she felt, or so her letters imply, would understand and sympathize.

If the private affairs of Douglass had suddenly grown turbulent, they were as nothing compared to the fear that roamed the highways and bridges. Beside every haystack something moved. Shadows darted across the roads at night and disappeared in the thickets. They came out of barns in which they had slept the daylight away, shook themselves and took out across the fields. Under a load of cornshucks something twisted, panting for breath. And a kind of code-like rapping at the back door of the Douglass house became a nightly ritual.

Those who rapped were never turned away. How could Frederick Douglass forget that he had been helped and hidden by David Ruggles when he fled? Even the child Rosetta had been told that story. She knew why it was that one of their nine rooms was reserved for guests about whom they did not speak before outsiders. Soon Julia learned the secret, however. She and the Douglasses worked together to assist and encourage fugitives bound for Canada by way of the Underground Railroad, and none of them had to be told that traffic was booming on the line as 1849 came to a close.

Even if they had not been located on the outskirts of Rochester, along one of the main lines of escape for run-aways, they could have guessed that the flight fever was spreading on the plantations of the South. Spokesmen for the slave states had begun plugging for a fugitive slave law which would enable them to recover their straying property. To the North this was presented as part of a compromise measure designed to reduce tension between the sections, and as such it received the endorsement of such antislavery men as Daniel Webster and Millard Fillmore as well as many church leaders. A coalition of these Northerners, anxious for an end of bitterness, with the Southern block produced the Fugitive Slave Law of 1850, but only the free Negroes of the North seemed to realize immediately what they had actually done.

Fugitives who had settled in western New York left their homes in disorder and headed pell-mell for Canada. Whether they had resided there a week or a generation made no difference. Only legal proof of emancipation could save them, and those who lacked documentary evidence had no choice but to race the authorities to the borders. Free-born Negroes and those who had been properly emancipated were made uneasy too. None in this group liked the idea of having to prove their free status to a judge, especially a judge—as the Law provided—who would collect ten dollars a head for each one he returned to slavery and only five dollars each for the ones he found to be free.

Douglass wondered, for example, how such a judge would regard the validity of his own free papers, remembering that they had been obtained *in absentia,* so to speak, with his former master being forced to settle for what he was offered or risk getting nothing. Under the circumstances, should he also make a dash for St. Catherine's? He was debating this question when Daniel A. Payne, a bishop of the African Methodist Episcopal Church and certainly one of the most influential Negroes of his day, hurried to Rochester to consult with Douglass.

What should they do, he and Douglass, Payne wanted to know. What should they as Negro leaders advise their followers to do? Somehow Douglass did not feel inclined to run despite the dark outlook. As long as men like Samuel Ringgold Ward and Henry Highland Garnet, both conspicuous preachers, stood their ground, he told his visitor, he thought he would stay at his post too.

But that was just the point, Payne remarked anxiously. Ward had fled to Canada. Other colored ministers had led their whole flocks across the border. Payne had seen Ward go across at Windsor. Not only were men like themselves in danger of being taken by the agents of the Law. Another peril had shown itself—kidnapping.

Douglass knew about that. The hooligan element. He had met it at Pendleton and at Harrisburg. Now it had found a way to make its crimes profitable. A look of dejection came into the visitor's eyes as Douglass looked at him. Was Payne going to stay or run, Douglass wanted to know?

"We are whipped," the bishop cried. "We are whipped, and we might as well retreat in order."

Suddenly Douglass felt tired and defeated. His own dismay resulted more from Payne's loss of heart than from the situation they were discussing, however. Here was an unusually intelligent man, a representative of a large element among the free Negroes of the North, a man of courage and resourcefulness, and there could be no doubt that he represented the best thinking of the people Douglass had undertaken to lead through his newspaper, through his public lectures and through the colored conventions in which he had participated. Douglass sighed. His position was like that of a besieged city, he mused, a city whose defenders had fallen at its gates.

Then abruptly his mood changed. There was another side to this picture, he reminded his visitor firmly. True, kidnappers were at work. They had hustled free-born Negroes into slavery. They had even been known to dispatch a few white people who could not furnish immediate proof of their whiteness. And he did not expect such villains to overlook the Douglass house or its occupants, but he had confidential news for the Bishop. Miss Griffith had assured him as had several Rochester neighbors that many stout-hearted antislavery friends were unprepared to surrender. Loyal defenders of freedom had already stood guard around his premises for several nights. If kidnappers come, he added ominously, thinking perhaps of John Brown's biblical fervor, they'll discover that there are "blows to take as well as blows to give."

That was his word to Bishop Payne and his AME constituents.

As if by command, the resistance began. On a Saturday morning in February 1851, a well-favored young Negro named Shadrack was waiting table at the Cornhill Coffee

House in Boston when two solidly built but tight-lipped citizens entered and ordered breakfast. Shadrack was about to oblige them when the deadpan expressions on the faces of the strangers suddenly changed. In another second they were out of their chairs, clamping powerful grips on each of the waiter's arms. Amid the rattling of coffee cups and other indications of surprise, if not consternation, among the guests, the muscular pair introduced themselves: Deputy Marshal Riley and ex-Constable Byrnes.

Guests breakfasting at the Cornhill need not be dismayed, they assured them. Everything was perfectly legal. A few moments later the three principals reached the courthouse, followed by a gathering crowd of interested, curious or disturbed observers, including other colored help employed at the Cornhill. A whisper ran through the crowd. Excitement spread. Within a few moments the courtroom was filled and a mulling throng surrounded the courthouse.

Shadrack was still wearing his waiter's apron when the arresting officers explained the case. They had taken the Negro into custody on the demand of a U. S. Purser at Norfolk, Virginia, who claimed ownership. They had scarcely completed their statement when five white men came forward. All five were known to the court, for they were members of the bar, but they were also known as members of a citizen's Vigilance Committee which had been organized in Boston to meet just such situations as this.

Without waiting for their defense, Shadrack promptly blurted out in the courtroom for all to hear. This court, his old master in Norfolk, citizens of the Vigilance Committee, U. S. marshals, constables, everybody concerned might as well know now as later that the waiter named Shadrack was not going back to Virginia—not alive anyhow. Despite this outburst, probably discounted by the Court as desperation talk, the friendly lawyers went ahead with their effort and arranged to have the case adjourned to give them time to prepare their defense.

The casual observer could see a long legal battle shaping up in the surprise arrest of Shadrack at the Cornhill Coffee House, but Shadrack's many friends, his fellow waiters and dishwashers, his Negro neighbors and cronies, saw nothing hopeful in this prospect. They did not have to be lawyers to know that the Fugitive Slave Law had stacked the cards against them in a situation like this. The Vigilance Committee, though its roster included more than two hundred names, some of them highly respected in Boston, would not be able to withstand the forces bent on putting Shadrack and other runaways like him back in slavery. It was perfectly plain to them that the power of Shadrack's foes was not limited to Congress, in which the laws supporting slavery were made. Through trade with Boston merchants the South was in a position to crack a whip too.

Shadrack was trapped. All of them were trapped. The glances they exchanged in the courtroom were to say that only one way was left, and that way was known to them all. The Negroes present began to huddle together. They moved toward the front where Shadrack stood between the deputy marshal and the one-time constable. This attracted no particular notice in the packed room. Everybody wanted to hear. Everybody was pushing. But when the presiding judge uttered the word "adjourned," a dark wall suddenly congealed around Shadrack. In another instant, overcome by a strange fury, the desperately united band shaped itself into a human wedge and began to drive toward the door.

The crowd fell away before it. Outside the courthouse the rescuers of Shadrack began to run. If they were followed, they didn't know it. When they looked back, the streets behind were clear. They could not help noticing, however, that the sky above was scowling, and none was simple enough to think that Shadrack was safe because they had snatched him from the law and hidden him in one of their own houses. No, their work was not done.

That night, as the storm began to roar, Shadrack began the long journey to Canada to join the twenty thousand refugee slaves who had already fled, and William Lloyd Garrison jubilantly wrote a headline for the next issue of the *Liberator:* "The Arrest—The Rescue—The Flight." "Thank God, Shadrack is free," his story began. "Nobody injured and nobody wronged, but simply a chattle transformed into a man!"

Six weeks later Thomas Sims, recently escaped from Savannah, Georgia, by stowing away on the brig *M. C. Gilmore,* was walking on Richmond Street in Boston when a man disguised as a city watchman ordered him to stop. Sims muttered softly. He was tired, very tired. Experiences on board ship had taken a lot out of him. He had been discovered in the forecastle nearly frozen as the vessel neared port and thereafter had been locked in a cabin. That night he had unscrewed the door with his pocket knife and left the boat at South Boston. Now he was caught again. Sims stepped back and prepared to use his fists.

His first blows staggered the policeman and caused him to turn away but others promptly came out of concealment and went to work on the fugitive. Sims was knocked down, overpowered and held. Later he was dragged into a carriage summoned for the purpose, and hauled off to the courthouse. As he was removed from the carriage, a spectator heard him mutter something about kidnappers. By the next morning the Vigilance Committee was on the job.

While the trial lasted, Horace Mann, Wendell Phillips and many others made passionate speeches in his behalf. On Sunday clergymen of Boston and vicinity received requests for special prayer signed by the mark of Thomas Sims and witnessed by S. E. Sewall and E. W. Jackson,

prayers for the deliverance of "a freeman . . . from his op-
pressor." So aroused were the antislavery forces, in fact,
and so fresh was the case of Shadrack in the memories of
the authorities, that a delegation of prominent men, led by
the marshal and including the mayor, entered the prison
room of the courthouse between four and five o'clock in
the morning of April twelfth, removed the captive and
marched him to the head of Long Wharf in the center of
a hollow square and placed him on board the brig *Acorn*.
At almost the same instant the paddles of the tugboat began shoving the *Acorn* downstream.

But if this episode seemed to turn the tables on Shadrack's friends, it did not make the South happy. A Savannah newspaper was quoted as saying, "If our people are
obliged to steal their property out of Boston in the night,
it would be more profitable to adopt a regular kidnapping
system at once, without regard to law." And the Augusta
Republic sneered bitterly. "We lost Shadrack and recovered Sims. A faithful execution of the law, indeed! When
costs have been subtracted, we should like to know how
much has been gained. . . . Sims was the fugitive slave of
Mr. Potter, beyond dispute; yet the case was kept in court
and before a commissioner for a whole week. It was necessary to guard him with a heavy police in the third story of
the Court House. The building was surrounded by a bar-
ricade of chains, and hundreds of the military had to be
kept on guard to prevent his forcible rescue. The whole
case looks more like a successful farce than anything else.
Look at some of the incidents. Mr. Fletcher Webster is
imprisoned; Marshal Tukey is held to bail in the sum of a
thousand dollars. Mr. Bacon and Mr. De Lyon, the agents
of Mr. Potter, were arrested on a charge of conspiracy to
kidnap, and had to give bail to the amount of $10,000—one
of the agents narrowly escaped being struck on the head by
a Negro named Randolph. If his arm had not been caught

by an officer, the life of a Southern man would have been sacrificed in an effort to recover a slave under the law of the country."

The cases of Shadrack and Sims were only two instances of many, but they suggest one thing. Whether free Negroes of the North were conscious of it or not, they were following Frederick Douglass in the spring of 1851, and the young leader, now in his thirty-fourth year, with the help of a bad law had put them in the field beside the radical abolitionists.

Nor did Douglass himself fail to see action as the wave of resistance mounted. When three dark strangers knocked at his door that year, it was as if lightning had struck twice in a single day, and Douglass showed them to the room reserved for such wayfarers, aware that something more than the Fugitive Slave Law was involved. A few hours earlier their story had come over the telegraph wires, and when the leader of the group gave his name as Parker, Douglass knew what he had on his hands.

These runaways were of the desperate kind. They had belonged to a determined man named Gorsuch who with his son had pursued them into Pennsylvania. At Christiana the owner had been joined by officers of the law, and together they had closed in on the escaped slaves. But Parker and his companions were prepared to fight, and when attacked they opened fire with a pistol. One bullet killed the old master. A second wounded the son. A third caused the officers of the law to retreat and gave the fugitives running space.

A widespread search of the Pennsylvania mountains began as the news flashed from town to town. Parker and his fellows were not just fugitive slaves. They were murderers in the eyes of the law and not to be trifled with. How they had managed to reach Rochester so soon after the tele-

graphed report puzzled Douglass, but Parker explained
that after the shooting at Christiana they had crossed up
their pursuers by not taking refuge in the mountains as
expected. Instead they had found friends who put them on
a train. They were tired now, after two days and nights of
grim flight, and in the brick house of Frederick Douglass
they slept like dead men.

While they slept, Douglass asked Julia to go to the
Genesee River landing, three miles away, and inquire casually about boats leaving that night for Canadian ports, if
any. Meanwhile he asked himself questions about the men
he harbored. Were they murderers? Well, he knew how the
law of the land regarded them. But what would Garrison's
answer to such a question be? How would John Brown
classify Parker? Neither answer was hard to guess. Nor was
Douglass's own conclusion evasive.

Parker and his friends were heroes and patriots in his
book. They had taken up arms against manstealers and
murderers. They had risked their own lives in the cause of
freedom which was more than personal, which was the
cause of all mankind. His duty, his challenge, was to speed
them to safety. Fortunately Julia brought good news. A
steamer was scheduled to sail for Toronto from the Genesee
River landing that very night.

A few hours later Douglass hitched the horses to his family carriage. Then he awakened his sleeping guests and
invited them to sit at the table with him. A meal cooked
by Anna was a treat which men prominent in the abolitionist movement could not forget, and she did her best for
the fugitives. But Parker and the two who fled with him
had to eat hurriedly. When they finished, Douglass led
them outside and across the shadowy drive. A moment
later, the whites of their eyes visible in the darkness, they
were in the carriage as Douglass gave the horses a touch of
the whip.

The three miles to the landing were long ones that night. Had anyone seen the trio approach the Douglass house? Would agents be at the river to check on the arrival and departure of the night steamer? Had the inquiry by Julia Griffiths been suspected? What if suddenly, from the roadside, marshals of the law were to appear and halt the horses?

Parker grunted. He knew the dangers. He and his companions had taken nothing for granted when they made their break. They were still ready for the worst. They had not thrown away the pistol that repulsed their pursuers at Christiana. Nor were they uncertain about the consequences of capture now. Their lives were for sale, not to be given away, and Douglass began to realize as he urged the horses ahead that his own security at the moment was linked with theirs.

Perhaps Parker sensed the same thing, for at the landing he was suddenly overcome by gratitude. Having waited in the carriage till the steamer tied up, Douglass decided it would be best to delay going aboard till the time of departure. Fifteen minutes passed. Then abruptly the four figures stepped down and hurried to the dock. Douglass went aboard with the others and waited with them till the order to haul in the gang plank was given. Then he turned and Parker, clasping his arm with a surprising warmth, slipped a heavy metal object into his hand. It was the pistol. Without speaking Douglass hurried back to the gangplank.

In his carriage again and on the more leisurely drive home he had a chance to contemplate Parker's gift, the weapon which had saved his life and the lives of his two companions, a symbol of the slave's will to freedom and of the common cause in which he and they were united.

For a moment the night seemed less black.

At home, however, life became increasingly complicated. The new baby, whom they had called Annie, would be a more delicate child than the older ones, Douglass could see, and perhaps more sensitive. Perhaps—perhaps little Annie would be *his* child in a way that none of the others were. The three boys and Rosetta were all strikingly like their mother in appearance, as nearly everybody noticed, and it was possible to discern in them still other traces of her personality. Her reticence, her unquestioning devotion, her down-to-earth simplicity had already marked her offspring. Five of a kind they were, but Annie—what would she be like?

Annie was two at the time Douglass put Parker and his companions on the Toronto steamer. She was three in 1852 when the house in which she had been born began to tremble. The smoldering quarrels between her father and mother, dating from the arrival of Julia Griffiths but mild and intermittent at first, reached a point of crisis that year. People around Rochester were talking more than ever. Even Julia's colleagues on the ladies' antislavery committee began to raise their eyebrows. Rosetta noticed the tension and sided with her mother against the strange woman in their house. Finally somebody put a foot down, a heavy, determined foot. Apparently it was long-suffering, sometimes unimaginative Anna. In any case, Julia Griffiths moved out of the Douglass residence in the fall of 1852.

Neither she nor Douglass dignified any of the innuendo by replying to it. They were in a crusade together. That was all. And when she moved into other quarters in the city, Julia continued to assist with the editing of *The North Star* and to collaborate with Douglass in his other antislavery work. She also continued to speak about him in correspondence with Gerrit Smith, the patron of their movement in western New York. Douglass's family difficulties and the state of his health were often in her thoughts.

Unfortunately her change of residence did not mean an

end of family problems for Douglass. The question of his children's education had arisen, for one thing. It had actually arisen the year of their arrival in Rochester, for Rosetta was at that time old enough to be admitted to Seward Seminary for girls, and Douglass had made the necessary arrangements. When the youngster came home and reported that she was being taught in a separate room, apart from the other little girls of that fashionable school, his first act had been a protest to the principal. The principal had agreed to put the issue to the other pupils and to their parents, and one parent had registered opposition to the presence of the colored child in the school. On the strength of this one vote Rosetta had been asked to withdraw.

A poorly equipped and poorly staffed Negro school was available in Rochester at the time, but Douglass had decided instead to send his young daughter to a school in Albany. After two years, the fast-growing youngster having reached an age at which she could be helpful as well as good company to her mother during his long absences, he had brought her home and employed a white governess, Phoebe Thayer, a Quaker, to continue the girl's education. Now Rosetta was thirteen and ready for secondary school, and her younger brothers were old enough to work as printer's devils in the shop in which *The North Star* was published, and the fact that the public schools were not open to them had become a serious inconvenience which rankled their father.

Well, at least the quarrels with Anna subsided. Not so, however, the bad blood which followed his defection from Garrisonianism. While the two principals and their respective friends continued to meet on platforms and at the big annual gatherings of the Anti-Slavery Society and to button up their lips on the subject that had alienated them, the offense remained. Behind the scenes blows were struck, and persons close to the two men could scarcely fail to see that Garrison and Douglass were feuding bitterly. Neither was saying anything good about the other, and in the early months of 1851 when, with Julia Griffiths' deft hand plainly at work in the background, *The North Star* had merged with the *Liberty Party Paper,* whose financial backer was Gerrit Smith, the embers of the controversy reddened. Help from Smith toward the costs of publishing *The North Star* was taken for granted as a result of the move, but to Garrison it was unholy. Douglass's paper, which in the future would be called *Frederick Douglass' Weekly,* had by that act transformed itself from an abolitionist journal to a political organ. Was there any greater sin?

The annual meeting of the American Anti-Slavery Society was held in Syracuse that year, close to the bailiwick of Smith's followers, and Douglass chose this time to put an end to whispers. With Garrison sitting behind him on the platform, he stunned the meeting by announcing in a "hesitating and embarrassed manner" that he was now convinced that the Constitution "might be consistent in its details with the noble purposes avowed in its preamble." Accordingly, he was resolved to counsel the use of political action along with moral suasion in the fight against slavery.

If to some persons present, such as the reporter for the Worcester *Spy,* this public confession of new faith seemed "manly and candid," to Garrison it was almost maddening. A piece of the sky fell on the "antislavery apostles," their friends and followers and the battered veterans of their righteous cause as the man who was the voice of conscience to many of them rose from his seat to reply with passion that "there was roguery somewhere."

The end of that dispute was scarcely in sight as another year faded to a close, and now Garrison was writing letters to abolitionists in England asking them to withhold support from *Frederick Douglass' Paper* on the grounds that it served no good purpose. Wendell Phillips was also saying however, "If there is anybody who does not like quarreling, I would advise him to join the conservatives, for he will find reformers always in a tempest," and this was good for a perspective.

Given a certain perspective, the differences between Douglass and the Boston group could be boiled down to a few points. The Constitution question was important, of course, because on it hung the crucial issue of union or separation. The resentment of Garrisonians against his paper was understandable and perhaps inevitable, human nature considered, but that too was related to the stand on the Constitution. Some of the group had accused him of calling George Thompson a drunkard. On that he would not comment, but perhaps all these together entitled him to voice a criticism or two of his own.

He did not have to retract any of the praise he had so often heaped on Garrison's head to point out that the editor of the *Liberator* had not actually begun the antislavery movement, as so many abolitionists seemed to take for granted now. Garrison's special contribution was the doctrine of immediate rather than gradual emanicaption, Douglass thought. Nor had he failed to notice certain flaws in his former friends. Such disciples of Garrison as Wright, Pillsbury and Foster, he charged, were infidels at heart. And the Negro Garrisonians were no better. While he was in the mood, he let them have a piece of his mind too.

Take Robert Purvis of Berry Hill, Pennsylvania. The wealth with which he was born was blood money. William C. Nell, the dapper postal employee who had presided at the dinner at which Douglass was honored in Boston on his return from abroad, who had later joined him in the publication of *The North Star* but who could not bring himself to part company with the Garrisonians, why Nell was a "tool" and "an enemy of the colored people." Charles Remond, for whom Douglass's youngest son was

named, and William Wells Brown, handsome young mulatto, a good speaker and a better writer, who had escaped
from slavery in Kentucky and started life as a freedman in
the office of Elijah Lovejoy—well, the less said about them
the better. They were going along with Garrison, and that
was unforgivable.

By spring of 1853, however, he had something more
wholesome to think about. Harriet Beecher Stowe wrote
him a letter.

Douglass's troubles in the years immediately following
the enactment of the Fugitive Slave Law reflected the fears
and frustrations of all the free colored colored people of
the North. His bitter, reproachful mood, on the other
hand, pointed up the Valley Forge ordeal of the whole
antislavery agitation. The abolitionist sects were falling
apart. Douglass's defection to the ranks of the political
group, an unappealing spectacle in terms of old allegiances
and personal friendship, was in reality a part of a widespread trend. It now appears that an actual majority of
Northern abolitionists came to the same conclusions Douglass reached in those years.

While the old line abolitionists stewed and fretted, however, *Uncle Tom's Cabin* swept the country, and for the
first time a significant segment of the general population
began to gnash its teeth over the sin of slavery. Of course
Uncle Tom's Cabin did not do the job alone. The cases of
Shadrack and Sims helped. Resentment against the slave
catchers produced more antislavery sentiment than Garrison and his followers had ever succeeded in arousing. Soon
hundreds of previously indifferent Northerners were ready
to speed runaways on their journey to free territory.

None of which can fairly detract from the positive effect
of the great agitation. The abolitionists had contributed
moral fervor, without which no social reform succeeds.

They had provided the forces opposed to slavery with a rationale for struggle. Indeed they had accomplished more than they dreamed, for at the moment of their deepest dejection and confusion they were actually being sucked into a wave so big they failed to recognize it. The acclaim which Harriet Beecher Stowe gained as a result of her disturbing book merely baffled them. Of course they were pleased by its popularity, but where did it leave them?

Mrs. Stowe was planning a trip to England, following invitations from prominent persons in Britain and a promise of a testimonial, when she wrote her note to the Negro leader. They had never met, but her letter was an invitation to him to spend a day at her house. Douglass could not imagine what prompted this cordiality, but the name of Harriet Beecher Stowe, the most talked about woman in America, made it exciting. Of course he would accept at once.

At the end of the long journey to Andover he was received into the Stowe home with warm friendliness, and the celebrated author, as fluent in conversation as in writing, promptly dispelled the mystery. "I have invited you here," she said, "because I wish to confer with you as to what can be done for the free colored people of the country. I am going to England and expect to have a considerable sum of money placed in my hands, and I intend to use it in some way for the permanent improvement of the free colored people, and especially for that class which has become free by their own exertions. In what way I can do this most successfully is the subject about which I wish to talk with you. In any event I desire to have some monument rise after *Uncle Tom's Cabin* which shall show that it produced more than a transient influence."

Douglass's ears fairly waved, but he did not interrupt. The author went on to mention ideas that had been suggested to her, including the establishment of a school.

What did Frederick Douglass, the recognized leader of the group she was most anxious to help, consider the best way to help the free Negro people?

His answer was on the tip of his tongue. Not a school, he blurted. At least not an ordinary school. Money spent to teach book learning would be wasted on his people at that moment. The root of all evil, where the recently emancipated were concerned, was the *want* of money. Free Negroes in the North were barred from all the lucrative occupations. The best employment they could hope to find was barbering, waiting table, driving horses—the poorly paid jobs. "Poverty keeps them ignorant and their ignorance keeps them degraded," he sighed. "We need more to learn how to make a good living than to learn Latin and Greek."

Which was to suggest what?

Perhaps a series of workshops would be possible, he proposed. A series of workshops in which colored people could learn handicrafts, iron, wood and leather work, while acquiring a simple English education which would serve their needs.

Harriet Beecher Stowe smiled as she listened. When he finished talking, she told him that she agreed with his ideas. She would use the money she expected to receive abroad to establish an institution in which Negro youth could learn trades while being taught to read, write and count. Would Douglass prepare a letter setting forth his plan in detail, a letter she could take to England with her and show to her friends there?

Back in Rochester on March eighth, he went to work on the statement. Amused by the figure he cut, never having had a day's schooling in his life yet boldly projecting a plan of education, he briefly analyzed the condition of his people and the discouragements they faced. Colleges were open to them, but lawyers, doctors, editors and the like needed a clientele. There was little that men in these professions could do for the bewildered ex-slaves of the country. Even well-educated ministers were wasted on congregations which valued strong lungs above high learning. Still he could more easily get his son into a lawyer's office to study law than get him into a blacksmith's shop to blow the bellows and learn the trade. No wonder John Russwurm, Henry Highland Garnet, Samuel Ringgold Ward, and other Negro intellectuals were giving up the struggle in the United States and looking beyond the country's borders to more congenial climates.

Having finished the letter and posted it, Douglass remembered another part of Mrs. Stowe's request. She wanted also, he recalled, the views of other free Negro people on the plan she and Douglass had discussed. He had promised to do something in this direction too. Suddenly he thought of an excellent way to get such a cross section of opinion.

Another colored convention had been called. Not since the Cleveland meeting, five years earlier, at which Douglass had been selected by the delegates as their leader, had representative free Negroes of the North assembled to exchange views and discuss their common problems. Much had happened to their group in those five years, as indicated by the wholesale flights to Canada after the passage of the Fugitive Slave Law, and all Northern Negroes felt less secure in their persons than previously. Much had happened to Douglass, the young man the representatives had elevated amid whisperings about John Brown and his admonition to free Negroes to carry weapons under their coats. While those wild dreams had faded, or at least remained dormant, there had been the break with Garrison, the founding of *The North Star,* the return of Julia Griffiths, the visit with John Brown himself in Springfield, the rapproachement with Gerrit Smith, the birth of little

Annie, the trouble about Rosetta's education, the family quarrels and the change in Julia's place of residence, the increased travel on the Underground Railroad, and the usual hardships of an editor compounded by all of these. And now, two months before the Rochester Colored National Convention was scheduled to meet, here was this thing in which Harriet Beecher Stowe was interested.

Certainly the work college came within the scope of the call, answered by one hundred and forty delegates from eight states, for "the development of means for the amelioration of the condition of the colored people," and Douglass had no trouble getting a favored place for it on the docket when sessions opened on July 6. Before it could reach the floor, of course, there was organizational business. While Douglass was not given the chairmanship of the Convention again, there was some evidence that this may have reflected heightened rather than lowered prestige. His old friend J. W. C. Pennington was tendered that honor. Douglass was named as one of the vice-presidents and appointed to the chairmanship of the vital Committee on Declaration of Sentiments, and before the sessions ended, he found himself guiding one or two other committees as well.

Before the deliberations were over, he also found himself clashing horns with a strong minority of his colleagues who seemed in no wise appalled by the reputation of their past-president. Always ready for a fight, Douglass shook himself and charged. Henry Bibb, who had made one of the principal addresses at the Boston reception honoring Douglass on his return from abroad, and Martin Delaney of Pittsburgh, whose name appeared with Douglass's and William C. Nell's on the masthead of the first issues of *The North Star,* brought the old, dog-eared question of colonization to the floor. Delegates sighed. The idea of solving the problems of the Negro people of the United States by colonizing the group elsewhere in the world had been advocated in some quarters for more than a quarter of a century. Since 1830 a majority of free Negroes and most white abolitionists had been firmly set against it. In 1832 Garrison had published his *Thoughts on African Colonization* in Boston, arguing against it in theory and pointing up the Negro's own resistance to the notion. But the new dilemma, some delegates felt, warranted a reconsideration, and Bibb and Delaney spoke for this point of view. Douglass was ready for them. He had spoken his mind on colonization many times before, and he still considered it the "twin sister of slavery." Born in the United States, generally of mixed ancestry, the American Negro had little in common with the African. He had helped to make this country and earned his place in it. "His attachment to the place of his birth is stronger than iron." Moreover, he had noticed that "the human race becomes indolent in a warm climate," and that was not for Douglass.

While such reasoning failed to sway Bibb and Delaney, both of whom continued for some time afterwards to advocate colonization as a way out for their American brethren, the main body of the Convention shared Douglass's point of view and Pennington spoke for them when he concluded, "We intend to plant our trees on American soil and repose in the shade thereof."

The question of a work college for free colored youth also had a history in the deliberations of colored conventions. The 1831 meeting in Philadelphia, many remembered, had heard and approved a comparable proposal, backed by the wealthy abolitionist merchant Arthur Tappan. The opposition of New Haven citizens to such an institution in their community, they recalled, had thrown cold water on that plan. Sponsored by Douglass at the Rochester Convention, twenty-two years later, with the figure of Harriet Beecher Stowe in the background, the project banged into surprising resistance at the very start, and oddly enough the opposition was led by Nell, Douglass's other associate in the founding of *The North Star*.

Nell was backed by those Negroes who had declined to follow Douglass out of the Garrison camp. The clean-cut Nell was beginning to question the Colored Convention itself on the grounds that all-Negro meetings and programs showed a kind of tacit approval of segregation. While he had not stayed away from them as some opponents had, he attended with reservations, and now he had begun to think, "of abandoning, as soon as possible, all separate action and becoming part and parcel of the general community" as the best line for Negroes to follow. But Douglass was not to be denied on this point, having gone so far with it in conversation with Mrs. Stowe and prepared such an elaborate letter for her use in England. When another former colleague, Charles Remond, lined up with the group who said the proposed venture was too costly to consider, Douglass struck back powerfully.

A strong argument could be made from facts with which all the delegates were familiar. While the old-line abolitionists accepted the Negro as a man and a brother, few of them had been known to open up work opportunities for him. The gossip was that even the Tappan brothers, stouthearted defenders of fugitives from slavery, had neglected to use their influence as businessmen to make jobs for Negroes.

And so the controversy grew. Eventually Douglass was named chairman of a committee to draw up the Convention's resolution favoring the school, and this was adopted by the full body, but the fight had been bitter and damage had been done. Nevertheless disinterested observers, the reporter for the New York *Tribune,* for example, were impressed by the level of the discussions, and the *Tribune* account stated that "not a word of nonsense was talked."

The delegates too felt that the meetings had been constructive. Douglass wrote a letter to Gerrit Smith in which he noted that the Convention had done something for "the current of feeling toward colored people in Rochester." On the tide of this elation after battle the Convention drew up a plan for a National Council, a permanent organization of twenty-one representatives from state societies. As the delegates adjourned, their own warm feelings convinced them that better days were just ahead for Negro people of the North.

These hopes faded quickly, however. The plan called for a meeting of the Council in New York in January of 1854. Some members gathered, including Douglass, but failing to number a quorum, no meeting was held. A second meeting was set for six months later in Cleveland. To this one Douglass did not go, and the bare quorum which gathered soon found itself floundering. Any single member could defeat measures he opposed simply by absenting himself and reducing the attendance below the constitutional requirement of eleven. The sessions, it was said, "stood constantly in need of a sergeant-at-arms." A call to another full convention in Philadelphia in 1855 drew only a small attendance. The colored convention movement, the framework for free Negro expression and leadership in the first half of the nineteenth century, had died.

Perhaps the seeds of its failure had been planted when it tried to make its way without the cooperation of the white reformers and abolitionists interested in the Negro's progress. And the proposed work college, which served by this time to symbolize its program, ran into rough sledding on other counts. Such a school was not considered educationally sound. Some Negroes thought a system of apprenticeships would be better. In England, where Harriet Beecher Stowe succeeded in collecting only a little over five hundred dollars and lost interest in the whole idea, it was pointed out that vocational schools invariably failed in that day.

Douglass's spirit sank, and Mrs. Stowe's decision to turn the small fund she had collected in England over to him personally as a contribution toward his own efforts in behalf of his people did not make much difference. Nothing was going well. His newspaper continued to struggle for its life, but subscriptions fell off badly. In 1855 Julia Griffiths decided that she had done her bit for the paper and its editor, if not for the cause of abolition in the United States. She returned to England with the promise to submit articles for publication from time to time. Though these did not show up as promptly as expected, the first one finally arrived and others followed now and then till the time of her marriage to H. O. Crofts, a British clergyman, four years later, and even after that her correspondence with Frederick Douglass continued. Indeed, in 1888, when all of this seemed long ago and far away, she recalled that "for 42 years our correspondence has been uninterrupted."

At the time of her departure, however, Douglass was in no reflective mood. Or if he was, the thing his mind went back to was the visit he had made to the home of John Brown in Springfield, in the early days of *The North Star*. He had occasion to recall that impressive meeting just a few months before Julia sailed, in fact, for in June of 1855 Douglass happened to be in Syracuse attending a meeting of the Radical Abolitionist party when Brown rose and appealed to the convention for "men and means to defend freedom in Kansas." Old John Brown was headed west, and there was fire in his eyes. The delegates gave him sixty dollars.

The following December the strange man passed through Rochester en route to the east and repaid Douglass's visit. Thereafter the two men found few opportunities for such cordiality, but Douglass followed the accounts of the Kansas troubles with a strongly partisan interest. No other course seemed to be advancing the Negro's cause. Maybe John Brown's fervent refrain, "without the shedding of blood there is no remission of sin," maybe—

Then in May of the following year the old man struck his first blow. Free-soil settlers of Lawrence, Kansas, had been attacked by proslavery forces. When the settlers appealed for help, John Brown stepped up, mustered volunteers and went after the attackers at Pottawomie Creek. He got five of them. But the Kansas affair tended to isolate itself, and by the next year old Brown was looking for another place to strike. He was out of money again, however, and to raise funds it would be necessary to return East. On the way he stopped in Rochester.

It was the first or second day of February. The leathery old party offered to pay lodging if the Douglasses would put him up. Douglass did not like the suggestion of payment, but Bown insisted, and being John Brown he had his way. While at the Douglass's home Brown spent most of his time writing letters. These turned out to be lengthy epistles to sympathizers on whom he counted for backing in a venture he was not ready to talk about to Douglass. To deepen the mystery he signed the letters *Nelson Hawkins*. Between letters he spent hours revising and recopying a constitution which he told Douglass he would put into operation when he gained power. The document consisted of forty-eight articles and seemed to revolve around a military chief.

While he kept his secret, Brown did not hesitate to talk about his general aims. He even gathered the Douglass children around him and illustrated with blocks the plan he had outlined to their father years earlier, the plan for guerilla warefare in the Alleghany Mountains. This visit with the Douglass family, intended as a very short stay, stretched to three weeks. Finally Brown proposed that he and Douglass meet again in Philadelphia, say a fortnight hence, at which time he might be able to clear up part of the mystery he had apparently caused.

Douglass consulted his calendar. That was agreeable. He had a lecture in Philadelphia about that time. On this note the old man departed for Peterboro and a visit with Gerrit Smith from whom he expected financial assistance. Within a few days, however, it became apparent that Douglass would not be able to reach Philadelphia on schedule, and he wrote Brown to ask that the appointment be changed to March 11, five days later than planned. This appointment Douglass kept and found himself in conference with Brown and Brown's eldest son, along with Henry Highland Garnet and William Still, a Negro Underground Railroad operator. But instead of detailing his plans Brown simply appealed to these well-known Negroes for money and men, and Douglass went home to Rochester as puzzled as ever.

Yet there was little doubt that the avenger was preparing to strike again. Three weeks later Brown and his son showed up at the Douglass home once more. This time the old man was bound for Canada where he had an appointment with Harriet Tubman, an amazing black woman who had been leading fugitive slaves by the score to freedom. Through wilderness and over mountain this hard-bitten creature with an animal's instinct for directions, with fang-like teeth and a horrible scar on her head, the result of a murderous blow dealt her in slavery by a crazed master, this shadowy woman had made trip after trip into the slave states to rescue people from bondage, even bringing out her own haggard old parents, and John Brown had a feeling she would be right for the operation he planned.

Eleven days after Brown and his son and another man departed for St. Catherine's Douglass heard from him. "I expect to need all the help I can get by the first of May," the letter said. But that date turned out to be premature, and Douglass got the impression that something he revealed to Brown might have been influential. One of Brown's followers turned sour and threatened to expose the venture if he were not provided with money.

The disgruntled individual was Hugh Forbes. Douglass had met him five or six months earlier and received an unfavorable impression, for Forbes had requested a little money at that time. An Englishman whose adventures had begun with Garibaldi of Italy, Forbes had promised to help Brown drill his men. Under the circumstances Douglass thought he could afford to draw up a little list of names of other friends of John Brown's cause at Forbes' request. But this was a mistake. Forbes at once commenced blackmailing these friends, and Douglass rushed this information to Brown.

The fact that Brown decided soon afterwards to return to Kansas and postpone whatever plans he may have had for May seemed to Douglass a consequence of this warning. Actually Forbes had already told Senators Hale, Wilson and Seward all he knew about Brown's plans, and Brown had received the same information from Senator Wilson through Samuel Gridley Howe, a trusted backer. This had been followed by a secret conference of five of Brown's financial supporters, including Gerrit Smith, Theodore Parker, George L. Stearns and Thomas Wentworth Higginson as well as Howe, and together they had decided that Brown must return to Kansas as a means of discrediting the charges of Forbes. Postponement was a bitter disappointment to John Brown, but he acted on the advice of his friends.

A year later, with a price on his head, John Brown came out of the West. He was ready to strike again, and this time Frederick Douglass was definitely in his plans. Douglass was

lecturing in Detroit in March of 1859 when he received a
letter from the hunted man. Brown had something to tell
him. In fact, Brown had decided to reveal his master plan
to Douglass in the hope of enlisting Douglass in the operation. But when Brown passed through Rochester a month
later, he was on his way to Peterboro and a visit with Smith
and had only a few hours to stop. His whiskers were long,
and he arrived in the morning when Douglass was working
at the shop. They talked intensely together for a while,
but this was not the show-down. There simply wasn't
enough time.

Again John Brown dropped out of sight. Five months
later his eldest son appeared in Rochester and asked for
Frederick Douglass. Douglass was away as usual, this time
lecturing in Niagara Falls, but he returned home the next
day and had a long talk with the young man. Their conversation has not been preserved, but young Brown went
away and when he returned again, six days later, Douglass
had already left for Chambersburg, Pennsylvania, about
twenty miles from Harpers Ferry. Perhaps it was to check
on this that the young man had returned.

On August nineteenth Douglass was led to an old stone
quarry by Shields Green, a runaway slave whom Brown had
met in Rochester during his three-week sojourn in the
Douglass home about seventeen months earlier. In his
pocket Douglass carried a letter to Brown from a colored
woman in Brooklyn, enclosing twenty-five dollars with
"best wishes for your welfare and prosperity." With Brown
in the quarry as Douglass and Shields Green entered was
his "Secretary of War," John Kagi, a young veteran of the
bloody business in Kansas.

John Brown told Douglass of his aim to seize the government arsenal at Harpers Ferry and to capture leading citizens whom he could hold as hostages. From that point the
campaign would follow the plan he had outlined to Doug-

lass in Springfield eleven years ago. What did Douglass think of it?

Douglass was stunned. He had come down to Chambersburg ready for bold measures. He did not shrink from the idea of forcibly emancipating slaves, but the suggestion of attacking the government arsenal seemed insane. It could only end in disaster, he gasped.

Brown was unimpressed by such warnings. If the effort failed, the attempt would still be worth while, he thought. Evils had to be dramatized before legislatures would be impressed. The whole country would hear about the action at Harpers Ferry. What more could you ask?

But Douglass only shook his head and repeated his willingess to join in any plan which aimed simply at emancipating slaves.

"Come with me, Douglass," the old man entreated. "I will defend you with my life. I want you for a special purpose. When I strike, the bees will begin to swarm and I shall want you to help me hive them."

Douglass was touched, deeply touched, but somehow he could not make up his mind to accept immortality, on those terms. Presently he turned to leave but paused to ask Shields Green what he was going to do.

"I be'lieve I go wid de old man," Shields drawled.

Evidently Brown did not take Douglass's rejection in the stone quarry as final, and he set about to bring pressure. Douglass received a most unusual letter a few weeks later, a letter signed by a number of colored men. It invited him to represent them at a convention being held "right away" in Chambersburg. The writers pledged themselves darkly to see "your family well provided for during your absence, or until your safe return to them."

Douglass did not elect to represent the men. Instead he continued his regular lectures. On October seventeenth he was speaking in National Hall in Philadelphia when the

news broke. Brown and twenty-one men, five of them Negroes, had attacked the arsenal at Harpers Ferry. Now
Brown had been arrested. Jolted by the reports, Douglass
immediately remembered letters he had received from
Brown and which, if found, would tend to link him with
the attack. His friends in Philadelphia were equally
alarmed. They crowded around him backstage and urged
him to leave town as fast as possible.

While they pondered, a dispatch addressed to the Philadelphia sheriff reached John W. Hurn, telegraph operator.
It called for the arrest of Frederick Douglass, believed to be
an accessory to the crime of which John Brown was
accused. But John W. Hurn, an antislavery man and an admirer of Frederick Douglass, delayed delivering the message. After three hours, when he was convinced that Douglass was well on his journey, he let the dispatch go through.

Even in New York, however, Douglass could not feel
safe as one of the biggest news stories of the century hit the
streets. He scarcely paused in the big city and began mak-
his way toward Rochester as inconspicuously as possible. As
he traveled, he read the *Herald*'s story under the headlines,
"Brown has made a full statement, implicating Gerrit
Smith, Joshua Giddings and Frederick Douglass." Apparently Brown had disclosed enough, it added, to "justify a
requisition from Governor Wise of Virginia, upon Governor Morgan, of New York, for the delivery over to the
hands of justice of Gerrit Smith and Fred Douglass, as
parties implicated in the crime of murder, and as acces-
sories before the fact."

Back in Rochester the disturbed traveler relaxed, but
not for long. It was hard for him to believe that his friends
and neighbors would let agents of the government send
him to Virginia for trial. But his Rochester friends themselves were less sure. Several hurried consultations were
held, followed by the burning of certain papers from Doug-

lass's desk. In desperation he packed his bags and fled to Canada.

He was scarcely across the border when the United States district attorney for western New York appeared in Rochester. One of the local newspapers hinted broadly that he was looking for Frederick Douglass.

VIII

DARK VICTORY

JOHN BROWN'S ATTACK on the Arsenal at Harpers Ferry touched off the Civil War. More precise historians, perhaps, have settled on the action at Fort Sumter as the starting point, but not Frederick Douglass. As an escaped slave and an abolitionist, as one so deeply involved in the conflict as to mark its progress by his own heart beats, he perceived, or thought he perceived, a sudden change in the air after Harpers Ferry. The great agitation had ended. War had begun.

Actually, feverish months lay ahead and many preliminary events were required before opposing armies could meet on battlefields to shed the blood needed, as John Brown believed, for the remission of the nation's sins, and Douglass lived this interlude dangerously. His first problem was to stay alive. Certainly the marshals of a government which had recently upheld the Dred Scott decision could not be expected to help him achieve this aim. Canada provided a healthier climate for the moment.

But should he have run? Had it been cowardly? Front page headlines had implicated him along with Gerrit Smith, Dr. Samuel G. Howe, Theodore Parker and Thomas Wentworth Higginson in John Brown's attempt, and the latest word was that John E. Cook, one of the men captured, had not only accused Douglass of letting the others down but blamed him for the failure of the plan. Douglass, Cook alleged, was to have appeared with arms and men. The others had waited several hours for him.

Should these charges and allegations remain unchallenged? Exactly where did he stand now on the John Brown insurrection?

Douglass decided to tell his side of the story. From Canada West on October thirty-first, twelve days after Brown's capture by troops under the command of Colonel Robert E. Lee, he wrote the Rochester *Democrat and American:* "I notice that the telegraph makes Mr. Cook denounce me as a coward—and to assert that I promised to be present at the Harpers Ferry insurrection. This is certainly a very grave impeachment, whether viewed in its bearings upon friends or upon foes, and you will not think it strange that I should take a somewhat serious notice of it. Having no acquaintance whatever with Mr. Cook and never having exchanged a word with him about the Harper's Ferry insurrection, I am induced to doubt that he could have used the language concerning me which the wires attribute to him." He paused to spin a metaphor:

> The lightning, when speaking for itself, is among the most direct, reliable and truthful of things; but when speaking for the terror-striken slaveholders at Harper's Ferry, it has been made the swiftest of liars. Under their nimble and trembling fingers, it magnified seventeen men into seven hundred—and has since filled the columns of the New York *Herald* for days with interminable contradictions. But, assuming that it has told only the simple truth, as to the sayings of Mr. Cook in this instance, I have this answer to make to my accuser: Mr. Cook may be perfectly right in denouncing me as a coward. I have not one word to say in defence or vindication of my character for courage. I have always been more distinguished

for running than fighting—and, tried by the Harper's Ferry insurrection test, I am most miserably deficient in courage—even more so than Cook, when he deserted his old brave captain, and fled to the mountains. . . . But wholly, grievously, and most unaccountably wrong is Mr. Cook, when he asserts that I promised to be present in person at the Harper's Ferry insurrection . . . my wisdom or my cowardice has not only kept me from Harper's Ferry, but has equally kept me from making any promise to go there. . . . So much I deem it proper to say negatively.

On the other hand, however, he wanted it clear that

In the denial which I have now made, my motive is more a respectful consideration for the opinions of the slave's friends, than from my fear of being made an accomplice in the general *conspiracy* against Slavery. I am ever ready to write, speak, publish, organize, combine, and even to conspire against Slavery, when there is a reasonable hope for success. Men who live by robbing their fellowmen of their labors and liberty, have forfeited their right to know anything of the thoughts, feelings, or purposes of those whom they rob and plunder. . . . If anybody is disposed to think less of me because of this sentiment; or because I may have had a knowledge of what was about to occur, and did not assume the base and detestable character of an informer, he is a man whose good or bad opinion of me may be equally repugnant and despicable. Entertaining this sentiment, I may be asked why I did not join John Brown—the noble old hero whose one right hand has shaken the foundation of the American Union, and whose ghost will haunt the bedchambers of all the born and unborn slaveholders of Virginia through all their generations, filling them with alarm and consternation! My answer to this has already been given, at least impliedly given: "The tools to those who can use them." Let every man work for the abolition of Slavery in his own way. I would help all, and hinder none. My position in regard to the Harper's Ferry insurrection may be easily inferred from these remarks, and I shall be glad if those papers which have spoken of me in connection with it would find room for this brief statement.

They did. The *Herald* reprinted it on November fourth. Douglass's own paper, now known as *Douglass' Monthly*, its third typographical change of face since it began publishing in 1847, carried in the November issue an angry Douglass editorial attacking the line of defense which some papers had taken in behalf of John Brown. These papers had gone along with the counsel assigned by the court to defend Brown and attributed his actions to insanity. To Douglass this was like calling the patriots at Lexington, Concord and Bunker Hill crazy. What kind of effeminate and cowardly age had the world drifted into? If further proof of the debauchery to the intellect caused by slavery were needed, this was it. Heroism, self-sacrifice, belief in the Declaration of Independence and in the Bible, the basis of John Brown's action, were now presented as madness. "But the future," he predicted, "the future will write his epitaph upon the hearts of a people freed from slavery, because he struck the first effectual blow."

Douglass also disclosed that he had made plans to go abroad, plans which had actually been delayed rather than hastened by the dramatic events of the past weeks. He mentioned it casually as an afterthought to his statement on the insurrection, for whatever those who accused him of cowardice wished to make of it, and he sailed from Quebec on November twelfth.

In the United States, meanwhile, things popped. There is no other way to describe the firecracker-like succession between John Brown's arrest and the beginning of military hostilities. While the trial of Brown and his companions was being rushed, unduly rushed, many charged, a feverish search for confederates and silent partners began. One of those named, Theodore Parker, a respected Boston pastor, was in Europe and out of the reach of American authorities. Traveling abroad for his health, he did not attempt to hide his sympathy for Brown or prior knowledge of the attempted raid. Dr. Samuel G. Howe, however, another who had aided and encouraged Brown, lost his nerve and issued a statement denying that his personal acquaintance indicated complicity in the other's plans, a statement which some historians have since called a misrepresentation. Even so, Dr. Howe and George Stearns and others under similar suspicion took the precaution of stepping across the Canadian border in order to view forthcoming developments with calmer detachment.

Gerrit Smith heard the news from Harpers Ferry and promptly lost his mind. He had to be taken to the Utica Asylum for the Insane. But Thomas Wentworth Higginson, a stouthearted Worcester clergyman, refused to run away or to deny the encouragement he had offered, and very soon it began to be apparent that he had chosen the wisest course.

Even before December 2, when John Brown was hanged, a change in the public attitude could be detected, but the effect of his death was electrical. Voices began to rise in defence of old "Osawatomie." Ralph Waldo Emerson's, a particularly strong one, predicted that John Brown's death would make the gallows glorious like the cross. Stearns and Howe, now assured that they would not be prosecuted in Massachusetts or extradited to another state, ventured to return home.

Meanwhile Douglass rested uneasily in the home of the Reverend Russell Lant Carpenter in Halifax. The Atlantic crossing had required fourteen days, so he had been in England about a week when John Brown went to his death in Charlestown, Virginia, remarking slyly but triumphantly as he marched between the lines of soldiers that reached from the porch of the jail to the gallows, "I had no idea that Governor Wise considered my execution so important." Eventually the news reached the British people, with all the sidelights by which it had been dramatized in the American press, and suddenly hosts of Englishmen were eager to hear about Douglass's connection with the plan. Before he knew it, he was launched on a series of lectures, and soon he had John Brown's own death-morning words with which to assail the emotions of his hearers: "I John Brown am now quite *certain* that the crimes of this *guilty land: will* never be purged *away;* but with Blood. I had *as I now think; vainly* flattered myself that without *very much* bloodshed; it might be done."

Brown's tragic victory was not the only reason for Douglass's uneasiness, however. He began his second sojourn of the British Isles with no assurance that he would ever be permitted to return to his native land, to his home and family and friends, to his newspaper and the other interests which made up his life. As far as he could see, the curtain had fallen. Equally crushing was the news from Rochester. Little Annie, it said, little Annie, the sensitive child, had taken her father's flight very hard. The whisperings about U. S. marshals, about the trial and hanging of the old man who had visited them in their home within her memory and the predictions that she might not see her father again terrified her. As a result she had not been well since he left.

Visiting with old friends in England, lecturing, talking about John Brown, renewing acquaintances made thirteen years earlier, Douglass kept thinking about Annie, the angelic child whose birth had followed his first trip abroad. Early in the new year Rosetta wrote that her ten-year-old sister had lost the power to speak or hear. In March little Annie died. When Douglass heard it, he felt something snap inside. Without pausing to ask whether or not it would be safe, he canceled his outstanding speaking engagements and rushed back to the United States.

He arrived quietly on the coast of Maine and proceeded to Rochester as inconspicuously as possible. He was at home with his grief-striken family for more than a week before it became generally known that he had returned. By then he had been able to reassure himself about the risks involved. The John Brown hysteria had definitely subsided. True, the Senate committee which had been appointed to investigate the insurrection and its background had not yet rendered its final report, but neither had it called any prominent witnesses nor held newsworthy hearings, despite the fact that its chairman was James M. Mason of Virginia.

Douglass tried to arrange the parts of the puzzle. His private conclusion was that the men conducting the investigation had decided against whetting a knife for rebels. He suspected that they were planning something in the nature of rebellion themselves, not in behalf of liberty but in behalf of slavery, and that they feared that such a weapon, should they sharpen it, would presently be used against them. Other observers attributed the committee's coyness to a similar but different reason. These felt that the pro-slavery senators merely shrank from providing a great sounding board against which men like Higginson and Parker might harangue the nation with the moral argument against slavery. For whatever reason, however, the committee walked softly and faded away. The report it gave a few weeks after Douglass's return was so restrained it passed unnoticed by nearly everybody, and Douglass went out of his house boldly and picked up his work where he had left it six months earlier.

Six months after his return from abroad, the Republican candidate, Abraham Lincoln, was elected President of the

United States. Within another four months Lincoln was inaugurated and the states of the deep South seceded. The new President began his administration by calling for volunteers to "maintain the honor, the integrity and the existence of our National Union."

The response to this call was expressed in a song. "We are coming, father Abraham, three hundred thousand strong."

To Douglass it was a war of liberation, pure and simple. In the May issue of his paper he let himself go. Amid sprawling drawings of the American flag and eagle he exulted, "Freedom for all, or chains for all." A few lines further on he added sardonically that his assurance could be traced "less to the virtue of the North than to the villainy of the South."

But since it was a war of emancipation, as he felt, he had a suggestion for the new president as to how it should be waged. "Let the slaves and free colored people be called into service and formed into a liberating army, to march into the South and raise the banner of Emancipation among the slaves." To his surprise, however, Lincoln failed to jump at the suggestion. Negro enlistments in the navy were accepted without question, in view of practice long established, but the president wanted to think about this army thing. What Douglass did not know at the time, of course, was the extent to which Lincoln's efforts to hold the border states in line and his behind-the-scenes struggles with other Republicans in the government accounted for his reluctance to change the Negro's status.

Marking time on the issue, Lincoln made small, token gestures. He authorized General Benjamin Franklin Butler to hold all runaway slaves who reached his lines. A couple of months later he signed a measure designed to counter any military or naval use the Confederacy might make of slaves. Neither of these acts seemed important to Douglass, and he began to feel let down and to talk about "the slow coach at Washington."

The President's hesitation also aroused the old-line abolitionists. Meeting in October of that year, the American Anti-Slavery Society, through its executive committee, petitioned Congress to declare slavery ended. Backing down somewhat from its burning idealism of other days, the Society approved "a fair pecuniary reward" to slaveholders who remained loyal to the government. Plainly Garrisonian abolitionism was finished. Perhaps it had been finished, in a sense, ever since men like Douglass and Gerrit Smith and Theodore Parker and Thomas Wentworth Higginson began listening to John Brown, but now even Garrison decided it was time for his followers to give up. The Society refused to disband, however.

A reminder of the glorious old days of the movement, of the shouting and the catcalls and the unmerchantable eggs and the demolished platforms, came to Douglass the following month in Syracuse nevertheless. He was booked to lecture there on the evening of November 14, but hostile groups placarded the city with threats against him. To meet the threats Mayor Charles A. Andrews appointed fifty special policemen and called out a company of soldiers. It was enough to stir the blood of old crusaders like Gerrit Smith and Samuel J. May. Taking tea together that afternoon, they remarked that the armed men were already at their posts around the hall where Douglass was to speak. Evidently leaders of the would-be mob saw and considered too. No disturbance occurred, though Douglass appeared as scheduled and spoke for ninety minutes.

Garrison was thrilled and wrote to May, "Honor to your city." But the event made little impression on Douglass, whose attention was focused on Washington. "It seems to me," he grumbled impatiently in a letter to May, "that our Government has resolved that no good shall come to the

Negro from this war, and that it means to convince the slaveholders that slavery is safer in than out of the union." To him it appeared that the government had resolved "that Negroes shall smell powder only in the character of cooks and body servants in the army." And when Lincoln's first message to Congress advocated colonization for Negroes, he lost all restraint. He told Smith he was "bewildered by the spectacle of moral blindness, infatuation and helpless imbecility which the government of Lincoln presents." Colonization—bah!

Two months later, in February of 1862, he took his feelings to the lecture platform, speaking in Boston before the Emancipation League, a group organized a year earlier by four men who had been mentioned in connection with John Brown's plans. A week later he was in New York, using the same subject, "The Black Man's Future in the South," and repeating his denunciations of the administration for failure to emancipate the slaves immediately.

Before he could repeat it again, however, straws of another kind, which Douglass could not fail to notice, began to appear in the wind. First, Lincoln refused to commute the death sentence of Captain Nathaniel P. Gordon, sentenced for commanding a slave ship, and the captain was hanged as a pirate on February 21. Before the middle of March the President put his name to a bill which forbade the army or navy to return runaway slaves. Then, sponsored by the Massachusetts senators Charles Sumner and Henry Wilson, a bill outlawing slavery in the District of Columbia went through both houses of Congress and was signed by Lincoln, and Douglass's hopes soared again. "Let high swelling anthems now roll along the earth and sky," he wrote in his *Monthly*. Finally, on September 22, Lincoln's preliminary proclamation, declaring that all slaves in any state or district in rebellion on January 1, 1863, would be free was issued.

Doubts followed this high moment of excitement, however, and Douglass anxiously devoted himself to writing and publishing a pamphlet called "Slave's Appeal to Great Britain," a plea to the British public not to recognize the Confederacy as a sovereign state. Even a letter from Henry Richardson assuring Douglass that his leaflet had not gone unnoticed, ("I have no doubt that it has appeared in whole or in part in very many English newspapers,") did not completely change the author's mood. Abolitionists began to question whether or not the actual proclamation would ever be made. Amid these doubts Negroes of Boston set the stage for an appropriate celebration of the historic event—should it happen.

Naturally Frederick Douglass was included in their plans. Under the sponsorship of the Union Progressive Association three huge meetings were scheduled for Tremont Temple on New Year's Day of 1863. As the afternoon speaker Douglass evoked a solemn mood with an address which inspired loud *Amen*'s and *Bless-the-Lord*'s. "The rosy dawning of the new truth of freedom" was to be greeted, his organlike voice announced. "We are here to rejoice."

But that was preliminary. The news over the wires was expected later. It would perhaps be evening before President Lincoln finished shaking hands with all the people who had come to the White House to extend New Year's greetings. Then he would have time to make good on his promise. The colored folks of Boston were not impatient. They understood.

Twilight had fallen when Douglass left his room again that evening and began walking slowly toward Tremont Temple. Snow covered the ground. Here and there holiday candles burned in windows. When would it happen? When would lightning strike the telegraph wires like a herald of the resurrection? When?

Never mind. The snow, the blue dusk, the fairy lights—

they were enough now. He would not hurry. Indeed it was nearly eight o'clock when he entered the hall, and the place was jammed. An usher showed him to the seat reserved for him on the platform. Someone explained that a line of messengers stretched from the telegraph office to Tremont Temple. Seconds after the news was received, it would be announced in the auditorium. Meanwhile, with well-known orators like William Wells Brown, Anna E. Dickinson, J. Sella Martin, Leonard A. Grimes and Frederick Douglass on the platform, the time need not be wasted.

An hour of speaking passed. Then two hours, and the audience began to show restlessness. Despite the oratory, the colored folks could not forget why they had assembled, and they knew there was a chance that they would be disappointed. But suddenly a door banged open. A half-crazy messenger leaped into the aisle and raced to the platform. "It's coming! It is on the wires!"

A moment later a deafening tumult rose outside on Boston Common. Presently a second messenger bounded through the door with the telegraphed proclamation in his hand. The sight of him was too much for the audience in Tremont Temple. It exploded. How long the cheers and shouting lasted no one was calm enough to measure, but when the uproar finally subsided, Douglass raised a song, "Blow ye the trumpet, blow."

Two hours later the celebration was unabated, but someone reminded the leaders that Tremont Temple had been rented just till midnight. Douglass favored continuing it at the Twelfth Baptist Church on Phillips Street and so did the Reverend Grimes, its pastor, and most of the others on the platform and in the audience. Within an hour after the crowd left Tremont Temple a fresh meeting was in full surge at Twelfth Baptist where the walls bulged and the rafters swayed. There were prayers and songs till morning, interspersed with refreshments.

Douglass was so elated he did not feel tired as he left
Phillips Street. In fact, he did not get tired during the next
thirty days in which he traveled more than two thousand
miles back and forth across the country making speeches to
enraptured Negro audiences and joining with them in the
celebration of the greatest event of their history in the
New world.

In his "Boston Hymn," composed on the day of Emancipation, Emerson wrote:

> I break your bonds and masterships,
> And I unchain the slave:
> Free be his heart and hand henceforth
> As wind and wandering wave.

This may have been part of the reason why Douglass remarked that his people have come to "a day for poetry and
song."

Such delirious joy could scarcely be expected to last, so
Douglass began to brace himself against a slump. Lecturing at Cooper Institute in New York City the following
month, he decided to air the unsettled question of using
Negro soldiers. What puzzled him about the controversy,
he said, was that those who opposed the idea sometimes
did so on the grounds that Negroes would not fight and
sometimes on the grounds that the same Negroes would
become dangerous if armed.

But before he could get steamed up over the problem
again, he noticed that popular sentiment had changed. The
attrition of war, including battle losses as well as desertions,
seemed to produce a more realistic attitude. Slogans like
"Every black man who joins the army enables a white man
to stay home" were heard more frequently, as were also
such jingles as

> In battle's wild commotion
> I shouldn't at all object
> If Sambo's body should stop a ball
> That was coming for me direct.

Previously Congress, by a special bill, had authorized the President to "garrison forts, positions, stations and other places, and to man vessels of all sorts in said service" by "persons of African descent." Lincoln had signed it on July 17, 1863, but nothing had happened. Now, marking the change of sentiment among the people, the advocates of using Negro troops began to speak up again. Governor John A. Andrew of Massachusetts was one of the foremost, and a petition by him to raise two regiments of Negro soldiers had remained for some time on the desk of Secretary of War Edwin M. Stanton. Now, quite suddenly, the petition was granted, and Governor Andrew asked George L. Stearns to undertake the recruiting.

Within a month Stearns was on a train to Rochester. He had come, he explained on arrival, to ask Douglass to serve as an agent. He was attempting to establish posts from Boston to St. Louis for recruiting. Would Douglass help?

Of course he would. Three days after Stearns' visit Douglass had a new issue of his *Monthly* out, carrying a lead article headed, "Men of Color, to Arms!" Setting up headquarters in Buffalo, Douglass put his goal at one full company and began by enrolling his youngest son Charles, now twenty years old. Soon afterwards he signed up Lewis, the oldest of his three boys. By the middle of April he had dispatched more than a hundred recruits to Boston, Negro boys enlisted in Albany, Syracuse, Buffalo and other towns of upstate New York. His expenses for the operation had amounted to $700.

Though he had reached his quota, Douglass was not satisfied with the number of young Negroes who had an-

swered his call to arms. In April and May he renewed his
efforts and did not stop till he had raised a second company,
arguing as he did so that citizenship carried its obligations,
that battle experience would enable the ex-slave to recover
his self-respect, and that in the last analysis this was a war
of emancipation.

Meanwhile at Readville, Massachusetts, Robert Gould
Shaw, a handsome young Harvard man and member of an
old Back Bay family assumed the command of the regiment,
known as the Fifty-fourth Massachusetts, and by the end of
May it was ready for action. When General David Hunter,
commander of the Department of the South, requested that
it be sent to South Carolina, Negroes throughout the North
were electrified. Douglass rushed to Boston to see the excitement.

Fearing that prejudice might still outweigh patriotism
in some American communities, the commanding officers
arranged to have the unit sent to the front by water instead
of by railroad. Accordingly, the regiment arrived in Boston
for embarcation on May 28, and the city rose to the occasion. Flags, streamers and bunting went up everywhere. A
compliment of one hundred reserve policemen was put on
duty—just in case bad actors should attempt to embarrass
liberty-loving Boston by a show of resentment against uni-
formed Negro troops. Aside from clearing the streets to let
the parade pass, however, the police were not needed.

Among the flags carried by the dark soldiers as they
marched through cheering crowds to the Common were
several of striking beauty. One was a national emblem, the
gift of a group of young colored women of the city. Another
was the state flag of Massachusetts, also the gift of a local
ladies' club. But neither caught the eye more suddenly
than the white silk regimental banners with the state's coat
of arms on one side, a golden cross and a golden star on the
other, and the blazing legend *In hoc signo vinces*.

John Greenleaf Whittier was among the thousands who came out to see the Negroes march. Considering his general attitude toward war and soldiering and the fact that it was the only regiment he came out to see during the whole conflict, this was a compliment. On Essex Street the parade passed the home of Wendell Phillips, where William Lloyd Garrison stood on the balcony, "his hand resting on a bust of John Brown."

Frederick Douglass was in the street following the soldiers, thrilled by the uniforms of orderly and sergeant-major worn by Charles and Lewis respectively. On the crowded Common he saw the troops pass before the reviewing stand on which Governor Andrew sat with the Mayor of Boston and Senator Henry Wilson. The reporter for the *Transcript* was impressed by the "ease and uniformity" of the marchers in "going through the manual." He liked the "general precision attending their evolutions."

From the Common the regiment paraded to Battery Wharf while its band played the John Brown song. Early in the afternoon the soldiers went aboard the *De Molay,* a new vessel about to make her maiden voyage to Port Royal, South Carolina. Still having fun, Frederick Douglass sought and secured permission to go aboard where he could stand and wave among the young soldiers as if he were one of them. The Fifty-fourth was his regiment; the two companies he had personally recruited and the two sons he had contributed were his stake in it. He did not leave the *De Molay* till the tugs left it far down the harbor. He returned to Battery Wharf on one of these.

Home again, he began urging other states to follow the lead of Massachusetts in recruiting Negroes, and less than three weeks after the Fifty-fourth sailed from Boston, citizens of Philadelphia were granted permission to raise colored troops. To their surprise and the surprise of Stearns, supervisor of enlistments, the Negroes of Pennsylvania seemed in no hurry to join up. Stearns thought he knew what to do about that. He arranged for Douglass to speak in National Hall on July 6.

But Douglass did not have to go to Philadelphia to learn the cause of the unexpected reticence. William Whiting, solicitor of the War Department, had taken the position that Negroes in the army should be given the wages of laborers rather than the pay of soldiers. Where white men in the Grand Army of the Republic received $13 a month plus clothes, he thought Negroes should be glad to buy their own clothes out of $10 a month. Douglass was as strongly opposed to this differential as anybody, but he did not think it should keep young colored men from enlisting, and in Philadelphia he said as much. In view of his painful, sometimes hideous, experiences in slavery, his involvement in the issues of this war, the Negro should accept the opportunity to fight even if he were not paid at all, he told his audience. To those who still looked up at him with puzzled eyes, he gave the clincher: "Once let the black man get upon his person the brass letters, U. S.; let him get an eagle on his button and a musket on his shoulder and bullets in his pocket, and there is no power on the earth . . . which can deny that he has earned the right to citizenship in the United States."

A few days after he came to Pennsylvania to help, Douglass learned that a second Massachusetts regiment of Negroes, the Fifty-fifth, was ready for service. Like the Fifty-fourth it contained many young men recruited by him, and the report gave him pride, but bad news followed. Evidently the differential in pay was just one of many discriminations suffered by black men under arms. White soldiers were given enlistment bounties. They were offered the inducement of advancement in rank. Neither was held out to Negroes. And in battle the enemy too made a difference. Whites captured were treated as prisoners of war. Often these were exchanged. But the South decided on a separate code of war for dealing with Negroes who fought against the Confederacy. In effect, slavery and death were promised to those captured.

The first report from the Fifty-fourth was also disturbing. Eager to the point of overconfidence, no doubt, the unit had assaulted Fort Wagner under a night sky in mid-July. Colonel Shaw, its gallant leader, had fallen in battle as had nearly half its officers and hundreds of the young recruits with whom Douglass had sailed down the bay in Boston less than two months ago. The trial by fire had been severe. The action had failed, and the only consolation Douglass could derive was that his own sons had come through unhurt and that the regiment had fought bravely, so bravely indeed that some recognitions would certainly be in order.

In the gloom that accompanied this crushing news Douglass began to ponder bitterly the grievances of colored soldiers. The glib answers he had been giving to Negro audiences and to prospective recruits who hesitated because of what they had heard now began to seem unsatisfactory to him. He could not go on excusing the government or its leader. Negro soldiers were not being fairly treated, and there was no good excuse for it. But what to do? Certainly he could not continue to invite young Negroes of Pennsylvania to the colors, despite the sharp rise of the Negro's stock as a fighting man following accounts of bravery at Fort Wagner. Instead he returned to Rochester and wrote a strong letter to Major George L. Stearns, giving up his recruiting work and stating the case for Negroes under arms with special emphasis on the threat of Jefferson Davis to treat captured colored soldiers as felons rather than prisoners of war.

Stearns, himself a man who had believed in John Brown, responded before Douglass could get a copy of the long, passionate letter into print. The government was aware of the wrongs to Negro soldiers which Douglass had pointed out and measures were already being taken to restrain the Confederacy from carrying out Davis' proclamation. "What ought to have been done at the beginning comes late, but it comes," Douglass sighed. Then, remembering John Brown, perhaps, he added, "It really seems that nothing of justice, liberty, or humanity can come to us except through tears and blood."

But Stearns also added a suggestion. In respect to the other grievances, why didn't Douglass go to Washington and make an effort to present them to President Lincoln in person? Douglass perked up. Indeed, why not? With such long-standing personal acquaintances as Senators Charles Sumner and Henry Wilson and Samuel Pomeroy, Secretaries Salmon P. Chase and William H. Seward in Washington, why should he not seek an audience with the President? Presently he was on his way.

It was Senator Pomeroy who actually accompanied him on his first visit to the executive mansion. When Douglass entered, Lincoln was seated in a low armed chair, his feet out-stretched, a hive of secretaries buzzing around him. The room had the clutter and disorder of piled up paper work. Everybody in it, including the President, showed signs of strain and fatigue. The deep lines on Lincoln's face impressed Douglass immediately, but he also noticed that the President's eyes brightened with interest when the name of Frederick Douglass was called. Lincoln rose, shook hands cordially.

"I know who you are, Mr. Douglass," he smiled, restraining Douglass's modest attempt to introduce himself. "Sit down. I am glad to see you."

Douglass expanded. Here was a man he could love, honor and trust without reservation, an honest man. "I was assisting to raise colored troops," he began quietly.

Abraham Lincoln nodded.

Douglass continued. In Massachusetts he had been very successful in getting men to enlist. Now, working in Pennsylvania, he was finding it harder. The men felt that the government was not dealing fairly.

Lincoln interrupted. Could Douglass be more specific?

He could. Three particulars might be mentioned. First, there was the question of wages. Negroes ought to get the same pay as white soldiers. Second, captured colored soldiers should be able to claim the same treatment as other prisoners of war, and it would seem that the United States government was in a position to compel such treament by announcing retaliation for murder of Negro troops. Finally, there was the question of promotion.

Lincoln listened silently with troubled eyes. When Douglass had stated his case as fully as he could, the President replied slowly. Douglass should not forget, he said, that the use of colored troops at all was a great gain, so great in fact that it could not have happened at the beginning of the war. The differential in pay was frankly a concession to popular prejudice and should not be allowed to obscure the fact that Negroes had much to gain from this war.

As to retaliation, that was an even harder problem. If he could get his hands on a Confederate soldier who had been guilty of mistreating a Negro prisoner, the matter would be simple, but the idea of retaliating against innocent Confederate prisoners was revolting. However, he thought the rebels would themselves drop such barbarous warfare. In fact, he had already received word that colored soldiers were already being treated as prisoners of war.

On the third point Lincoln's comment was short and emphatic. He would sign any commission to a colored soldier his Secretary of War would present.

How long the conference lasted Douglass did not know. Certainly he felt it had been unhurried, and if he was not altogether pleased with the President's views on the first two propositions, he was thoroughly pleased with the man himself. Lincoln's human qualities stood out above all issues.

Douglass left the room exhilarated. That he would resume his work of recruiting Negro soldiers went without saying.

But the part of the interview that stuck in Douglass's mind was the President's assertion that he would sign any commission to a Negro which his Secretary of War would present. In fact, he decided to do something along that line forthwith. Leaving the Executive Mansion, he headed directly for the War Office and asked to see Assistant Secretary C. A. Dana, an acquaintance from the old abolitionist days whom Douglass had first met at "Brook Farm." At Douglass's request Dana ushered him into the presence of the Secretary of War.

Douglass imagined he sensed immediately a difference in the attitudes of Edwin M. Stanton and Abraham Lincoln. He thought the Secretary of War showed annoyance as he looked up from his work to acknowledge the introduction. Every line in Stanton's face seemed to ask, "Well, what do you want?" and to insist, "Come on, get it over with." Of course the Secretary of War was terribly busy but not more so, Douglass thought, than the President had been. Putting his feelings aside, however, Douglass repeated the statements he had made to Lincoln.

As he spoke, he saw, or thought he saw, a change come over the face of the Secretary. "Contempt and suspicion and brusqueness had all disappeared," and Stanton took time to give a careful defense of the government's policies toward Negro soldiers. While Douglass was not impressed by the reasoning, neither was he inclined to change his resolve to return to the work of recruiting which Lincoln had influenced. At this point he sprang the idea that had

brought him to the War Office. Since he was definitely committed to the work of recruiting, and in view of the President's willingness to sign commissions to Negroes, would
it not be appropriate for the Secretary of War to submit
Douglass's name?

A little surprised, no doubt, and perhaps feeling trapped,
Stanton agreed. He would make Douglass an assistant adjutant on the staff of General Lorenzo Thomas who was then
engaged in recruiting Negroes in Mississippi. That sounded
fine to Douglass. He would take no more of the Secretary's
time.

Traveling back to Rochester he had many hours for
contemplation. Was his work done? Was the uniform of a
commissioned officer in the Grand Army of the Republic
the climax of his thirty-years' war against slavery? If Douglass thought so, even for a moment, he must have decided
quickly that *climax* was not the right word. The climax of
his struggle, anyone who reviewed his life could see, had
occurred in the stone quarry near Chambersburg, with
John Brown, Shields Green, John H. Kagi and himself
sitting on broken rocks and John Brown intoning, "Come
with me, Douglass; I will defend you with my life. I want
you for a special purpose. When I strike, the bees will
begin to swarm, and I shall want you to help me hive
them." Believing that John Brown was indeed in a position
to offer him immortality and world renown, he had nevertheless turned away and rationalized, "The tools to those
who can use them. . . . He could die for the slave; I could
only live for him." That had been the climax. His next
step had to do with the conclusion. For this the uniform
seemed right.

But now was no time for fantasy. Army service, even on
the staff of an adjutant general, would put an end to civil-
ian activities, to a way of life. Douglass's endless lectures,
for example, would have to cease. That was an agreeable

thought. He was tired of them anyway. Then there was his paper, *Douglass' Monthly*. He sighed with relief. Another good riddance. He would make the next issue, August 1863, the last.

But weary as he was of the physical discomforts of filling lecture engagements in all parts of the country and of the trials of a struggling editor, he could scarcely drop either without emotion. He was a born orator and performer. He lived on applause and the tumult of audiences. Moreover the lecture platform had paid him well—was still paying him well, better than ever, in fact. His was the golden age for lecturers. But a man gets tired. In the forty-seventh year of his life Douglass had begun to feel that he had had his fill of that dish.

His editorial work recalled the break with Garrison and the excitements of his first sojourn in the British Isles. Then there was Julia Griffiths–Croft, who came with the gift of money from England, so to speak, and was thus linked with his newspaper ventures. The first issue of *The North Star* had gone out in December of 1847. Nearly sixteen years of unbroken publication had followed. It had reported in its pages an astonishing cavalcade of American history. Most vividly Douglass remembered the great Free-Soil Convention in Buffalo, the Nomination of Martin Van Buren, the Fugitive Slave Law, Daniel Webster's seventh of March Speech, the Dred Scott decision, the repeal of the Missouri Compromise, the Kansas-Nebraska bill, the Border war in Kansas, the deeds of John Brown, and the beginning of war between the North and the South. Begun in a year when the end of slavery seemed as remote as a dream, Douglass's papers had continued to cry against the institution till Emancipation was proclaimed and until the triumph of the Union seemed assured.

But Douglass had never been interested in journalism for its own sake. To him writing and publishing had been means to a definite end, namely, the suppression of slavery. Because of this, perhaps, the relative smallness of his circulation, fluctuating between two and four thousand copies an issue, had dismayed him only insofar as it related to solvency. Thanks to Julia's devotion and shrewd management, however, to festivals and fairs conducted by the Western New York Anti-Slavery Society in its behalf, to continuing subsidy from friends like the Reverend Russell Lant Carpenter and his wife in England, to the same from Gerrit Smith, Chief Justice Salmon P. Chase, Senator Charles Sumner, Horace Mann, William Seward, Samuel May, Joshua Giddings, John G. Palfry and others in America financial worries had disappeared. Evidence of the paper's influence beyond its actual circulation had never been lacking. Men in public life all over the country turned to it for the free Negro's point of view, and this was especially true of editors of more widely circulated journals. No serious question as to the worth of the effort had ever arisen, but now suddenly everything was changed. Now he could go home and put the final issue to bed.

Back in Rochester he sat down at his desk and undertook to state the case for his readers. Hard times were not driving him to the wall, he would have them know. Nor had the day of agitation ended. Neither were they to assume that the editor was merely hankering for a change of occupation. But with the rise of other periodicals in which the aspirations of colored people could be expressed, the *Independent* and the New York *Tribune* and the *Anglo-African,* for example, his *Monthly* was no longer essential. As a sort of afterthought he let the cat out of the bag. "I am going South to assist Adjutant General Thomas in the organization of colored troops."

That revealed, and the issue mailed, he settled back to wait for the commission to come through. Finally a letter from the Adjutant General's office arrived. It was dated

August 13 and it ordered Douglass to report to Thomas at Vicksburg and to help in "any way his influence with the colored race can be made available." Everything about the letter was impressive and terribly official, but Douglass could not fail to note the neglect of the War Department to enclose the promised commission, and he pointed this out in his reply. His next communication came from Stearns, who may have been drawn in at this point because of his known zeal in the Negro's behalf, and it went into the matter of salary, subsistence and transportation without, however, touching on the commission.

Douglass was not merely disappointed. He was embarrassed and angry. A promise made to him in good faith by the Secretary of War and the President of the United States, he felt, had not been kept. Naturally he had no intention of going to Vicksburg or of doing anything else related to military affairs. Perhaps they thought they had him anyhow, after he had announced his intention and apparently burned his boats by terminating the publication of his paper. Perhaps someone else convinced one or the other of the men involved that a commission for a Negro in the Union Army was too far in advance of public sentiment in the North. However it had come about, his own course was clear. Douglass began booking lectures for the winter months ahead.

But no advance booking was necessary for his appearance on the platform of the annual meeting of the American Anti-Slavery Society the following December. Seeing him in the audience, the old-line Abolitionists, including Garrison, Phillips, Foster, May, and Lucretia Mott as well as Senator Wilson and Henry Ward Beecher, promptly beckoned him to his accustomed place among the speakers. For most of the veterans of their movement the thirtieth anniversary of the Society was mainly a victory celebration.

They had lived to see slavery crushed, and their speeches were hymns of triumph. Now it could be told how they had helped runaway slaves, how they had warmed to their mission in the days when the risks were great.

When Douglass's turn came, he decided to strike a new note. So now the slave was free. Well, what next? His proposal was that the Society turn its efforts toward the advancement of the Negro toward full citizenship. The next step was suffrage. It would be argued, of course, that the freedman was not ready to vote, but Douglass had no patience with this point of view. "If he knows an honest man from a thief, he knows more than some of our white voters. If he knows as much when sober as an Irishman knows when drunk, he knows enough to vote."

His own sights had been lifted in regard to the War and its aims. "We are fighting for something incomparably better than the old Union. We are fighting for unity; unity of idea, unity of sentiment, unity of object, unity of institutions, in which there shall be no North, no South, no East, no West, no black, no white but a solidarity of the nation, making every slave free, and every free man a voter."

Apparently most of the members of the Anti-Slavery Society did not feel that he was talking about their war, their thirty-year struggle, and they showed no inclination to accept the new challenge. Many of them were old. They had done their work. Yet they did feel one more obligation. They drew up a petition to Congress calling for a constitutional amendment abolishing slavery forever in the United States.

Moreover their convention had provided Douglass with a theme for his lectures in 1864, and a month later his appearance packed Cooper Institute in New York, a tribute paid to no other speaker but Wendell Phillips that winter. Early in February the *Transcript* covered his speech on "The Mission of the War" in Boston and noted the "long

applause" with which it was received. But by spring his
spirits sank with the general despondency in the North.
With General Grant hacking his way painfully through
the wilderness toward Richmond, a line he proposed to
follow "if it took all summer," with war-weary elements in
the North suggesting that peace was now possible—without
emancipation—the assurance of victory had begun to fade.

Then in August an invitation from the White House
perked him up. With Senator Samuel Pomeroy from Kansas he was called to a conference. He went gladly, but he
found the President's mood anything but cheerful. Opposition to the War troubled him, especially that part of the
opposition which stemmed from the abolition crusade.
Lincoln, Douglass gathered, thought he might be forced
by public opinion to conclude a peace which would compromise the slavery issue by leaving in bondage all slaves
who had not escaped to the Union lines. This in turn had
caused him to observe that "the slaves are not coming so
rapidly and so numerously to us as I had hoped."

Douglass remarked that he was not surprised. Probably
very few slaves had heard about the Emancipation Proclamation.

"Well, I want you to set about devising some means of
making them acquainted with it, and for bringing them
into our lines," Lincoln said. Specifically he had thought
of an organized band of scouts, composed of colored men
but copying somewhat John Brown's plan for guerrilla
warfare. These would go behind enemy lines, carry the
news of Emancipation and urge slaves to run to their freedom.

If the plan itself failed to excite Douglass, the conference
was important for another reason. Lincoln's words and the
tone of his voice convinced Douglass that the President felt
deeply about the moral implications of slavery and was

genuinely disturbed by the prospect of peace without victory on this issue.

Nothing came of the idea, of course, for almost immediately the fortunes of the Union took a turn. The Wilderness campaign succeeded. Atlanta fell. Equally important, the political picture in the North began to clear up. A split in the Republican party was composed by the withdrawal of John C. Frémont from the race and the presidential campaign narrowed to a contest between Lincoln and General George B. McClellan, the Democrat.

Douglass, sold on Lincoln since his first meeting, had not joined his friends Phillips and Elizabeth Cady Stanton in their Cleveland convention which nominated Frémont, and now that the air was clearer, he hurried to Syracuse where a National Convention of Colored men had been called. Selected as president of the Convention, Douglass joined the group in expressing thanks to the government in Washington for benefits received, the abolition of slavery in the District of Columbia, the recognition of Liberia and Haiti, for example, and with the other delegates stressed the absolute necessity of the franchise for Negroes. Gloomily he foresaw, as did they, that an aftermath of the War would be "a sullen hatred toward the National Government . . . transmitted from father to son as 'a sacred animosity.' " And with the Convention he stood up for Lincoln's re-election, thus beginning a long affiliation of Negroes with the Republican party.

After Lincoln's re-election Douglass resumed his lecture schedule, but he managed to be in Washington for the second innaugural. In fact he was in the crowd waiting for the opening of the ceremonies when he saw Lincoln touch the Vice-President at his side, say something and direct the other's eyes toward Douglass. It would have been cause for a moment of pride had not Andrew Johnson frowned. Douglass turned to the colored woman who stood beside him and whispered, "Whatever Andrew Johnson may be, he certainly is no friend of our race."

Neither the Vice-President's frown nor the fact that at first he could find no Negro friend in Washington with nerve enough to accompany him kept Douglass from attending the grand reception that night at the executive mansion. He considered carefully what he was about to do. Negroes had never ventured to present themselves at such functions before, but were not things different now? Had not freedom been proclaimed? Negro men were dying on the battlefields. Why shouldn't a Negro offer his congratulations to the re-elected President along with the other citizens—especially a Negro who had worked for his election?

It was reasonable and logical that he should attend, Douglass concluded, even though there might be doubt as to his welcome, and eventually he convinced Mrs. Thomas J. Dorsey, the woman who had stood beside him at the inaugural, to go along. Together they joined the procession moving toward the entrance. At the door two outraged policemen pounced upon Douglass. His arms clamped firmly in their hands, he heard them explain, with obvious insincerity, that they had been ordered to admit no Negroes.

Instead of delivering his usual lecture on the meaning of democracy, Douglass calmly told the guards he did not believe they had any such orders. Mr. Lincoln would certainly not approve, he ventured. When the policemen attempted to rush him and Mrs. Dorsey into the exit, he decided to be as willful as they were. He was there to congratulate the President, not to be tricked and insulted. Seeing a familiar face in the line, he asked the individual going in if he would kindly inform Mr. Lincoln that Frederick Douglass was at the door—detained.

The response came quickly, and Douglass and Mrs. Dorsey were ushered into the East Room. Towering over the crowd, Lincoln saw and greeted the highly visible Douglass from a distance. "Here comes my friend Douglass. I am glad to see you. I saw you in the crowd today, listening to my inaugural address. How did you like it?"

Douglass hedged. He was reluctant to hold up the line. "There are thousands waiting," he said.

"No. No. You must stop a little," Lincoln insisted. "I want to know what you think of it."

Douglass' voice trembled. "Mr. Lincoln, that was a sacred effort."

"I'm glad you liked it," Lincoln murmured.

By then Douglass and Mrs. Dorsey were moving along again, but the brief incident had not escaped notice. The next day it was widely discussed. Frederick Douglass at the Presidential reception . . . Lincoln chatting with him while others waited. But to Douglass it was simply confirmation of the opinion he had already formed of the Emancipator's attitude. He returned to his lectures with mounting esteem for the President.

He had just reached Rochester again when the crushing news came from Washington. Lincoln was dead, assassinated by John Wilkes Booth, a half-mad actor, and on the following night Douglass went mournfully to the city hall to pay homage. In the course of the tributes, perhaps the first memorial service for Lincoln in any American city, he was called upon to speak.

The citizens of Rochester may have been too shocked to report all the words spoken on that occasion, but Jane March Parker thought that Douglass, more than all others, "gave utterance to the fullness of our sorrow." On the funeral day, she recalled, "unconsciously we gave him the place of chief mourner." "Many of us can remember how all eyes followed him as he passed down the Main street. . . .

He had no word of greeting, only a hand pressure for his nearest friends."

Charles Sumner, based on his record in the Senate, loomed as the Negro's strongest friend in government after Lincoln's asassination, and Douglass wrote him on April 29 of that spring to say that they were relying on him, more than anyone else, for "the final settlement of our national troubles." But somehow this hope failed to fill the void that Lincoln's death had left. Douglass had been hard hit by the tragedy, and when Mrs. Lincoln sent him the President's walking stick, saying that Lincoln had spoken to her of sending Douglass some token of his personal esteem, his grief was compounded.

Then suddenly he realized that the War was over. Lee had surrendered to Grant at Appomatox, and a page of history had turned. That the Negro's struggle would also enter a new phase seemed obvious. The war of liberation had been won. The task ahead was to win the peace—a peace of liberation. When the historic Thirty-ninth Congress met the following December, one of the first pieces of business was the appointment of a Joint Committee on Reconstruction, and in no time at all there was an uproar caused by the Radical friends of abolition, advocates of measures favorable to freedmen, and the followers of Andrew Johnson, supporters of easy terms of readmission to the Union for the states that had seceeded.

Theodore Tilton, editor of the *Independent,* became a mouthpiece for Radical sentiment, while Thaddeus Stevens spoke for the same forces in Congress. The public controversy that followed aroused in Douglass a fighting spirit comparable to his youthful zeal in the days of the 100 Conventions. Already on record as favoring suffrage for the freedmen of the South, he now advocated it with increasing fervor. By February of 1866 he was expressing the view that without it emancipation was nothing. Lecturing that season on "The Assassination and Its Lessons," he had no trouble centering his remarks on the importance of the vote to the ex-slave, and there are indications that his argument was followed with interest by significant elements of the public. At the Brooklyn Academy of Music, where he was at first barred by directors who later yielded to pressure, "every seat was occupied," and Tilton, serving as chairman, wisecracked in his introductory comments. It was rumored, he alleged with a twinkle, that the names of the five directors who had to be outvoted before the lecture could be held were to have their names "written on shells and deposited in the Brooklyn Historical Society's collection of Long Island fossils."

Douglass's swing through the East included appearances in Philadelphia and Washington, Chief Justice Chase presiding at the latter, but the highlight of his stop in Washington had no connection with the public lecture. While there, he was appointed by a colored convention to a committee of well-known and respected Negroes, including the wealthy and civic-minded John Jones of Chicago, which was asked to call on President Johnson and try to get his views on current political issues of interest to them. The convention wanted to learn particularly through their delegation how Johnson stood on the Freedmen's Bureau Bill, the Civil Rights Bill and the proposed Fourteenth Amendment, and of course Douglass was anxious for the President to know his own views on suffrage for the freedmen.

The President was prepared for the little group. Douglass and his companions had scarcely indicated the burden of their visit when Johnson began making a speech to them. According to Douglass it lasted more than three quarters of an hour, and when it was finished, the President announced that the interview was over. He would hear no replies. That was all. As the squelched Negroes passed from his presence, they heard the echo of his parting remarks, "I have great faith in the people. I believe they will do what is right."

Outside the executive mansion Douglass announced to reporters in equally lofty tones, "The President sends us to the people, and we go to the people."

A representative of the Radical Republicans in Congress caught up with the delegation as it left the White House and invited the colored men to meet some Congressmen in the anteroom of the House of Representatives. But Douglass discovered that he and his Negro friends were not precisely in step with the men in Congress who seemed to favor their cause. The Radical Republicans, the Negroes felt, pushed Negro suffrage as a way of punishing the South and of retaining for themselves the control of government. Their attempts to keep whites from voting in the South were similarly motivated, but these sentiments were not shared by Negroes, who are on record as favoring the enfranchisement of former Confederates at this time.

Nevertheless Johnson's attitude and the set of his mind left Douglass and the men with him sick at heart. And the fact that the President's long statement, which he would not allow them to interrupt or comment on, was ready for the press at the time he received them was doubly discouraging. But Douglass had an idea left. Why should they not issue their own statement to the papers—tonight? If they hurried, they could get it out to the same editions that carried the President's.

The others nodded, and Douglass dashed to his room and wrote out a rejoinder to Andrew Johnson's remarks. To three points he took sharp exception. First, Johnson had based his opposition to Negro enfranchisement on alleged hostility between former slaves and poor whites. "We admit the existence of this hostility," Douglass fumed, "and hold that it is entirely reciprocal. But you obviously commit an error by drawing an argument from an incident of slavery, and making it a basis for a policy adapted to a state of freedom. The hostility between the whites and blacks of the South is easily explained. It has its root and sap in the relation of slavery, and was incited on both sides by the cunning of the slave masters. Those masters secured their ascendency over both the poor whites and blacks by putting enmity between them. They divided both to conquer each." The poor whites, he recalled from his own dark past, were put to work as slave catchers, slave drivers and overseers by the slave owners. What other result could you expect? But slavery was now abolished. Was it logical to legislate for freedmen from slaveholding premises?

The second point was connected. Even granted that enmity between the two classes persisted in freedom and was so monstrous a fact that it had to be considered, was it just for a president to put power, in the form of the ballot, in the hands of one group to be used without limit against the other which remained disarmed politically? If the poor whites and the Negroes were hostile, the obligation to give freedmen ballots with which to defend themselves was that much greater. "Men are whipped oftenest who are whipped easiest," he went on, quoting himself. The way to tranquillity was through equal justice.

Finally, Johnson had mentioned colonization. Perhaps the answer to this should have been ho-hum, considering the thoroughness with which it had previously been debated, but in February of 1866 Douglass felt obliged to point out that Negroes had not only labored to help build the nation but had recently died on battlefields to defend it. This tendency to think of them as strangers and to deal with them as aliens began to seem absurd.

The members of the committee reassembled that evening, checked the wording of Douglass's statement, added their names to it and gave it to the editor of the Washington *Chronicle*, and in the days that followed it was reprinted elsewhere and became part of the general discussion of reconstruction measures.

Two months later Congress finally overrode Johnson's veto of the Civil Rights Bill. Three months after that it put into law a second Freedmen's Bureau Bill, but neither Douglass nor his Negro friends were naive enough to think that "Andy Johnsonism" was licked. The fight was just getting hot.

The place of the Negro leader was on the sidelines, however. If occasionally a spotlight fell on Douglass, as occurred in Philadelphia that fall at a gathering of the Radicals when the disturbing symbolism of his marching from Independence Hall to the National Hall arm in arm with Theodore Tilton gave the party wheel horses as well as their opponents a scare because of its possible influence on the vote, or when the New York *Tribune*'s reporter, still in town for the political hullabaloo, picked up the "touching" incident of Douglass's meeting in the street with Lucretia Auld, daughter of his former owner and one of the people who had befriended him in slavery, or when he took the stump for the Radical candidates and then exulted in their victory in an article contributed to the *Atlantic Monthly*, the light did not linger. The times were mixed up, and scenes changed rapidly.

During most of 1867 Douglass was lecturing for fees of from fifty to one hundred dollars a night and keeping busy. After a three-month tour of the West he returned to Rochester for a short interlude and then doubled back to Indiana for two more months. A proposal that he give a series of lectures gratis for the benefit of the widow of Abraham Lincoln drew his attention briefly. Mrs. Lincoln was in financial distress, and Elizabeth Keckley, the colored woman who had been her personal maid, took the lead in the plans. It fell through when Mrs. Lincoln, whose efforts to raise money by disposing of her furs and shawls through a broker had been called undignified, decided to turn it down. A more spirited interest was awakened in Douglass that summer when a stranger named Carter Steward called at his home in Rochester.

Douglass was out of town as usual, but his son Charles wrote him a letter to say that the visitor had come from Washington—from the White House, in fact. Two weeks later there was a follow-up. A letter from William Slade, personal friend of Andrew Johnson, wanted to know Douglass's availability as Commissioner of the Freedman's Bureau. "If I secure the appointment," he asked, "will you accept?" Slade implied that the present commissioner was weak-kneed and that this was the reason the President had decided to replace him.

Douglass's eyes bulged. He did not have to be told that the Commissioner of the Freedman's Bureau occupied a significant post in the government. The salary of $3,000 a year was medium, but the authority and responsibility of the Commissioner were indicated by the fact that over two thousand employees came under his supervision, that among them were two Civil War generals, Clinton B. Fisk and Rufus Saxton, serving as assistant commissioners, and that its Congressional appropriation for the year ending June 30, 1867 was $6,940,450. Douglass agreed to think it over.

What immediately disturbed him about the offer was the unfavorable reference to the incumbent. Douglass happened to know something about General Oliver Otis Howard. He knew as did every other informed Negro that the General's record and reputation were unblemished. Negroes as well as whites held him in the highest esteem. Even his enemies in government acknowledged that he was a "very good sort of man." Why would Andrew Johnson want to remove the blameless General Howard and replace him with a Negro? Certainly not for any good reason, Douglass thought. He had never been convinced by any of Johnson's assertions that he meant well toward Negroes. Nevertheless it took him two weeks to reject the enticement. When he finally sat down to the task, he made his position clear, "I could not accept office with my present views of duty."

In a personal letter to the editor of the *Independent* he gave a fuller explanation. He was as unwilling to be a party to the move against General Howard as he was to "place himself under any obligation to keep the peace with Andrew Johnson."

Even had he not been troubled by the moral implications, Douglass could not have played his cards better. Tilton gave him a big cheer in the *Standard*. "The greatest black man in the nation did not consent to become the tool of the meanest white," he shouted. And soon Douglass had more substantial reason for being pleased with his decision. The plan to replace Howard by a prominent Negro was part of a larger scheme to get rid of Secretary of War Stanton. Radicals could not safely oppose the highest appointment ever offered a Negro in government, and this circumstance was counted on to muffle their protests against the Stanton ouster. But bad days for Andrew Jackson's political career were just around the corner. Republicans in the House of Representatives started impeachment proceedings against him soon thereafter, and his prospects of renomination faded. A long Republican reign had begun. And Douglass's rejection of Slade's offer left him in good and regular standing.

He began buzzing around Republican conventions, and his ability to pick winners must have surprised even himself. He supported the nomination of Ulysses S. Grant while his old Abolitionist friend Gerrit Smith was behind Salmon P. Chase, and in the election that followed Douglass did much to swing Negro votes to Grant and away from Horatio Seymour, the New York Democrat. His argument was simple. The Democrats had favored the rebellion and now opposed suffrage for the Negro. The Republicans had opposed the former and now favored the latter.

The result was 450,000 votes for Grant from Negroes. His popular majority was 300,000. Was this not reason enough for the Radicals to go all out for Negro suffrage? They seemed to feel that it was, and in '69 they proposed a constitutional amendment to the effect that neither the national government nor any state should be permitted to deny the ballot to a man because of his race or color. In so doing, they gave Douglass another pointed issue with which to take the road.

To his surprise, he failed to win support for the idea in one expected quarter. Long the special pet of the women's righters, who had seen in slavery a likeness of their own problem, he went to his old friends Susan B. Anthony and Elizabeth Cady Stanton to enlist them in the new crusade. At the Boston Woman's Convention, attended by Garrison, Whittier, Higginson, Julia Ward Howe, Bronson Alcott and others of comparable reputation, he stated the case vigorously. The question of Negro suffrage was preliminary to the question of woman suffrage, he urged.

The women of the Equal Rights Association could not see it that way. As a matter of fact, the failure of the proposed Fifteenth Amendment to include a clause outlawing political discrimination against women was interpreted as another insult to their sex. They were against it. Indeed, to make their position completely clear, they took the occasion to change their name from the Equal Rights Association to the National Women's Suffrage Association. Nor were they dismayed later in the year when another group, calling itself the American Woman Suffrage Association, with Henry Ward Beecher as president, came out for priority to Negro suffrage.

Where Negroes were concerned now, it seemed that everything hinged on the constitutional amendment. So pressing was the issue, in fact, a number of them decided to hold one of the old-fashioned conventions, the kind at which they had gathered in times past to cry out against slavery. This one was called in Washington in '69 and got under way by electing Douglass president. While it added nothing new by way of insights or direction to the representative men assembled, the convention was emotionally satisfying. The delegates congratulated Congress, praised Grant, appointed a committee to ask the Senate Committee on Military Affairs about regular veterans' bonuses for Negroes who had fought in the War, and predicted forward steps for the Negro in politics.

The prediction was sound. Early in the following year Hiram R. Revels, an Oberlin educated mulatto, came to the United States Senate from Mississippi to occupy the seat in which Jefferson Davis had sat ten years earlier. The following month, March 30, 1870, the Fifteenth Amendment received the number of state ratifications required to put it into the Constitution, and a chorus of rejoicing such as had not been heard since the Emancipation Proclamation suddenly rose throughout the land.

"The most important event that has occurred since the nation came into life," President Grant wrote.

"We have washed color out of the Constitution," Wendell Phillips intoned.

The American Anti-Slavery Society called its final meeting. Its work was done. One more love feast and they could all go home. All of the old-timers were there except Garrison, and Douglass went among them shaking hands and speaking softly of the battles they had survived together.

In many cities celebrations were held. Perhaps the greatest of these was the one in Baltimore in the latter part of May. Weeks of hard work went into the preparations. Finally the parade started. Behind twenty carriages of distinguished guests marched regiments of Negro soldiers, drum corps, contingents of secret lodge members, and other clubs and groups of marchers to the number of 20,000. At Monument Square the line came to a halt and the tired marchers dispersed—all but about six thousand who stayed for the speechmaking.

Letters from Charles Sumner and William Lloyd Garrison were read by the chairman. Then John Mercer Langston, handsome, scholarly professor of law at Howard University, gave the oration of the day. The Postmaster General of the United States added a few words. Then one of the bands began to play fervently. Frederick Douglass was taking the platform. When the music subsided, he told the upturned faces what it takes to implement citizenship: the cartridge box, the ballot box, and the jury box. He recalled the struggle for the first two. "Now we want the jury box," he concluded.

More addresses followed, and it was late when the chairman rose to read the resolutions, but the audience remained. No one stirred as he concluded:

> Resolved, That in recognizing in Frederick Douglass the foremost man of color in the times in which we live and proud to claim him as one "to the manner born," we do here most respectfully, yet earnestly, request him . . . by the power of his magnificent manhood help us to a higher, broader, and nobler manhood.

IX

THE SUN-DOWN HILL

Exactly what he had been promised and by whom is not clear, but after Grant's first election Douglass allowed himself to hope for the postmastership at Rochester. By 1871 he knew better. Instead, apparently as consolation, he was offered a pleasant ocean voyage. He was invited to go along as one of the secretaries to a commission appointed to visit Santo Domingo and try to measure the sentiment of the people toward a proposed treaty of annexation to the United States.

The voyage itself, made aboard the American battleship *Tennessee,* with a battery of newspapermen and a detachment of scientists in the party, was a fine one, and Douglass enjoyed sitting at the captain's table with Ben Wade, former Ohio senator, President Andrew W. White of Cornell University and Samuel G. Howe, one of John Brown's financial backers. It gave him a lift to go ashore and breathe the air on the spot where Columbus had stood. But he came down with a thud when he discovered that the letters from President Grant and Secretary of State Hamilton Fish, delivered by the commissioners to the Dominican officials, contained no mention of himself. His connection with the commission, he now learned, was purely honorary. He had no duties.

As if that were not indignity enough, the steward on a mail packet, to which the commission transferred at the mouth of the Potomac, on the return voyage, refused to allow Douglass to enter the dining room. His blood boiling, Douglass went ashore and carried the incident directly to the President. Grant ignored it. Moreover he forgot, or purposely omitted, Douglass when inviting members of the commission to dine at the White House three days later.

What made it worse, where Douglass's feelings were concerned, was that he could not strike back as he had been accustomed to do in the old antislavery days. This was politics, and he was committed to the Republican party. So he carried his wounds to the home of Charles Sumner, who had scars of his own to show for encounters in the same arena. But Douglass neither renounced the Republicans nor gave up the quest for political appointment. The Republican party, he moaned in anguish, "is the deck. All else is the sea." And in 1872 the National Committee hired him to campaign for three months for Grant's re-election.

Negroes generally were less inclined to forgive the snubs to their leader than was the leader himself, and Douglass had much explaining to do as he took the stump that year. In a campaign pamphlet called "Ulysses S. Grant and the Colored People" he swallowed hard but exonerated the President of all blame. Congress had provided for only three commissioners. That fact, plus the circumstance that the three had been invited to the White House informally during a conversation with Grant, accounted for Douglass's failure to dine with them on the occasion in question. Certain other members of the expedition to Santo Domingo had also been omitted.

He now had to reckon with another factor of concern to Negro voters in the North. The Democrats had selected Horace Greeley as their candidate, and Greeley's antislavery record was definitely good. Indeed the Democrats had counted on his reputation to cut into the solid Republican vote of Negroes, and this expectation had helped to swing his nomination. To Greeley's bid for Negro support Douglass replied simply, "Where is a Democratic President who ever invited a colored man to his table?"

Even so, debate continued, and Douglass was forced to repeat in writing and on platforms his excuses for Grant's behavior. He admitted that Grant had not been "educated in the Gerrit Smith school." Certain shortcomings were therefore understandable. But Grant had made a fine statement after the ratification of the Fifteenth Amendment. He had given Negroes a number of high appointments. He had provided some protection against the Ku Klux Klan. And Douglass's personal contacts had convinced him that the President was essentially free of prejudice.

While he stumped New York, Massachusetts and Maine for Grant, Douglass was astonished, if not amused, to learn that his own name had been placed on a ticket for the vice-presidency of the United States. An oddly arresting feminist named Victoria Woodhull was responsible. Having successfully combined an interest in spiritualism with speculation on the stock market, thanks in part to friendly tips from Colonel Cornelius Vanderbilt, she could see nothing fantastic in her ambition to swing from the editor's desk of *Woodhull and Claflin's Weekly* to the presidency of the United States. To simplify the preliminary bother she availed herself of a meeting of the National Women's Suffrage Association to organize her party and have herself nominated. Within another hour her 668 followers had passed over Ben Wade, Wendell Phillips, Theodore Tilton and other prospects and named Frederick Douglass as her running mate. According to the report in her own paper, the mention of his name touched off half a dozen eulogies in quick succession.

Everybody present was happy about the slate, the Cin-

cinnati *Commercial* reported, ladies showering kisses on their candidate and men passing their arms around "women who were not their wives." All this was accomplished, her followers boasted, without a spittoon in sight or a whiff of tobacco smoke in the air. Borne upward on their pink cloud, they began to plan their campaign. The first step was the notification and the acceptance by Mrs. Woodhull. The stage was thus set for Douglass to reply, but he was too seriously engaged even to take note of what was going on. Nor did he pay any attention to the subsequent deflation of toy balloons. When *Woodhull and Claflin's Weekly* ran out of funds and had to suspend publication from the middle of June till the early part of November, when election day found Mrs. Woodhull and her sister-partner in jail for alleging in their paper that Henry Ward Beecher had stolen the affections of Theodore Tilton's wife, Douglass was too busy working for Grant's election to become interested.

Indeed, with Sumner advising that Grant should be impeached rather than re-elected, with many representative Negroes inclined toward the same point of view, mainly on the strength of the trust they placed in Charles Sumner, the fight for the Negro vote had turned out to be a rough one in every way, but Douglass's commitment was such that it had to be won for the Republicans if he was to maintain his influence, to say nothing about his deferred hopes for an appointment in government. He pulled all the oratorical stops within his reach and began bleating feverishly from platform to platform about the sword of Grant which "cleft the hydra-head of treason" and the great heart of this man to whom Negro Americans owed the ballot.

Again it worked, and the Negro vote went to Grant in a block. To be sure, other significant batches of ballots contributed to the Republican victory in that election, some of them traceable to the "fat cats" or patronage dis-

pensers of the party, but Horace Greeley was particularly
disappointed by his failure to convince colored people. "I
was an Abolitionist for years when to be one was as much
as one's life was worth even here in New York," he mused
bitterly, "and the Negroes have all voted against me." A
month later, insane with disappointment as well as grief
over his wife's death in the midst of the campaign, Greeley
died.

Meanwhile the Republican State Committee met at
Utica and selected the New York presidential electors. On
the suggestion of Thurlow Weed, Douglass was named an
elector-at-large, along with Gerrit Smith, and when the
electors assembled, they designated Douglass to go to Washington and present the thirty-five electoral votes of the
State. Proud of this honor, but still hoping for a more
tangible reward from the Republicans, he headed for the
nation's capital.

En route he meditated. He could not overlook the fact
that no particular district had chosen him for its elector.
While a Northern community, predominantly white, had
been an ideal base for antislavery agitation, it could not
promise a Negro leader much in the way of a political
career.

Nor was his mission to Washington wholly responsible
for these thoughts. While he stumped New York and New
England for Grant's re-election, Douglass's nine-room
home on the edge of Rochester was destroyed by fire. He
had been too preoccupied to give the disaster the attention
it merited at the time, but now he felt he would have to
decide whether or not to rebuild it, and the question of
his future in politics, if any, began to impress him as an
important factor.

Another circumstance also had to be considered. Anna
was lonesome in Rochester. Never having learned to speak
the language of Douglass's crusading friends, never having

hobnobbed with the neighbors, she seemed doubly deserted now that the children had begun to marry and leave home, and Douglass wondered if colored friends and a colored neighborhood might not cheer her. To him this was a more important consideration than the kindly desire of Rochester people, now quite proud of him, to restore his home that he might grow old in their midst.

On still another side there came urgings from Negroes themselves, some of whom thought he should go South and seek election to Congress or the Senate from one of the states in which Negro votes could be decisive. This counsel Douglass rejected automatically. The very idea of taking up residence among people merely to get their votes seemed to him cheap and unworthy. Somewhere along the way he concluded that Washington would be the best place for him, and nothing happened on that trip to change his mind. Soon afterwards he and Anna moved into a small brick house on A Street, S.E. and settled back to wait for something to happen.

Of course Douglass was not idle. While he waited for his reward from Grant's second administration, he listened to a group of men with a proposition. They had a weekly Negro newspaper called the *New National Era*, which was not doing well. Published in the nation's capital for the purpose of guiding the new citizens as they emerged from slavery, it needed the name of Frederick Douglass to give it prestige. It required Douglass's editorial experience. Unlike his former publishing venture, the men promised this one would not keep him on the road raising subscriptions. His associates would do that. Nor would he have to worry about keeping the expenses and the income in balance. Douglass would be paid a fixed salary as editor in chief. His name and prestige were the capital he was asked to contribute to a partnership involving George T. Downing, J. H. Hawes, J. Sella Martin and other well-known

Negroes. Would he agree to associate himself with the project?

Douglass listened and nodded. God knew he had had his fill of newspaper work, but another thought flickered in the back of his mind. His sons were all married now, as was his daughter Rosetta. Charles, the youngest, had been the first of the boys to settle down, and now in his twenty-seventh year, the fifth year of his married life, he held a clerkship in the Treasury Department of the government. But the older sons Lewis and Frederick had both waited till they were nearly thirty to find wives and even yet had failed to find employment adequate to the support of families. Douglass had not yet given up hope, however, and it occurred to him now that this might be a chance to put them on their feet. Both Lewis and Charles had been apprenticed in the Rochester shop and had helped to print *The North Star*. If he could use his connection with the *New National Era* to make jobs for them, Douglass reasoned, it might be worth while. He continued to nod. He would accept.

But not all that happened in the next few months was according to plan. Douglass sighed as he discovered the realities behind the dreams of his associates. Publication of the *New National Era* demanded more of him than his name and reputation. To begin with, it required work, sweaty, coatless work in a shop similar to the one in which he had put out *The North Star,* and Douglass found himself saddled with more and more of the routine operations as days passed. As weeks and months passed, the failure of the paper's agents in the field became as conspicuous as the shortcomings of the staff. Soon the *New National Era* was indebted to Douglass for his salary as well as loans he had been asked to make. By then however his connection with the publication was so generally known that Douglass was unwilling to see it discontinued. He decided instead to buy out his associates and turn the whole concern over to Lewis and Frederick. A few years later, the paper's indebtedness to him having approached $10,000, Douglass withdrew his backing and let it fold.

Meanwhile he listened to still another proposition. The Freedman's Savings and Trust Company, familiarly known by Negroes as the Freedman's Bank and incorporated by Congress in 1865 with fifty prominent trustees, including General Howard, Gerrit Smith and George L. Stearns, was not thriving. Though the *New National Era* and other Negro newspapers continued to carry its ads, urging the newly emancipated folk to "Cut off your vices—don't smoke —don't drink—don't buy lottery tickets," fewer and fewer colored people were heeding the advice to "Put the money you save into the Freedman's Savings Bank." At first they had responded to such admonitions. Informed that Lincoln himself endorsed the bank, they had at one time deposited as much as $57,000,000 in branches scattered over all the Southern states. Now a strange shyness had come over depositors, and in the spring of 1874 the trustees decided that this was a problem for Frederick Douglass.

Knowing far less about banking than about journalism, Douglass nevertheless felt a warm glow as the trustees assured him that his influence was needed to save the Freedman's Savings and Trust Company. The opposition of white Southerners to the bank was well known, and no one denied that on its own responsibility the bank had blundered in a score of ways. Bad loans had been made, including one to a speculator named Jay Cooke for half a million dollars. Declining values of certain real estate securities had also hurt, but there was nothing wrong with the bank that restored public confidence would not cure, the majority of the trustees agreed. Accordingly they voted to make Douglass president.

Douglass was touched by this evidence of their confidence in him, despite the fact that John Mercer Langston, one of the most respected men among the trustees, opposed the action and had to be outvoted. But Douglass was too old and too experienced to hesitate because of mild opposition. The air was always charged with opposition. A man became philosophical about it. Moreover a vision floated before his eyes. He recalled one of the most favorably situated buildings in Washington, a handsome structure with black walnut woodwork inside and marble counters. Douglass had passed it on the street many times, peeping through the plate-glass windows to admire the "elegantly dressed Negro clerks, with their pens behind their ears and button-hole bouquets in their coat-fronts." Seeing them, he had felt his eyes enriched. He was in no mood to decline the appointment merely because he knew nothing about banking, as John Mercer Langston had pointed out.

So for a few enchanted weeks he sat in a luxurious chair, gold spectacles on his nose, and smiled as people addressed him as the president of the Freedmen's Bank. His thoughts were generally far away, however, for he could not dismiss the image of a young slave from his mind. The boy called Fred on Colonel Lloyd's plantation, the brat in the tow linen shirt, kept running in and out of his reverie. Was this a reality or a golden dream? Douglass ran his eye down a list of the bank's assets. Millions. Anyone could see it was solid.

Within a few days it became necessary for him to convey this same assurance to all the branches throughout the South. Down there depositors were nervous. Some of them wondered why they had experienced difficulties when attempting to withdraw money. At his shiny new desk Douglass drafted a telegram to each branch. All was well with the Freedman's Bank, he wanted them to know, and all deposits were secure. Let patience prevail. All would be well.

To the Senate Committee on Finance he also directed a communication. Public confidence was the ingredient needed. Given that, the bank could continue, he thought. He advised that certain branches be closed to reduce expenses. Then he settled back to wait for the results.

The reaction from the people was good. Negroes took his word for gospel and confidently waited for the bank to settle its affairs. Those who knew more about such matters were less sure, however. Presently Douglass learned with dismay that many of the trustees of the Bank had withdrawn their own money and deposited it elsewhere. Aroused like a lion in a trap, Douglass hurriedly called the group together and insisted on an explanation. Finally they told him the truth they had been withholding. The bank was hopelessly insolvent, and Douglass lamented, "I have married a corpse." He promptly recommended to John Serman, chairman of the Senate Committee on Finance, that the bank be closed. In June of 1874 the trustees placed the bank's accounts in the hands of a liquidating commission.

Depositors were repaid less than fifty cents on the dollar, and all eyes turned toward Frederick Douglass. Hadn't he wired assurances to the branches just three months ago? What did this mean? Douglass became the target of withering criticism and denunciation. Though his own connections with the enterprise were completely aired during the controversy and all evidence brought forward to show that he had been unaware of the true condition of the bank when he accepted the presidency, had in fact lost about $1,000 of his own money in it, the resentment of those who had lost deposits did not fade readily, and Douglass was as near disgrace as he had ever been.

So it was back to the lecture platform and the old and

weary ordeal of trains that did not run on schedule, poorly
ventilated and badly lighted halls, and women with crying
babies in the front seats. Though it continued to provide
him with a comfortable income, lecturing had completely
lost its appeal, but his experiences with the *New National
Era* and the Freedman's Bank left Douglass no choice—
pending a possible appointment in government. Now even
the hope of an appointment began to seem remote. Apparently his public career was near a bad end.

"I sometimes try my old violin; but after all, the music
of the past is sweeter than any my unpracticed and unskilled bow can produce. So I lay my dear, old fiddle aside,
and listen to the soft, silent, distant music of other days,"
he wrote sadly.

The mood lasted about two years, and historical events
in the United States during that time were plainly not designed to counteract a Negro leader's feelings of shame and
bitterness. These were years in which the Supreme Court
sought to establish a curious distinction between rights
based on national citizenship, which could not be abridged
constitutionally, and those growing out of state citizenship,
which could. They were years of atrocious guerrilla warfare
by the Ku Klux Klan against the newly emancipated citizens and their defenders, years in which Douglass, still
unable to retire from lecturing, reminded a Philadelphia
audience that "today in Tennessee Lucy Haydon is called
from an inner-room at midnight and shot down because she
teaches colored children to read." He pointed to Louisiana
and Alabama where "the black man scarcely dares to de-
posit the votes which you gave him for fear of his life."

As the terror spread in the South and hopes faded in the
North, Charles Sumner was stricken, and Douglass was one
of the friends who hastened to the sick man's house and
waited in the study till death came. At the funeral he

marched at the head of a Negro guard of honor in tribute to the statesman who ranked next to Lincoln in their affections. Soon afterwards Vice President Henry Wilson, a true friend of Douglass's since the abolitionist days in Boston, also died, and Negroes recalled that Wilson had been one of those who urged Lincoln to proclaim Emancipation, that as Senator he had introduced many antislavery measures. The Senate remembered too, for it named Douglass along with Robert Purvis and James Wormley, two other prominent Negroes, to accompany Wilson's body to Natick in Massachusetts.

Leaves were falling from the trees in Washington when they returned, and Douglass found a gloomy, disillusioned companion in P. B. S. Pinchback from New Orleans. A devilishly handsome mulatto, Pinchback had emerged from political storms in Louisiana as lieutenant governor, acting governor, and finally United States Senator-elect. But certain aspects of the elections in his home state came up for dispute in the Senate's Committee on Privileges and Elections, and a long argument began over the validity of Pinchback's election. While it raged, the capable but resentful Louisianan took up residence in Washington and frequently dined with Douglass. Knowing perhaps, as the Senate seemed to suspect too, that there had been corruption in both parties' elections in Louisiana, he was unable to hide his cynicism as public sentiment divided sharply on the case and the Senate, reflecting this division, voted 32 to 29 against seating him while compromising to the extent of voting him a senator's pay for the period of the drawn-out controversy. The rumors of strange influences behind the Senate's decision, together with the fact that some Republicans had joined the Democrats against Pinchback, contributed to the gloom the adverse action produced in Negro communities and further darkened Douglass's own outlook.

Even so, there were those who thought that Douglass's address at the unveiling of the freedman's monument to Abraham Lincoln that year marked the high point of his effectiveness as a public speaker. Part of his inspiration, on that anniversary of Lincoln's asassination, no doubt came from the impressive crowd, which included President Grant and his cabinet, Supreme Court justices, many senators and congressmen, for a joint congressional resolution had declared the day a general holiday to enable those who wished to attend. But an equal part came from within. Out of humiliation and hope deferred, the aging champion of the freedman's cause, the "imperial Douglass," as Higginson described him, suddenly recaptured the amazing power and exaltation of which he was sometimes capable.

But this was no more than an artistic triumph. It changed nothing in Douglass's life and brought him no nearer to the rewards which had been denied. If it helped to erase the memory of his unfortunate connection with the Freedman's Bank and the failure of the *New National Era,* that was its value. Nevertheless Douglass embalmed the occasion among his memories and surrendered himself again to his recurring reverie. The times were out of joint. Even the presidential elction of 1876, hotly contested by Hayes and Tilden, seemed less important than former elections. When it ended indecisively, he was not too concerned. What difference did the outcome make, after all?

To his surprise, however, it made a lot of difference. The voting between Democrats and Republicans was so close in the decisive states of Louisiana, Florida and South Carolina, and so irregular—each state having sent in two different sets of returns—an electoral commission had to be created to look into it. The commission, composed of seven Democrats and eight Republicans, returned an eight to seven verdict in favor of Hayes, the Republican candidate, in each of the disputed states. Naturally the Democrats were not satisfied and had to be appeased. The solution involved a promise to withdraw occupying Federal troops from South Carolina and Louisiana. And since such a move in turn left the way clear for the disfranchisment of Negro voters in the South, some act of appeasement to Negroes was indicated, an act, as *The Nation* thought, "of vicarious atonement for the abandonment of the Fifteenth Amendment."

Without admitting any such connection, of course, Hayes appointed Frederick Douglass marshall of the District of Columbia. The action touched off an immediate uproar. Anti-Negro elements in Washington were offended, as expected. Many Negroes were elated. Those who along with the editors of *The Nation* discerned the hidden play were nevertheless restrained in their comments and echoed that publication's opinion that the appointment was "a pleasing event for those who were fond of poetic justice and dramatic denouement." Douglass himself saw no reason why he should not accept the honor.

If he needed a defense for his course, the hostile Southerners in Washington provided it. He had merely to point to outraged local sentiment to prove that he was still on the firing line, still championing the cause of the Negro citizen. Moreover he could not help feeling, as did *The Nation,* that the appointment was no more than he deserved. The motivation behind it on the part of the newly elected President neither changed that fact nor quieted the angry people of the District who saw in their nightmares the towering, white-maned Douglass "in white kid gloves, sparrow-tailed coat, patent-leather boots, and alabaster cravat" introducing the aristocracy of the nation to the President in the Executive Mansion.

Douglass played up his opposition, chuckling over Washington's fears that he would appoint only Negro deputies, bailiffs, messengers and jurors and thus Africanize the courts of the capitol. Senator Roscoe Conkling of New York, who led the fight for confirmation of the appointment by the Senate, if he did not chuckle, certainly was not dismayed by the opposition. The North was as tired of the aftermath of Civil War as the South was of the occupying army. Reacting to all the elements and pressures, the Senate promptly confirmed.

Following the appointment, Douglass began looking for a suburban home suitable to his new station in life, his prestige as a Negro leader and his flocks of grandchildren. In 1878 he found the place he liked across the Anacostia River. It was an eye-catching estate about a mile beyond the bridge. A twenty-room house, snuggled by oaks and hickories as well as cedars, looked down from a stately hill. The grounds covered fifteen acres. Cedar Hill was its name, and from its broad portico, which stretched across the entire front, an excellent view of the nation's captitol unfolded. When Douglass learned that this handsome property had once been owned by Robert E. Lee, that still earlier an original owner had specified that no Negro or Irishman should ever acquire title, he knew that he would feel at home here, that the ghosts of Cedar Hill, if any, would not have the advantage of being unfamiliar to him.

He and Anna moved in and opened the gates to their progeny. At sixty-one, his eyes still bright, his skin coloring healthy, his beard and hair completely white, it occurred to Douglass that he could no longer take his robust health for granted. He formed the habit of walking the five miles to City Hall each morning, and two years later he renounced the use of tobacco.

Unfortunately his devoted Anna was not so blessed. Rheumatism became an increasing torment, and her Anacostia years were marked by "faithful constant care and nursing." If she could not go out with her husband or her grown children, however, she had no occasion to feel lonely. A steady procession of friends came to the home of America's and the world's most renowned Negro, and all showed a special tenderness toward the helpless old woman who had never been beautiful, who had never learned to read or write, but from whom the brilliant and handsome Douglass had somehow drawn strength.

Conspicuous by his absence from the lawns and paths of Cedar Hill was one Nathan Sprague, husband of Rosetta. The black sheep of the clan, Sprague was often in trouble; if he was not opening other people's letters in the Rochester postoffice, where Douglass had secured a clerkship for him, he was involved in questionable business deals. If not thus entangled, he was hounding Douglass for money to help support Rosetta and their seven children. Douglass had disapproved of the marriage from the first, and he showed no inclination to accept the trifling son-in-law now. The fine feeling he got walking down his hill and crossing the Anacostia bridge in the morning definitely had its limits.

"Our children marry in this country without much deference to the wisdom and advice of their parents," he lamented. But his resentment did not extend to the Sprague youngsters, nor did he cease to love the daughter who continued to defend the father of her children. Where she and his three sons were concerned, his expectations were modest. When he tried to place Rosetta in the fashionable Seward Seminary in Rochester thirty-two years ago, when he employed a Quaker governess for her after the failure of that attempt, when he sent her to the preparatory department of Oberlin College 1854, and finally when he succeeded in having the Rochester public schools opened to colored children, including her and her brothers, he had dreamed great dreams for all of them. Now—now he found himself unconsciously transferring these hopes to the grandchildren who came to roll on his lawns, climb his trees and riot in the little shady groves.

Of his three sons only Lewis, the eldest, had no children, but Lewis and his wife Amelia, the daughter of Jermain W. Loguen, a Negro abolitionist minister of Syracuse and an early acquaintance of John Brown, were frequent visitors at Cedar Hill. Fred junior and Charles came with their forces. Eventually these numbered seven for each, and Douglass cherished them all. His special favorites among the grandchildren, however, were Rosetta's Hattie and Charles's boy Joe. Joe was beginning to play the violin.

Was it in his grandchildren that a man looked for the reappearance of his own dominant traits, for the fulfillment of secret dreams? Certainly his own sons had reflected little of Douglass's image, little of his vision or capacity. All of them had learned printing in the shop in Rochester, and Lewis and Charles had fought with the Union Army during the Civil War while Fred junior engaged in recruiting. After the hostilities Charles had been employed first with the Freedman's Bureau while Lewis and Fred tried to find work in Washington as typographers. Rejected by the local union because of their color, the young men remained at loose ends till their father took over the *New National Era*. That enterprise having run its course, Douglass now secured small-salaried positions for each of them in the government. Charles meanwhile had stepped from the Freedman's Bureau into an appointment as U. S. consul at Puerto Plata, Santo Domingo. In the year his father moved to Cedar Hill however, his wife's illness had brought him back to Washington, and now she was dead and he was at home with the five children and available for another job, if one could be found.

Even at Cedar Hill at this relatively tranquil moment anxieties were not all suspended. Though Douglass's duties as marshal were definitely not exhausting, consisting mainly of such activities as escorting the President and the President-elect from the Senate Chamber to the east front of the Capitol and, when Garfield was innaugurated, of leading the march through the corridors and rotunda of the Capitol to the spot where the Chief Justice delivered the oath of office; though the salary permitted him to retire in comfort from the tediousness and strain of the lecture platform, though his crusading newspaper days were over, Douglass had no reason to suspect that he had come to an end of struggle. Garfield's election itself posed a problem. It marked the termination of the appointment as marshal. Would it be renewed? Garfield was said to have told Senator Roscoe Conkling, Douglass's warm supporter, that it would, but was that a promise?

Evidently not. Garfield appointed one of his own friends to the job, but he thought enough about the matter to designate another post for the prominent Negro leader. He appointed Douglass recorder of deeds for the District of Columbia, and Douglass showed his gratitude by giving reasons why he found this new position more appealing than the other. He refrained from mentioning that the recorder of deeds had no such social responsibilities as were associated with the marshal's post.

One of the copyists in the recorder's office, interestingly enough, happened to be the niece of the white man whose estate adjoined Cedar Hill, and the cordiality of good neighbors did not fail in the work relationship. Miss Helen Pitts, Mount Holyoke, '59, was austere, refined, but compatable. Descended from Captain Peter Pitts, first settler in the township of Richmond in western New York, she was eligible for membership in the Colonial Dames of America and in the Daughters of the American Revolution. Among her closer kin were abolitionists with whom Douglass had worked in Rochester. Plain, fortyish and efficient, she was a useful person in an office. It was a comfort to rely on her.

Within a few months after Douglass assumed his duties in the recorder's office, he found himself in accute need of compatability and comfort. Anna's rheumatic infirmity suddenly grew worse. In the summer of 1882 she died.

The expressions of sympathy that filled Douglass's mail in the days that followed often struck a quaint note. Old companions of the abolitionist campaigns tried bravely to incorporate all their impressions of this naive woman in comments about her good cooking, her tidy house and the extremely domestic picture she made with her head tied in a bandanna handkerchief. But few of them succeeded in hiding a still stronger feeling which her death revived: admiration for Douglass who, while outgrowing Anna outlandishly, had never so much as hinted that he felt unequally yoked. His devotion had been steadfast. So now sorrow was added to the public figure of the slave-born leader.

Perhaps Douglass's later years are best understood when one thinks of him as a popular hero rather than a leader in the sense of pointing a way and commanding the steps of followers. That he had been and done. Now Negroes of America tended to think of him as the foremost champion of their Emancipation. More than Lincoln or John Brown he symbolized their new birth of freedom. He had been more than an advocate. He was the slave himself, risen and transfigured. Nothing could ever detract from that renown. Well, almost nothing.

Less than a year and a half after Anna's death, on a cold January evening in 1884, Douglass and his secretary, driving in Douglass's carriage behind magnificent white horses, were joined by the Senator from Mississippi, Blanche K. Bruce, and Mrs. Bruce. Douglass directed his coachman to the home of a prominent Negro clergyman. A personal friend of Douglass's, the minister was nevertheless surprised by his late callers. He sent word downstairs for them to wait. A few moments later, upon request of those concerned, the Reverend Mr. Francis J. Grimke joined Frederick Douglass and Helen Pitts in marriage, the Bruces witnessing.

A complete secret up to the moment of the ceremony, the news broke a few hours later like a thunderclap. The storm followed promptly, highlighted by distorted newspaper accounts and insulting editorials. A hurricane of outraged letters hit Cedar Hill. Negroes and whites seemed equally offended. The venerable Douglass, white-haired and sixty-six, should not have married again at all, some thought. Others shouted that Negro womanhood had been disparaged by the implications of his choice. Could he not find among the many complexions within the race, all the exciting varieties and mixtures that pass as Negroes under the American definition, a colored woman good enough for him? In the South, of course, criticism found its most picturesque expression. Douglass was a "lecherous old African Solomon" in the eyes of the Franklin, Virginia, *Gazette*. An Atlanta letter writer told the Reverend Grimke that as payment for his part in it "a Little Tar and Fetters would be good."

Douglass's own children joined in the howl. How could he do this to them—and without consultation? Rosetta and her ne'er-do-well husband were the most incensed, and Sprague's sister, to whom Douglass had given employment for ten years as housekeeper, packed her bundle and switched out of the back door of Cedar Hill, her chin in the air. Douglass watched the whole demonstration with a twinkle in his eye.

He showed his amusement by keeping a scrapbook of the opprobrium heaped upon him and his white wife. When confronting interviewers, he slyly observed that in his first marriage he had paid his respects to his black mother, in his second to his white father. "Love came to me," Helen crooned when questioned, "and I was not afraid to marry the man I loved because of his color." For the resentment of his children Douglass was prepared, and his retort was neither witty nor pleasant. There wasn't one of them who wasn't at least partially dependent on him for support. They swallowed hard and crept away.

Douglass and Helen began playing croquet on the lawns of Cedar Hill. The place was quieter now. His health was wonderful. Douglass actually began to feel young again, and presently the ugly noises began to fade in the distance. None of his close friends, he discovered, had actually turned their back on him and Helen.

When calmness was restored, he watched his chance to strike back at his critics. White Americans were not really opposed to the mixing of the races; they only opposed honorable marriage between members of the two groups, he charged. Let doubters examine the facts. Let them count the mulattos in the South. Negro Americans, on the other hand, should think twice before allowing themselves to draw a color line. He had not abandoned his people by marrying a white woman. The marriage was on the contrary a most dramatic challenge to color prejudice in America.

Perhaps few minds were swayed, but not many were inclined to revive the issue publicly.

Meanwhile a new president took office, and in the year of Douglass's marriage to Helen Pitts the Democrats and Grover Cleveland won a hotly contested, mud-slinging victory over James G. Blaine and the Republicans. The assumption was that Douglass would be immediately replaced as recorder of deeds. Cleveland waited till January of 1866 before asking for the resignation, however. Civil service reforms, supported by the new President, were pending, and the delay struck Douglass as part of a maneuver to win support for the reforms before exercising the more traditional prerogatives of winners in a struggle for control of the government.

Miffed by the tactics, Douglass muttered a few uncomplimentary words about the new occupant of the White House, but Cleveland's personal attitude toward the Douglasses destroyed any real basis for complaint. With more courage and grace than Hayes, Garfield or Arthur had shown, he extended to Douglass "and the ladies of his family" invitations to his large, official receptions. Douglass and Helen attended without embarrassment.

But the reign of the Republicans was ended, or at least interrupted, and Douglass did not have to be told a second time that he was out of a job. Now—now he could devote himself to the good woman who had admired him as a public figure since she was a child, whose admiration had turned to affection on closer acquaintance, and who had unhesitatingly given him her love when the circumstance permitted. What he had in mind was in no sense a delayed honeymoon, but it was just as exciting. For forty years he had dreamed of a leisurely tour of Europe. With time on his hands now, with the children grown and out of the way, with money no longer a problem, and with Helen at his side, why should he not indulge his dream?

Within six months after he submitted his resignation as recorder of deeds, Douglass was writing letters, applying for passports, buying clothes and preparing to travel. Never in his life having been frustrated by inability to make decisions, he did not find it necessary to ponder this one long. Nor did he stop to ask who the Negroes of the United States would look to for leadership during his absence. It was almost as if his retirement from the appointment in the recorder's office included putting down this burden too.

Had he thought anything about dynasties and successions of leaders that year, however, he might have found the activities of two young men extremely interesting.

Booker Taliaferro Washington, who was giving his age as twenty-seven or twenty-eight, was actually thirty years old in 1886. Confused as to the date of his birth, the mind of that country schoolteacher was on all other matters pertaining to the South just about the clearest in the nation. As Douglass drove around Washington checking on the addresses of friends in the British Isles, arranging for his son Lewis to look after Cedar Hill and transact necessary business in the father's absence, Booker Washington was graduating his second class of Normal students at Tuskegee and preparing to add cabinetmaking to a curriculum which already included carpentry, brickmaking and printing.

When Douglass and Helen boarded the *City of Rome* in New York harbor that August, William Edward Burghardt Du Bois, age sixteen, his heart on fire, was writing poetry on a train bound for Nashville, Tennessee. By the time the Douglasses reached Liverpool, he had entered Fisk University and been assigned to a dormitory room in the large, newly constructed Livingston Hall. Seeing the South for the first time, after a Massachusetts boyhood, he had promptly begun to absorb new and exciting impressions, among them the notion that one of the girls at his table in the dining room was the most beautiful creature in the world.

While homespun teacher and youthful poet had both been "discovered" and marked as individuals worth watching, neither had come to the notice of Frederick Douglass before he and Helen went abroad. The fact that each was a warm admirer of his was not particularly significant. Admiration for Douglass was general among young Negroes. His struggle and example were settling into the folklore of the people. Without taking the rôle too seriously, however, Douglass began showing his sheltered Yankee wife the Irish slums which had facinated and horrified him forty years ago.

Ireland had changed but little in that span. Beggars still

swarmed to the dockside and followed the travelers to their rooming house. The natives still halted abruptly and turned to gape at the exotic Douglass. Now more than before, perhaps. With the graying of his hair he had grown even more striking. Accompanied by his modest white wife, he seemed even more picturesque. But there was nothing unpleasant about the stares, no hint of disrespect or disapproval. Irish eyes merely feasted.

After a week of visiting art galleries and the public library, Liverpool's great shipping piers and mechanical displays, and of twilight walks through the city the couple began a five-week tour of the British Isles which brought them by the first of October to the little town of St. Neots, about fifty miles from London. Along the way Douglass found occasion to reflect more than once on Emerson's *English Traits,* which he had begun reading aboard the *City of Rome,* and Helen uttered little occasional gasps at the "begrimed and tattered" children in the streets, at the drunkenness of women in Glasgow and Liverpool. Both took time in the evenings to keep diaries, and at St. Neots an old and very dear friend of Douglass's came to the gate to throw her arms around them.

She was Julia Griffiths-Crofts whom Douglass had not seen for thirty-two years and who had been widowed for nearly a decade. Supporting herself and occupying her time by running a girls' school, Julia made the visit of the Douglasses an event of first importance in the little world in which she now lived. The cozy ritual of tea welded the trio of friends in the first hour, and the next morning they walked to church together through the autumn lanes of St. Neots' cemetery. Thereafter they rode in Julia's carriage to neighboring villages, Douglass driving, and explored the countryside. One day was given to a visit to nearby Cambridge, including services at King's Chapel, and an afternoon to Julia's school, where Douglass spoke to the girls.

Between times Douglass and Julia reminisced. Warmed by the memories, she suddenly asked if Frederick remembered a certain afternoon in March of 1847? It was at a sociable, she reminded him, that "Eliza Wigham pinned a white camelia in your coat." Douglass could not remember. Nor did he or his wife question aloud the mood that brought the episode back from Julia's subconscious. But the moment became grave with memories, and after five heart-warming days the Douglasses set out for London.

Moving half-solemnly among the monuments of Anglo Saxon culture and history, Douglass found himself suddenly trembling with excitement in Parliament. Mr. Gladstone had the floor. The venerable statesman was speaking in the interest of home rule for the Irish, and it sounded good to Douglass, mighty good. As an experience it was worth all the voiceless relics in the kingdom.

Of course neither Douglass nor Helen could leave England without seeing Anna and Ellen Richardson, the women who had raised money to buy his freedom following his first sojourn abroad, so to pay his respects and to introduce his new wife Douglass called on his aging friends in Newcastle. The visit was not prolonged, for by that time Paris was beckoning from the Continent. Paris! City of light! No lad from the provinces could have been more bewitched by its reputation than was Douglass as he and Helen embarked for Calais.

The customs officers irritated him, mainly because of their delaying tactics, but all that was forgotten as they reached the city and immediately fell among old acquaintances. One who greeted them was Elizabeth Cady Stanton's son Theodore. Another was Theodore Tilton. The fact that his mother was a foremost feminist, a pioneer in the women's suffrage movement in the United States and an unusually dominant woman may not necessarily have accounted for Theodore Stanton's living abroad, but the scandal which charged Henry Ward Beecher with stealing the love of Theodore Tilton's wife did have something to do with the latter's residence in Paris at the time. In any case, both were fond friends of Douglass, and they tried to outdo each other's hospitality.

Following one or the other as guide, the Douglasses touched all points of historic or literary interest, pausing respectfully before the statues of Lamartine and Dumas and whispering their admiration for the formal dress of the French senators in session. Douglass was equally impressed by the tempestuous spirit of these well-attired gentlemen once they warmed to their work. He was thrillingly reminded of the uproar in the U. S. Congress when James G. Blaine tangled with Benjamin Harvey Hill of Georgia on the issue of amnesty for Jefferson Davis, and meeting Victor Schoelcher afterwards put a final touch on the experience.

Eighty-two years old and still full of fight, Schoelcher was in a sense the Garrison of France. He was known as the man who had drafted the measure emancipating slaves in the French colonies, the measure which Alphonse de Lamartine had signed. Schoelcher invited Douglass to his home, and the two veteran abolitionists exchanged memories. The Frenchman showed Douglass his collection of relics, including chains, fetters and iron-pronged collars once worn by slaves in the overseas lands of France. He also revealed that he was at the moment writing a biography of Toussaint L'Ouverture, the black hero of the Haitian revolution.

Returning to his room, Douglass pondered the difference between the French and the Anglo-Saxon attitude toward people of color. Certainly it was unmistakable. How could it be explained? Was the absence of minstrel shows wtih their damaging ridicule of Negroes a factor? Was it that slavery had been confined to the colonies of France, so that Parisians had seen Negroes, when they saw them at all, as scholars or artists or perhaps tourists? Or was it, he wondered, a difference in the religion of the people? He concluded that it was. The Catholic Church, he observed, "welcomes to its altars and communion men of all races and colors."

In this mood, eleven wonderous weeks having slipped away, he and Helen turned their faces toward Avignon. They were content to travel slowly, and when they saw the room in which the Court of Inquisition had sat in the ancient Palace of the Popes, when they visited Avignon's feudal castles, it was as if they had wandered into the middle ages. But now Rome was their destination. Arles, Marseilles, the Château d'If, setting of Alexandre Dumas' *Monte Cristo*, Nice, Genoa and Pisa were all on the route, and Douglass passed a traveler's judgment on them all. The beautiful women, promised by the guide book, did not show at Arles. The old island prison which had inspired Dumas seemed "anchored in the sea." Nice was shockingly expensive, compared to the other cities visited, and Genoa was the place where Douglass stood bewitched as he looked at Paganini's violin in the museum. Pisa had the leaning tower and cathedral associated with Galileo's observations on falling bodies.

Douglass was transported.

Back in Paris Theodore Stanton began writing an article which he called "Frederick Douglass in Paris," and the editor of *The Open Court,* a fortnightly journal, scheduled it for publication in the April 28 issue of the following year. Equally impressed by his association with the Negro leader, Theodore Tilton, whose published writings include much poetry, began sorting the phrases and images which eventually went into a little volume of *Sonnets to the Memory of Frederick Douglass.* A wake was forming behind the blithe traveler and his wife. This was its visible shape.

In the black belt of Alabama the results of Douglass's

leadership found their best expression in the medium-sized, generally unnoticed figure of Booker Washington, a country schoolteacher riding an old mule without a saddle. Having easily overcome white opposition in the little town of Tuskegee, his strange, one-man crusade had clashed with rustic Negro preachers, the backwoods Baptists and Methodists of Macon County who resented him as a man and ridiculed him as a teacher. Though it was not in his mind at this time to write a biography of Frederick Douglass, (which he later did), the courage and example of the exceedingly charismatic Douglass were seldom out of his consciousness. To him as to most Negroes who heard about it in the United States the picture of Douglass traveling abroad was simply a portrait of Douglass victorious, Douglass enshrined.

He was too shrewd not to see, however, that his job, the task of doing something with the barefoot human material that shambled in the dusty wagon paths, that gawked at him from the roadside, the ragged, unfed and spiritually undernourished millions whose right to freedom Douglass had championed, had to be started from scratch. His was a fearful assignment, but somehow he did not feel fearful. He knew what ailed these listless, grinning folk whose embarrassment he noticed as he slid off his mule and began signing them up for school. And he knew the cure too, for he had been in the same condition nine years before he came to Tuskegee. And nine years before that he had fought with pigs for choice bits of garbage from his master's kitchen. The requirements of the new job seemed perfectly obvious to him.

Reading Greek at Fisk University, attending the recitals of the Mozart Society, debating, writing and delivering orations, young Du Bois was not too detached to be aware of conditions like those in Macon County, Alabama. Even the carefully selected and in some ways unrepresentative

student body at Fisk was suggestive. Most of his fellow
students were much older than he. Almost none of them
had backgrounds similar to his New England high school
experience. And he was by no means sure he knew the
nature of the larger problem, let alone the answer. Tem-
peramentally inclined toward skepticism, he had assumed
a questioning attitude and resolved—well, he had resolved
to learn, to learn everything if possible but certainly everything about his people, his puzzling, unfamiliar people.

Already the small energetic youth had discovered history
and begun to wonder whether a near or distant focus
offered a better view of a problem like the one confronted
by the emancipated people of the South. One conclusion
he had reached. An understanding of the complexities facing a young Negro in the United States in that year demanded the best possible training. The gods willing, he
would get such a training. After Fisk he would try for
higher degrees. Harvard was in his mind. He was even
dreaming vaguely of study in Germany. Was the thought
of Frederick Douglass abroad awakening these wishes?

The Douglasses arrived in Rome and began another
round of Americanized pilgrimages to holy, near-holy and
unholy places. In St. Peter's, to which they hurried first,
Douglass's "speechless admiration" did not inhibit amused
comment on the blackness of the statue whose big toe he,
fortunately, could kiss without color prejudice, but presently dreamy relics and monuments were flowing together
before his eyes like a montage. The robed priest-guide
reverently showing the jewelled treasures of the cathedral,
the visit to the Vatican, the walk on the Appian Way, the
tour of the Coliseum, the unbelievable baths of Titus and
Diocletian, called to Douglass's mind the letters of the
Apostle Paul as well as secular histories he had read. And
his chance meetings with Edmonia Lewis in Rome did not
shatter the mood.

The oddly dressed woman, whose colthes had a masculine touch, materialized suddenly before the Douglasses as the couple strolled on Pincian Hill. If not herself a relic or a period piece, Edmonia at least belonged to another world, and that is where she was. Douglass had met her before. She had attended Oberlin and may have been present when he and Garrison debated President Asa Mahan. Apparently she had been on the campus while Lucy Stone was a student, but storms had driven this daughter of an Indian mother and a free Negro father. At Oberlin suspicion had fallen on her following the poisoning of two of her white classmates, her best friends. She had been defended by John Mercer Langston, foremost Negro lawyer, and exonerated, but the ordeal had been harrowing. Scarcely less devastating to the emotions had been her childhood encounters with slave hunters and the John Brown affair. By the time she took up sculpturing in Boston as a young woman, she was known for her personal peculiarities. Now a recognized sculptress, the first Negro American to achieve such recognition, she had lived in Rome more than twenty years and almost forgotten how to speak English.

Sarah Remond, also living in Rome in 1887, aroused somewhat different feelings in the travelers. Sarah was the sister of Charles Remond, the antislavery lecturer with whom Douglass had been associated in abolitionist days and for whom he had named his third son. Perhaps it was because she shared the bitterness which was so noticeable in her brother that Sarah chose to live abroad, for she too had lectured against slavery, and now she was old and finished with fighting. If Douglass needed a reminder of his own age, a reminder that sometime within the next few weeks, as he calculated, his seventieth birthday would fall, he had only to count the years since the abolitionist conventions.

What did it mean—this eager journey among the ruins

of the ancient world? Douglass himself did not pause to
answer. All he knew was that he felt hurried. He could
not stay too long in Rome this time. Perhaps he would
tarry on the return trip, but now he must press onward—
or rather backward. With the lonely sculptress clinging to
the visitors from home, the three met in Naples and went
to the museum together. More monuments and old places
waited here. Then there were Mount Vesuvius, the site of
the ancient city of Pompeii, and the tomb of Virgil. All
these inspired, but none seemed ultimate. Somewhere beyond, across water and deeper into the past was Egypt.
Douglass had not planned it this way, but now that he and
Helen had reached southern Italy, he felt strangely impelled to go farther. He could not stop. On February 13,
1887, he and Helen sailed for Port Saïd.

Had he been awake or dreaming when his mother called
him her Valentine? Certainly it was too late now ever to
be sure. She had been with him only at night when his
eyes were heavy and he floated dimly from one level of
consciounsness into the other, and now sixty-five years had
intervened. A life of struggle had ensued, a life which many
people considered remarkable in nearly every way. As an
old man Douglass recalled the little endearment spoken by
his tired slave mother, and it suggested something else to
him. Perhaps it meant that he had been born on St. Valentine's day.

In any case, he was on the Mediterranian the fourteenth
of February that year with nothing to do but to walk the
deck, gaze at the water and make notes in his diary. Their
vessel reached Port Saïd two days later and began sailing
down the canal toward Ismalia. A hush fell upon the ship.
It was as if silence had been communciated from the bar-
ren and voiceless country through which the canal passed.
Douglass, who was accustomed to uproar, was appalled by

it. He wondered if silence like this had anything to do with religious faith and began to suspect that it did. Inner perceptions became sharper, the soul could "hear quicker" amid such silences.

Cairo was six hours from Ismalia, through the Land of Goshen, and in Cairo they had a fortnight in which to move among the mosques and tombs of Mohammedanism. When his sightseeing was interrupted by a parade of British troops, he could not help noticing that "the people were not pleased with the sight." Finally, to cap the tour, he and Helen arranged to visit Gizeh.

This was the site of the great pyramid of Cheops. To it Douglass had been drawn as if by a magnet, and his discovery that most Egyptians, by American definition, seemed to be mulattoes and Negroes only heightened his excitement. Not only did he have to see the ancient monument which through centuries and milleniums had become a symbol to the whole human race, he also felt that he had to climb it.

At Douglass's age the 470 foot ascent was not easy. With the help of four Arabs, however, two pushing and two pulling, as he smilingly observed, he finally reached the top. Breathless from the climb and so spent it would probably take him weeks to recover, he nevertheless knew at once that it had been worth the exertion. One view of the Sphinx, the River Nile and the desert was reward enough for three score and ten years of pain and effort.

He would not try just now to express what this moment summarized for him, perhaps it would never be necessary, for he knew in his heart what he had seen and perceived. Now he was content. He could go down and meet Helen on the sand and return again by way of Italy, France and England to his home at Cedar Hill.

X

L'ENVOI

THE BITTERSWEET MOOD of introspection was never quite shattered thereafter, but the return journey of the Douglasses began as planned. A five-day trip to Alexandria followed, and it was from there that they arranged passage to Athens. Twelve days had been allotted to Greece, and the couple found it thrilling to stand upon the spot where the Apostle Paul was said to have preached from Mars Hill. Equally unforgettable, as Douglass recalled the experience in his updated *Life and Times* in 1892, was the view from Lycabettus, "overlooking the plains of Marathon, the gardens of Plato, and the rock where Demosthenes declaimed against the breezes of the sea." The Parthenon, the Temple of Theseus, the Temple of Wingless Victory and the Temple of Dionysius stirred him equally.

From this point on he and Helen would be retracing steps already taken, but now they felt less hurried. Two weeks did not seem too long for Naples after Athens, and in Rome there was more, much more to engage them. Easter services at St. Peter's, for example. At another time they watched the unveiling of a monument to Galileo. Meanwhile Douglass confided to his diary that he received a call from a woman who had introduced herself as Mrs.

John Biddulp Martin. The name did not ring a bell, but his puzzlement was dispelled when the caller turned out to be none other than the famous and former Victoria Wood-hull.

Meanwhile, too, Helen described in a letter to Jennie Pitts, dated April 25, 1887, a reception given by the American Minister in Rome, which the couple attended. As usual the elderly, white-haired Frederick Douglass promptly became a center of attention. "Many wanted to be presented to him," his wife reported shyly.

With activities and events such as these, a month slipped by in Rome, and then it was on to Florence where the first thing they did, again according to his reminiscences, was to seek the Protestant cemetery where the celebrated Unitarian clergyman Theodore Parker had been buried. Douglass remembered standing beside his mound with Helen and recalling that Parker "had a voice for the slave when nearly all the pulpits of the land were dumb." Their five days in Florence also included moments before the tombstone of Elizabeth Barrett Browning, whose devotion and commitment to freedom they silently celebrated, and a respectful pause at the burial place of the author of *Despotism in America,* a book both remembered for its strong attack on slaveholders.

The beauty of the Arno River won their hearts, but in mid-May it was on once more to Venice, Milan and Lucerne. Arriving in Paris near the end of the month, they were greeted by news that Helen's mother had become seriously ill at home in the United States. So they quickly paid their respects to the Stantons and Senator Schoelcher, who was remembered for kissing Douglass on both cheeks, called on Tilton, only to learn that he was out of town, and arranged passage back to America for Helen.

Douglass would have returned with her, except that they had made plans to visit various British friends, and some of these amounted to promises. Parting with his wife, Douglass went to England, but he avoided London where the city was bustling with joyous crowds celebrating Queen Victoria's jubilee. Instead he went direct to his friends in Newcastle, Edinburgh and Glasgow. At Carlisle he wrote to Helen on June 28, 1887, that he had found the cottage of Eliza Barlow "a place of rest and sweet repose."

In the days that followed Douglass was the guest of Julia for nearly a week at St. Neots. At Bridgeport, too, old friends warmed his heart. These included Mary Carpenter and her brother Russell Lant Carpenter and Russell's wife. Then there was Helen P. B. Clark, the eldest daughter of John Bright, who had contributed a preface to the English edition of Douglass's *Life and Times.*

There was more of the same in Dublin where Wilhelmina and Susanna Webb were expecting him. A letter from Helen written from Honeoye reported that her mother had improved and that it now seemed safe to leave her and return to Cedar Hill. Douglass's thoughts turned homeward. He missed Helen more than he had sometimes realized. He also felt revived concern about affairs of business he had for so long put out of his thoughts.

It was early August when he embarked for home, recounting as he did so benefits he felt had been realized from the long journey. There had been the exaltation of moments at the shrines of art and history. After these he placed the meetings with friends old and dear and "lost awhile." And to cap it all, there had been the stimulation one got from escaping the color line, at least temporarily, and walking "as a man among men."

Even so, it was now, as it had always been in the past, a joy to sail for home. And when he arrived in Washington, he found that his black admirers had prepared a public reception to honor him at the Metropolitan A. M. E. Church, a reception at which the Reverend R. E. Stewart presided and another minister, Walter Brooks, read an original poem written for the occasion.

Thereafter, the events of Douglass's remaining years took on a ceremonial aura not unlike activities of a returned hero or a retired commander. More precisely, his situation commanded a deference such as might be shown to a bold chieftain or leader of a subject tribe whose spirit had remained unbroken despite crushing blows to his people.

Not all of these activities were without interest, however, and one of them had in it the seeds of profound embarrassment. The aging leader found himself somehow supporting a white aspirant in a congressional election against an eminent and respected black candidate in Virginia.

John Mercer Langston, indeed, was second only to Douglass himself in the esteem in which he was held in black America, and in formal scholarship and legal experience he was far superior. Unfortunately, the two had never quite set horses, so to speak. Langston (the great-uncle of the poet Langston Hughes) had opposed, out of understandable conviction, one feels, Douglass's appointment to the presidency of the Freedman's Bank. He had differed with Douglass on the question of Negro migration within the United States and he had resented Douglass's favorable comments on Cleveland's inaugural address. Douglass, for his part, similarly sincere, was convinced by an array of circumstances that he was obliged to support Judge R. W. Arnold, the white candidate, in his bid for the congressional seat from the fourth district of Virginia, even though black voters outnumbered whites in the district. The contest was heated, but miraculously both Douglass and Langston managed to emerge relatively unscathed politically. Langston was elected and became the first (and only) Negro to represent Virginia in Congress.

In the aftermath, for reasons best known to himself,

Douglass requested reappointment to his former post as recorder of deeds. President Harrison took the request under advisement, and Douglass's later statements permit one to assume that his own self-esteem needed a favorable response at that point. While the President delayed, at least one concerned young Negro of prominence, R. R. Wright, offered the suggestion that Douglass be made a member of Harrison's cabinet.

Harrison did not respond to that, and he did not reply to the request of Douglass for reappointment to his old job. Instead, on July 1, 1889, he announced the appointment of Frederick Douglass as minister resident and consul general to the Republic of Haiti. Douglass accepted joyously. "President Harrison has done more and better for me than I asked," he exulted, "and has done it without my asking." But the President hadn't finished yet. Two months later Harrison added the post of chargé d'affairs for Santo Domingo to Douglass's assignment.

As surprised as he seemed by this turn of events, Douglass remembered that twenty years earlier he had been mentioned for such an appointment after Grant's first election. At that time he had deferred to another Negro, Ebenezer Bassett of Connecticut, who had studied at Yale and who was then a high-school principal, and Bassett had become during Grant's two terms the first Negro appointed minister to a foreign government by the United States. And John Mercer Langston had served two appointments to the same post after Bassett.

Despite this precedent, there were those who grumbled that the Haitians did not want a black representative from the United States. Douglass brushed such comment aside, and almost immediately the Haitian President, Louis Modestin Florvil Hyppolite, began to disabuse his mind further on that point. As he presented his credentials, Douglass spoke of the "opportunities for the exercise of a generous spirit of forbearance and concession, favorable to peace and fraternal relations" between the two nations. And Hyppolite pulled out even more stops in his response. Douglass was the incarnation of Haitian ideals, he said, "the moral and intellectual development of the men of the African race by personal effort and mental culture."

Nevertheless the tour of duty in that troubled island was not always that gracious, though the warm esteem in which he was held by the Haitians remained constant. Requests by Americans for him to settle claims they had against the Haitian government and vice versa were part of the routine, and not all of these were stimulating. Yet Douglass invariably handled them earnestly, including one from the Clyde steamship lines which wished to initiate a service between New York and seven Haitian ports, as well as to have the tonnage and port duties on American vessels reduced. Douglass's negotiations with the Haitian Secretary of State for External Relations resulted in the approval of both these requests, and the elder Clyde thanked him warmly.

Douglass was more in his element when speaking at a New Year's celebration or attending the opening session of the Haitian legislature or attending state funerals of prominent Haitians or transmitting the first cable message from Haiti to Secretary of State James G. Blaine. To this Blaine replied, saying, "Congratulate President Hyppolite that the two Republics are nearer today than they have been."

Eventually this pleasant exchange tied in with another that became bitter. The United States, in fact, was at that very time involved in some tension growing out of its need for a naval base and a coaling station in the Caribbean, and this situation was accentuated as plans for the building of a canal connecting the Atlantic and Pacific oceans were advanced. For this purpose the United States wished to secure Môle St. Nicolas, a port at Haiti's northwest tip.

Douglass favored such a lease, and he was told by Secre-

tary Blaine that President Harrison wished him to cooperate with Admiral Bancroft Gherardi, commander of
the North Atlantic fleet, in its furtherance. Considering,
however, the political situation in Haiti; namely the debt
which the Hyppolite government appeared to owe the
United States for past favors, including certain kindnesses
in Hyppolite's overthrow of his predecessor, François Legi-
time, not to mention the American Admiral's seeming in-
sensitivity, the native opposition to the idea of letting an
elephant, no matter how ingratiating, put his trunk in the
hut of a peasant, as well as a few other obstacles; the success
of the project was by no means assured in advance.

When the Haitian government turned down the request,
after months of diplomatic reticence, Douglass blamed the
outcome, confidentially, on all these negative factors. Much
of the American press tended to blame Douglass. As a result
Douglass promptly asked the State Department for a leave
of absence. Back in Washington he sent in his resignation
on the last day of June 1891, and the question arose as to
whether or not he was quitting under fire. But actually
eight months earlier he had written friends that a year in
Haiti had aged him more than two in America, and he now
repeated the same complaint to an interviewer for the
Baltimore Sun. He was indeed past seventy now and his
health seemed to require attention. The climate in Haiti
had favored neither him nor Helen, and during their final
months there the wife had suffered from a fever.

The news of his resignation reached Haiti slowly, but
when it did, twenty-three members of the faculty of the
Haitian College expressed a general regret by signing a
statement in which they made it plain that they had regarded him as Haitian at heart and one of the "greatest
champions of liberty, justice and equality" in the tradition
of their revered liberator Toussaint L'Ouverture.

Meanwhile, in the United States, at least two well-known

Negroes, T. Thomas Fortune and Mifflin W. Gibbs, hearing that Douglass was about to resign the ministership, wrote to ask Douglass if he would help them to secure the post. But meanwhile a more interesting letter came to him from a young man named Paul Laurence Dunbar, who modestly introduced himself by saying, "I have been somewhat successful in practical literary work." Dunbar was requesting Douglass to "use your influence" to help him get a job as a teacher of English literature in the public schools of Washington, D. C.

The brightest event of Douglass's declining years, however, was his subsequent appointment as Haitian commissioner at the World's Columbian Exposition at Chicago in 1893. The post had been proffered in recognition of his friendship and association with Haiti, and he had accepted in the same spirit, after being assured that his function would be mainly advisory and that someone else would handle correspondence and related chores. Under this arrangement a Haitian Pavilion was erected. In the course of his remarks at the dedication, after delivering encomiums to Hyppolite and to the Haitian people, Douglass observed, "We are situated upon one of the finest avenues of these grounds; standing upon our verandah we may view one of the largest of our inland seas, we may inhale its fine and refreshing breezes, we can contemplate its tranquil beauty in its calm and its awful sublimity and power when its crested billows are swept by the storm." On this crescendo he invited the general public to come one and all and savor "a generous taste of our Haitian coffee, made in the best manner by Haitian hands."

Black Americans were proud of the Haitian Pavilion and pleased with the Negro who served as its voice, but otherwise the Chicago world's fair, called the first of its kind, left much to be desired from their point of view. Lack of representation on its National Board of Commis-

sioners was the first complaint. Next there was the failure
of the fair to employ Negroes. No Negro guards were seen
and only three blacks in minor clerical jobs. But worse than
either was the enormity of overlooking the Negro's contribution to American life and culture. "All classes and
conditions are represented except the American Negro,"
they protested. These snubs, as well as the failure of a petition by them to Congress to create a ripple in that body,
prompted an eighty-one page pamphlet in 1893 called:
"The Reason Why the Colored Man Is Not Represented in
the World's Columbian Exposition."

To mollify this unrest, the managers of the exposition
designated August 25, 1893, as "Colored American Day,"
and Douglass was quick to understand why black Americans would not take kindly to a one-day observance as a
substitute for a full-blown exhibit depicting the advance
of the Negro since Emancipation. But he bit his tongue
and declined to support those who clamored for a boycott
of the fair at that moment. The fiery young composer
Will Marion Cook (father of Mercer Cook) saw in the
"Colored American Day" proposal something more than a
sop, however, and appears to have persuaded Douglass to
deliver the main address on the occasion. The fact that
Douglass and Cook had a strong bond in common (love of
violin music) may have been influential, but in any case
the "Day" became memorable. In addition to Douglass's
address, his grandson Joseph played a violin solo, Dunbar
read several of his poems, and the personable and gifted
young Negro baritone Harry T. Burleigh drew encores
from the large, wildly applauding audience. A dissertation
could be written on the events of that day and the subsequent careers of the eager young black people who were
present or participated. A provocative comparison might
also be made of the meaning and aftermath of that event
and the same of another at the exposition in Atlanta two

years later, where a speech by Booker T. Washington galvanized American attitudes with regard to black and white
elements in the nation's bloodstream.

However, a few weeks after the "Colored American Day"
at the fair, Douglass decided that eight months had been
enough for him and terminated his connection as commissioner. The Haitian government sent a check of
$2,012.50 for his services. Hyppolite sent him a rather regal
photograph of himself in presidential ribbons and stars,
and Bishop Theodore J. Holly, a scarcely less prominent
figure in Haitian life, wrote him, "The services in conducting Haiti's part in the Columbian Exposition you have
rendered to the cause of spurned and downtrodden humanity reflects the beautiful halo of a golden sunset over
your long, brilliant and glorious career."

Generally regarded as wealthy in his later life, Douglass
did not need the money, but such expressions as Bishop
Holly's were clearly satisfying. Douglass was as aware as
anybody of the lengthening chain of his years, and presently he began to have premonitions. This did not prevent
him on February 20, 1895, from attending a Woman's
Council (Liberation) meeting at Metzerott Hall, and when
he entered, the presiding officer, Mary Wright Sewall,
promptly suspended business of the Council in order to
allow Susan B. Anthony and the Reverend Anna H. Shaw
to escort him to the platform as the membership rose spon-
taneously and, waving handkerchiefs, gave him a standing
ovation.

He told Helen about it at dinner that evening at Cedar
Hill. It was five o'clock, and they were not hurried because
there was enough time to relax before his speaking engagement scheduled that evening at a local church. When
suddenly he rose from the table and turned toward the
stairs, his wife thought he was about to dramatize the events
of the afternoon, as he so often did, but she was petrified

with shock when he bowed and began to sink lower and lower.

Later descriptions of the moment differ, but in one of them he is reported as saying, as he fell to his knees, "What is this?" If he received an answer, he did not divulge it. He never regained consciousness. He was dead when the carriage arrived to take him to his speaking engagement.

The body remained at Cedar Hill till the morning of February 25, when the family gathered in one of the parlors and the Reverend Hugh Stevenson came and read Scriptures and prayed. Then the body was taken to the Metropolitan A. M. E. church to lay in state for four hours while the public walked down the aisle to take the last look. The black public schools of Washington had been closed for the day, and parents lifted their children for a better view. Others in the long, unbroken procession brought a flower, a fern leaf or a bouquet which they silently placed on the casket. "Howl, fir-tree," the preacher intoned, "for the cedar of Lebanon is fallen."

The doors of the church were closed at 1:30, and the service proper began. The faculty of Howard University, of which Douglass had long been a trustee, sat together in a body. Senators and justices of the Supreme Court were among the crowd in the tightly packed church. On the platform to eulogize or pray sat Alexander Crummell (later to be the subject of an essay by W. E. B. Du Bois), Susan B. Anthony, Bishops J. W. Hood and A. W. Wayman and other prominent figures. John E. Hutchinson of the famous Hutchinson family of abolitionist singers, the last survivor of the group, a tearful old wisp of his former self, was somehow able to summon back a recognizable likeness of the voice that had once been famous as he sang an emotion-charged solo. Someone read an original poem.

Following the service the body was placed on an early evening train bound for Rochester, New York. Helen and the three surviving Douglass children—Rosetta, Lewis and Charles—composing their differences for the length of the journey, at least, boarded the train to accompany the body. At Rochester flags were at half-mast, and the body lay in state at the City Hall as children, dismissed from the public schools in the custody of their parents, passed by. That afternoon the mayor and the aldermen were among the notables of the city who were there to speak for Douglass as "one of Rochester's most honored and representative men," whose memory "will remain a bright one on the gilded scroll of history."

Bands played dirges as the procession, leaving the Central Church, moved through crowded streets to Mount Hope cemetery. And so was buried the once furious slave, the intrepid giant whom Thomas Wentworth Higginson called "the imperial Douglass," born of a rage to live, spent by struggle, but free at last.

A NOTE ON SOURCES

When I first inquired, the log of the Frederick Douglass career seemed hard to assemble. Now it is easy. A reference library can list, if it wishes, forty or fifty cards under his name. Events have brought about the change, of course. There was the Supreme Court decision of 1954 which tended to turn attention to Douglass's role. Later the efforts by young people to arouse feelings that might work toward implementation of that decision became a factor. One way and another the tall shadow of Frederick Douglass was caused to reappear on the screen of the American past.

Almost the first discovery I made was that none of the three autobiographies Douglass wrote (*The Narrative, My Bondage and My Freedom* and *The Life and Times*) cancels the others out. All must be read to fill out his story. Nor can the correspondence and fugitive writing, now available on a rather poor microfilm, be spared.

The running accounts of his activities reported in William Lloyd Garrison's *Liberator* and in his own newspaper the *North Star* have likewise become more accessible. Naturally this has made librarians and other interested parties less inclined to brush aside the old biographies written before his death and shortly thereafter.

Despite the decay of his home in Anacostia and the misuse of the memorabilia left there, sources for reconstructing some aspects of his life have survived, and a fair amount has been picked up and preserved in later dissertations and scholarly publications, not to mention a few fictional and semi-fictional writings. Even so, the sometimes honored, sometimes neglected Douglass saga, continues to intrigue and perhaps to point a direction.

INDEX